NEPHILIM, FI

AND ALIENS

WHAT DOES THE BIBLE SAY?

Dr. Cathy Burns

Sharing

212 East Seventh Street (N-1)

Mt. Carmel, PA 17851-2211

TABLE OF CONTENTS

1. Let's Start with the Scriptures 5

2. The Serpent Seed Doctrine 8

3. "Ye Are of Your Father the Devil" 21

4. Is Cain Missing from Adam's Lineage? 26

5. The Nephilim 30

6. Why Was the Flood Sent? 53

7. "As in the Days of Noah" 77

8. What Is the "Neshama"? 86

9. The Golem 93

10. What About Daniel 2? 106

11. Who Are the "Watchers"? 114

12. The Nephilim, Cloning, and the Antichrist 120

13. Is the *Book of Enoch* Scripture? 149

14. Is the *Book of Jasher* Scripture? 164

15. Conclusion 180

Glossary 183

Endnotes 188

Index 216

1. LET'S START WITH THE SCRIPTURES

A popular theme today is talk of the Nephilim, fallen angels, aliens, greys, UFOs, Anunnaki, golems, genetic engineering and manipulation, cloning, and hybrid races. These topics can be found in many books, TV programs, videos, and movies within both the secular and the religious realms. Many evangelicals have written books on these subjects and these ideas can be frequently heard on talk radio shows.

What has caused the current interest in such phenomena? Why is it gaining so much popularity currently? Why is there an increased fascination with these issues?

In this book we will discuss some of these topics, but our source for truth must be a reliable guide. If we have a reliable reference on which to base our beliefs, then we'll be able to compare our research with that authority and be able to recognize false teachings should they arise. My starting point and source of truth is the Bible—the Word of God. Psalm 119:89 says that God's Word is forever settled in heaven. We are all aware that there are many false doctrines in the world. The only way we will be able to know the true from the false is if we have a true guide. The Bible happens to be that guide. John 17:17 says: "Thy word is truth."

If we study the real and know the real thoroughly, then we'll be able to spot counterfeits. "Federal agents don't learn to spot counterfeit money by studying the counterfeits. They study genuine bills until they master the look of the real thing. Then when they see the bogus money they recognize it."[1]

We need to do the same thing with the Word of God. For instance, if we study the Bible and then we hear a Mormon say that Jesus and Lucifer are brothers, we'll know that this is a counterfeit religion because the Bible says that Jesus was the ONLY BEGOTTEN Son of God (John 3:16). When we hear "As God now is, man may become and as man is now, God once was," we know this is a counterfeit teaching because the Bible says "from everlasting to everlasting, thou art God" (Psalm 90:2). When we read a book promoting reincarnation we can know it's false because Hebrews 9:27 says that "it is appointed unto men **ONCE** to die, but after this the judgment."

If you had a test coming up in school, you'd study the textbook. You wouldn't go to outside sources and then try to reinterpret the textbook.

As Christians we need to do the same thing. The Bible says that we are going to be judged by the Bible (John 12:48) and therefore we need to study it.

I remember one banking class I took and when the teacher asked a question I gave an answer. He then asked the class how many thought I was wrong. Every hand in the class went up. I knew I was correct because I had read the book and I gave the answer from the book but I didn't have to defend my answer because the teacher said "Well, she's correct." If the others in the class would have read the book, they, too, would have known the correct answer.

We need to do the same thing with the Scriptures. We should spend more time studying the Bible and getting to know what it says because, as the Bible warns us "there shall arise false Christs, and false prophets, and shall shew great signs and wonders; insomuch that, if it were possible, they shall deceive the very elect" (Matthew 24:24; see also Mark 13:22).

Because individuals are not grounded in the Word of God, they are often "tossed to and fro, and carried about with every wind of doctrine" (Ephesians 4:14). James 1:8 also says: "A double minded man is unstable in all his ways." Knowing God's Word will help us to become established and settled in our faith.

LESS CONFUSION

If people knew God's Word better, there would be a lot less confusion about the Nephilim, Anunnaki, aliens, UFOs, etc.

However, if we fail to accept the truth of God's Word, we will be an easy prey for deception and the lie. II Thessalonians 2:10-11 says because people received not the love of the truth, a strong delusion would be sent and they would believe a lie. Hosea 4:6 reminds us: "My people are destroyed for lack of knowledge: because thou hast rejected knowledge, I will also reject thee...."

Remember, too, we can't incorporate occult teachings into Scripture without tampering with the Scriptures. If our research doesn't line up with Scriptures, then we need to question the research. What is even worse is when the Scriptures tell us something clearly but we then go to other sources, find a different interpretation, and come back and try to reinterpret the Scriptures to fit with the new idea. We can't change God's Word but II Peter 3:16 warns us that the Scriptures can be wrested (or perverted)—**but it's to our own destruction if we do so.**

Throughout this book we will look at the topic of the Nephilim and fallen angels but we need to start with the idea of the "serpent seed" in order to lay a foundation for the other issues.

A glossary is included for those who may not be familiar with some of the terms found throughout this book.

2. THE SERPENT SEED DOCTRINE

The theory of the "serpent seed" has been promoted by the KKK, neo-Nazis, Identity groups, the Aryan Nations, Adolph Hitler, William Branham, Sun Myung Moon and the Unification Church, and many others. It is often used as a rationale to promote racism and hatred of certain groups.

There are various aspects and perspectives to this belief, but basically the "serpent seed" theory teaches that when Eve partook of the tree of the knowledge of good and evil in the Garden of Eden, she had actually engaged in a sexual relationship with the serpent or Satan and from this illicit relationship Cain was born.[1] Cain, therefore, is referred to as the seed or the offspring of the serpent, hence the "serpent seed."

Sherry Shriner asserts:

"Here is what really happened in the garden of Eden: Eve lost her virginity to 'the serpent,' whom was that 'Tree of the knowledge of good and evil in the midst of the garden,' and who is none other than Satan himself."[2]

Gnostic Scriptures go so far as to claim that Eve was actually raped by the serpent.[3]

Before delving deeper into this issue, we need to spend a little time checking the verses before and after this passage in Genesis 3. Let's start with Genesis 2:8-9:

"And the Lord God planted a garden eastward in Eden; and there He put the man whom He had formed. And out of the ground made the Lord God to grow every tree that is pleasant to the sight, and good for food; the tree of life also in the midst of the garden, and the tree of knowledge of good and evil."

Now let's go to verses 15-17:

> "And the Lord God took the man, and put him into the garden of Eden to dress it and to keep it. And the Lord God commanded the man, saying, Of every tree of the garden thou mayest freely eat: But of the tree of the knowledge of good and evil, thou shalt not eat of it...."

So far we see that God created the trees in the Garden and they were for food. The trees are literal trees and the tree of the knowledge of good and evil is specifically listed.

Now, Genesis 3 gives the account of the serpent tempting Eve. He told her that if she would eat of this tree, she would not die. Verse 6 says:

> "And when the woman saw that the **tree was good for food,** and that it was pleasant to the eyes, and a tree to be desired to make one wise, she took of the fruit thereof, and did eat, and gave also unto her husband with her; and he did eat."

Two verses later we see that God is walking in the garden so Adam and Eve now hide themselves among the trees of the garden.

SYMBOLISM CAUSES PROBLEMS

If we start to symbolize this, we run into LOTS of problems. First of all, the verses right before and right after Eve partakes of the tree show that the trees are **LITERAL** trees. God created the trees and when Adam and Eve tried to hide from God they hid among literal trees. Why would we try to symbolize the other reference to the tree? Notice also that when Satan discussed this tree with Eve, she looked at it and saw it was good for food. This is exactly why it was created so there's no reason for symbolism here. Furthermore, we see that Eve gave this fruit to her husband so if we symbolize this tree to mean sex, we not only have Eve having sexual relations with Satan but we may also have Adam and Satan participating in a homosexual act since Adam also "ate" of this tree.[4]

Not only do we find that the tree of the knowledge of good and evil was a **LITERAL** tree, but we also know that this tree **DID NOT** represent a sexual act because Genesis 1:27-28 states: "So God created man in His own image, in the image of God created He him; male and female created He them. And God blessed them, and God said unto them, **BE FRUITFUL, AND MULTIPLY....**"

If the tree of the knowledge of good and evil represented a sexual relationship, then God would have contradicted Himself by telling Adam and Eve to be fruitful and multiply but forbidding them to partake of the "fruit" that would allow them to do so. By trying to symbolize the tree of the knowledge of good and evil to mean a sexual encounter, we not only need to reinterpret the Bible but we would also have a God who is demanding disobedience. If Adam and Eve would obey God's command to be fruitful they would have to disobey His other command by eating of the "fruit" of the tree. If they would obey God's command to not eat of the tree of the knowledge of good and evil, then they would be obligated to disobey His command to be fruitful. I Corinthians 14:33 says that "God **IS NOT** the author of confusion...."

Furthermore, if "eating" would represent a sexual relationship,[5] how do you explain Genesis 2:16? "And the Lord God commanded the man, saying, Of EVERY tree of the garden thou mayest freely EAT." Adam and Eve were put out of Eden so that they would not EAT of the tree of life. In fact, the word "eat" is used 17 times just in Genesis 3. It's obvious that these other references CANNOT be referring to sexual relations, so why would we assume that this one instance does?

We also need to realize that when we begin to symbolize Scripture without appropriate reason, we have no way of knowing where to stop. If partaking of the tree of the knowledge of good and evil symbolizes a sexual act with Satan, how can we be sure we shouldn't also symbolize the virgin birth, or Christ's death, or His resurrection, or heaven, or hell, the flood, and so forth?

TREE OF LIFE

Returning to Genesis 3, we see that right after this encounter with Satan, God curses the serpent and puts Adam and Eve out of the garden. He did not want them to eat of the tree of life and live forever in a sinful state. God put up a protective barrier to keep them from the tree of life. Isn't it strange that God would go to all this effort to protect these trees if these trees were only symbolical? Of course, we know that the tree of life is a literal tree because it is mentioned 3 times in Revelation (2:7; 22:2, 14) and we are told that this tree is in the paradise of God and only those who "do His commandments...have right to the tree of life, and may enter in through the gates into the city" (Revelation 22:14).

After Adam and Eve are banished from Eden the Bible says in Genesis 4:1-2a: "Adam knew Eve his wife; and she conceived, and bare Cain, and said, I have gotten a man from the Lord. And she again bare his brother Abel." The sequence is clear that Eve only conceived **AFTER** they were expelled from the garden so Satan was not the father of Cain.

People such as Dr. Joye Jeffries Pugh[6] and Jerry Gentry[7] claim that Eve was referring to Satan when she said that she obtained a man from the Lord but the word "Lord" is Jehovah and refers to Almighty God. With over 140 references to Jehovah in the book of Genesis, EVERY SINGLE ONE of them referred to God. Why would JUST THIS **ONE** OCCURRENCE in Genesis 4:1 be different? Of course, it isn't. However, once we reject the clear teaching of the Scripture, we'll have to go to outside sources to get another explanation and this is where the teaching of the "serpent seed" comes in.

For instance, some people like Sherry Shriner try to use the *Dead Sea Scrolls* to bolster their "serpent seed" theory.[8] They say that the Bible is incorrect in Genesis 4:1 and should actually read:

"And Adam knew his wife Eve, who was pregnant by Sammael (Satan), and she conceived and bare Cain, and he was like the heavenly beings, and not like the earthly beings, and she said, I have gotten a man from the angel of the Lord."

There just happens to be a problem with this explanation. According to Michael S. Heiser, a scholar in Near-Eastern Semitic Languages, Koine Greek, and Sumerian studies,[9] we find that

"Genesis 4:1 was NOT found among the textual remains of the Hebrew Bible among the Dead Sea Scrolls. It is important to realize that much of the biblical material from Qumran is partial and fragmentary. Only the book of Isaiah can be said to be virtually complete (99% of it was found at Qumran). There are portions and scraps of every other OT book except Esther. Genesis 4:1, the account of Can's (sic) birth, is not in the Dead Sea Scroll material."[10] [Emphasis in the original.]

If this verse is NOT found in the *Dead Sea Scrolls,* then how can it be translated to mean that Satan fathered Cain? Of course, it can't.

So, WHERE did this idea originate?

Heiser continues:

"Since we already know the name doesn't occur in the biblical scrolls,...I thought I'd look for it among the other scrolls material—sometimes the other material has commentaries on the biblical material. A computer search for 'Sammael' (or the alternate spelling Samael) yields ZERO occurrences in the non-biblical texts from the Dead Sea Scrolls. This is more proof that this 'account' is not only absent in the biblical Dead Sea Scrolls; it isn't present in the scrolls that covered other subjects besides copying and commenting on the Hebrew Bible."[11] [Emphasis in the original.]

The name "Sammael" (or "Samael") does appear in the *Pseudepigrapha* but not in the sense that he had relations with Eve and fathered Cain. This idea is only found in one Targum (namely the *Targum Pseudo-Jonathan)* and some later rabbinic writings.[12] The word "Targum" means "translation" or "interpretation" and is the Aramaic translation of the Hebrew Bible.[13] The *Targum Pseudo-*

Jonathan was written about 1500-2000 years AFTER Genesis. Furthermore,

> "Targums can be very elastic translations, adding material quite freely with no Hebrew manuscript evidence at all. Everyone who does Aramaic knows this about the Targums—they can play pretty fast and loose with the text of the Bible; they INSERT all kinds of things into the translation, without regard to any prior textual manuscript history for support. IN (sic) plain language, the Targums often add made up material to the biblical text. Having Samael in Genesis 4:1 is a classic example—it was added at least 1500 years after the fact, and no other prior ancient Jewish material supports it."[14] [Emphasis in the original.]

CUNNINGLY DEVISED FABLES

The Bible is very specific about these rabbinical writings. Paul warned Titus: "Wherefore rebuke them sharply, that they may be sound in the faith; Not giving heed to **JEWISH FABLES,** and commandments of men, that TURN FROM THE TRUTH" (Titus 1:13b-14). There are several other similar references:

☞ "Neither give heed to **FABLES** and endless genealogies, which minister questions, rather than godly edifying which is in faith..." (I Timothy 1:4).

☞ "For we have not followed cunningly devised **FABLES,** when we made known unto you the power and coming of our Lord Jesus Christ, but were eyewitnesses of His majesty" (II Peter 1:16).

☞ "Wherefore the Lord said, Forasmuch as this people draw near Me with their mouth, and with their lips do honour Me, but have removed their heart far from Me, and their fear toward Me is taught by the precept of men..." (Isaiah 29:13).

☞ "For the time will come when they will not endure sound doctrine; but after their own lusts shall they heap to themselves teachers, having itching ears; And they shall turn away their ears from the truth, and shall **BE TURNED UNTO FABLES**" (II Timothy 4:4).

☞ "But evil men and seducers shall wax worse and worse, deceiving, and being deceived" (II Timothy 3:13).

☞ "But there were false prophets also among the people, even as there shall be false teachers among you, who privily shall bring in damnable heresies, even denying the Lord that bought them, and bring upon themselves swift destruction. And many shall follow their pernicious ways; by reason of whom the way of truth shall be evil spoken of. And through covetousness shall they with feigned words make merchandise of you..." (II Peter 2:1-3a).

☞ "But refuse profane and old wives' **FABLES,** and exercise thyself rather unto godliness" (I Timothy 4:7).

Strangely, in addition to the rabbinical writings, some Luciferians also teach that Samael (or Satan) fathered Cain with Lilith.

> **"Samael** was called the **Prince of Demons** and whose name meant roughly, **'Poison of God,'** and is a spirit of the Air (astral plane, dreaming). Samael, as being the same as Lucifer, Ahriman, Set, Azazel is by all accounts the fallen seraphim whose desire for individual thought and the ability to guide his own destiny resulted in the fall."[15] [Emphasis in the original.]

LILITH IS "THE BRIDE OF THE DEVIL"

Luciferians also honor Lilith as a goddess and Luciferian Michael Ford refers to her as "the Bride of the Devil."[16] In fact, Samael, Lilith, and Cain are considered to be the "Luciferian Trinity" in the Black Tradition.[17]

Ford wrote a book entitled *Liber HVHI.* "HVHI is called the incommunicable name of Samael, the Opposer/Adversary."[18] Elaborating on this idea of Cain being fathered by Satan, Ford claims:

> "In certain rabbinical literature, the Daughters of Cain were those who joined in sexual union with the Fallen Angels, the Watchers, and gave birth to the Nephilim, the Giants who were war like and brutal. They were said to have populated the earth in

plenty, and attacked the children of Seth. In Manichaean lore, the Queen of Demons and spiritual initiator of Cain, Lilith-Az, taught the fallen angels to form physical bodies and join with others sexually. It is suggested also by writers Kaufmann Kohler, W. H. Bennett and Louis Ginzberg that the Children of Cain spent their days at the foot of a mountain (Eden?) practicing in wild orgies with the music of Lucifer through that created by Jubal. Women, the first Pairikas or Faeries/Witches, in their beautiful appearances, invited the sons of Seth (children of god) and copulated with them, bearing other children. This Jewish Folklore presents the earliest forms of the Witches (sic) Sabbat as a Luciferian celebration and practice of sexual magick....

"Herein we can see that Cain is thus a flesh and blood embodiment of the Luciferian Path itself, he is the Son of Satan and Lilith, the dark essence which is deeply connected with Eve, the wife of Adam. Cain is not only the patron father of Witches, also the symbol of the initiate upon the antinomian path."[19]

Nathaniel Harris, a witch, writes: "It is said within the dark traditions [Satanism, witchcraft, etc.] that **the Bible is mistaken with regards to Cain's true parentage.**"[20] [Emphasis mine throughout unless otherwise stated.]

Why would evangelicals promote an idea that is foreign to the Scriptures but accepted by the Satanists and witches?

SATAN IS THE FATHER OF LIES

We know that Satan is an intelligent creature but he is also the father of lies. Why would I want to go to sources that have demonic inspiration to try to find the truth? If Satan lied to Eve, don't you think he'd also lie to his followers? I cannot go to occult sources to find truth.

It is understandable that occultists do not believe or accept the Bible but it is hard to comprehend why evangelicals, who claim that the Bible is the inspired Word of God, do not accept the simple truth of Scripture.

For anyone who claims that the Bible is God's Word yet holds to the serpent seed theory, we find that Scriptures MUST be overlooked, reinterpreted, or ignored. To believe that Cain was LITERALLY the son of Satan, we need to symbolize Genesis 3.[21] We need to ignore or ADD to Genesis 4:2a where it states that "Adam knew Eve his wife; and she conceived, and bare Cain...." We also need to ignore another verse of Scripture which says in Acts 17:26 that God "hath made of ONE BLOOD **ALL** nations of men...." There are not separate bloodlines in the sense that one lineage is from Adam and another lineage from Satan.

Some people even seem to resort to intentional manipulation and lying. For example, Willie Martin and Sherry Shriner in their attempt to justify their viewpoint that Cain was Satan's son, turn to several commentaries. Both quote from Matthew Henry: "IT SHOWED THAT HE (Cain—W.M.) was the firstborn of the serpent's seed...."[22] [Emphasis in the original.] The truth, however, is that both Martin and Shriner left off the rest of the sentence which states: "even he, the **ELDEST SON OF THE FIRST MAN,** was of the wicked one."[23] The partial quotation makes it **APPEAR** as though Matthew Henry believed in the serpent seed theory but that obviously is not the case. Of course, Martin, as well as Arnold Murray and others, believe that the Jews are the "descendants of Satan through Cain..."[24] which is another unscriptural teaching.

One way people try to change the Scripture is to claim that Eve was already pregnant from Satan when "Adam knew Eve..." but that isn't what the Bible says at all.[25] Malachi 2:10 asks: "Have we not all **ONE FATHER?** hath not one God created us?"

Furthermore, if you recall, this idea SUPPOSEDLY comes from the *Dead Sea Scrolls* but we've already discovered that this isn't the case, either.

SATAN HAS A SEED

Thomas Horn, a former minister with the Assemblies of God, also believes that Satan has a seed. He writes:

"Daniel's prophecy, coupled with Genesis chapter 3, provides an incredible tenet—*that Satan has* <u>*seed,*</u> *and* <u>*it*</u> *is at enmity with Christ!*

"'And I will put enmity between thee and the woman, and between thy seed and her seed; it shall bruise thy head, and thou shalt bruise his heel' (Gen. 3:15).

"The word translated here as 'seed' is the Hebrew word *zera,* which means 'offspring, descendants, children.'"[26] [Emphasis in the original.]

While it is true that "seed" can mean "offspring, descendants, children," the word is **NOT** limited to such a meaning. It can be used figuratively and it also refers to seed such as grain which is used for planting. Here are a few verses with this same word ("zera") highlighted.

✳ "And God said, Let the earth bring forth grass, the herb yielding **seed,** and the fruit tree yielding fruit after his kind, whose **seed** is in itself, upon the earth: and it was so" (Genesis 1:11).

✳ "While the earth remaineth, **seedtime** and harvest, and cold and heat, and summer and winter, and day and night shall not cease" (Genesis 8:22).

✳ "And the house of Israel called the name thereof Manna: and it was like coriander **seed,** white; and the taste of it was like wafers made with honey" (Exodus 16:31).

✳ "And all the tithe of the land, whether of the **seed** of the land, or of the fruit of the tree, is the Lord's: it is holy unto the Lord" (Leviticus 27:30).

✳ "In the morning sow thy **seed,** and in the evening withhold not thine hand: for thou knowest not whether shall prosper, either this or that, or whether they both shall be alike good" (Ecclesiastes 11:6).

✳ "He that goeth forth and weepeth, bearing precious **seed,** shall doubtless come again with rejoicing, bringing his sheaves with him" (Psalm 126:6).

JESUS HAS A SEED

It is quite obvious that the word "seed" ("zera") does not always mean children. Furthermore, according to Isaiah 53 we see that Jesus, too, has a seed. "Yet it pleased the Lord to bruise Him [Jesus]; He hath put Him to grief: when thou shalt make His soul an offering for sin, He shall see His **seed,** He shall prolong His days, and the pleasure of the Lord shall prosper in His hand" (Isaiah 53:10). We know from Hebrews 7:3 that Jesus does not have any descendants so we know that Jesus' seed are those who believe in Him and trust Him as their Lord and Saviour. I John 3:1-2 declares: "Behold, what manner of love the Father hath bestowed upon us, that we should be called the **sons of God:** therefore the world knoweth us not, because it knew Him not. Beloved, now are we the **sons of God....**"

✝ "But love ye your enemies, and do good...and your reward shall be great, and ye shall be the **children of the Highest...**" (Luke 6:35).

✝ "Blessed are the peacemakers: for they shall be called the **children of God**" (Matthew 5:9).

✝ "And it shall come to pass, that in the place where it was said unto them, Ye are not My people; there shall they be called the **children of the living God**" (Romans 9:26).

✝ "Thus said the Lord, Israel is **My son,** even My firstborn..." (Exodus 4:22).

✝ "For as many are led by the Spirit of God, they are the **sons of God....**The Spirit itself beareth witness with our spirit, that we are the **children of God**" (Romans 8:14, 16).

✝ "For ye are all the **children of God** *by faith in Christ Jesus*" (Galatians 3:26).

✝ "And because **ye are sons,** God hath sent forth the Spirit of His Son into your hearts, crying, Abba, Father. Wherefore thou art no more a servant, but a son; and if a son, then an heir of God through Christ" (Galatians 4:6-7).

Satan has "children" in the same sense as Jesus has "children." Isaiah 1:4 says: "Ah sinful nation, a people laden with iniquity, **a seed of evildoers, children that are corrupters:** *they have forsaken the Lord,* they have provoked the Holy One of Israel unto anger, they are gone away backward."

We also find in I John 3:8, 10:

"He that committeth sin is of the devil; for the devil sinneth from the beginning. For this purpose the Son of God was manifested, that He might destroy the works of the devil....In this **the children of God** are manifest, and **the children of the devil:** whosoever doeth not righteousness is not of God, neither he that loveth not his brother."

It is clear that Satan's seed are those who are living in sin and Christ's seed are those who are living righteously. This idea is brought out in Romans 6:

"Know ye not, that to whom ye yield yourselves servants to obey, his servants ye are to whom ye obey; whether of sin unto death, or of obedience unto righteousness? But God be thanked, that ye **WERE** the servants of sin, **BUT** ye have obeyed from the heart that form of doctrine which was delivered you. Being then made free from sin, ye **BECAME** the servants of righteousness....For when ye were the servants of sin, ye were free from righteousness....But now being made free from sin, and become servants to God, ye have your fruit unto holiness, and the end everlasting life. For the wages of sin is death; but the gift of God is eternal life through Jesus Christ our Lord" (Romans 6:16-18, 20, 22-23).

This thought is also found in Ephesians 2:

"That at that time ye were without Christ, being aliens from the commonwealth of Israel, and strangers from the covenants of promise, having no hope, and without God in the world: **BUT NOW** in Christ Jesus ye who sometimes were far off are made nigh by the blood of Christ....For through Him we both have access by one Spirit unto the Father. Now therefore ye are no more strangers and foreigners, but fellowcitizens with the saints, and of the household of God" (Ephesians 2:12-13, 18-19).

"Wherefore come out from among them, and be ye separate, saith the Lord, and touch not the unclean thing; and I will receive you, And will be a Father unto you, and **ye shall be My sons and daughters,** saith the Lord Almighty" (II Corinthians 6:17-18).

DEVIL'S CHILDREN CAN BECOME GOD'S CHILDREN

It should be clear that the devil's "children" can become the Lord's "children" through faith in Jesus Christ. "To open their eyes, and to turn them from darkness to light, and **from the power of Satan unto God,** that they may receive forgiveness of sins, and inheritance among them which are sanctified by faith that is in Me" (Acts 26:18).

In spite of the clear teaching of Scripture, people still insist that Satan had a literal son by the name of Cain. Trying to "prove" their theory, they will point to John 8:44 where Jesus said: "Ye are of your father the devil."

We will look at this verse more closely in the next chapter.

3. "YE ARE OF YOUR FATHER THE DEVIL"

The idea of the "serpent seed" has some variations in beliefs. As already mentioned, the idea that Satan was literally the father of Cain is unbiblical. However, some groups that believe this lie claim various lineages from Cain. According to the Unification Church (Moon's group), the Communists and Atheists are Cain's descendants. The Nation of Yahweh claims that the Whites are Cain's offspring.[1]

Other groups (such as the Christian Identity Movement) teach that the Jews are the descendants of this supposed "demonic" lineage of Cain.[2] Hitler was one who believed that the Jews were of the "serpent seed."[3] This idea is now quite prevalent in some churches. Willie Martin claims: "Lilith-Kali-Isis-Ishtar is the wife of Cain in Genesis 4:17, the ancestral mother of the Serpent race of Jews. It is a counterfeit race not created by God."[4] Another ministry states: "Jesus identified these so-called Jews as the descendants of Cain."[5] They go so far as to state:

> "Cain's race is not on (sic) the Book of Life....There is absolutely no sense in preaching to the physical Serpent's seed as they are not among God's creatures or creation. They may be nice folk and good citizens—church-goers; even preachers—pay their tithes and sing in the choir, but they will never be in the Kingdom of God and they have no Kinsman Redeemer."[6]

Trying to justify their viewpoint from the Bible, they will point to John 8:44 where Jesus said: "Ye are of your father the devil."[7]

We can make the Bible say a lot of things such as Ephesians 4:28 where we are told "Let him that stole steal" (which could "justify" stealing) and Psalm 14:1 and 53:1 say: "There is no God" (which could be taken as a promotion of atheism). The problem with these verses is that I only gave you part of the verse. The first verse actually says "Let him that stole steal **no more**" and the second verse says **"The fool hath said** in his heart, There is no God." We need to be careful not to pull phrases out of context. As someone has said, "A text without the context is a pretext."

"WE BE ABRAHAM'S SEED"

This is the case with John 8:44: "Ye are of your father the devil." Jesus did say this but we need to look closer at this chapter. In John 8 we see Jesus talking about His father and the Jews asked who His father was. He said that He was from above but that they were from beneath. As He spoke to them, many believed on Jesus. "Then said Jesus to those Jews which believed on Him, If ye continue in My word, then are ye My disciples indeed; And ye shall know the truth, and the truth shall make you free" (John 8:31-32). The Jews then responded: **"We be Abraham's seed,** and were never in bondage to any man: how sayest Thou, Ye shall be made free?" (John 8:33). Jesus explained that whosoever committeth sin was the servant of sin and He added: "If the Son therefore shall make you free, ye shall be free indeed" (John 8:36).

Now, watch the following exchange starting in verse 37. Jesus CLEARLY says to these Jews: **"I know that ye are Abraham's seed."** Jesus was revealing to the Jews that He was referring to an earthly **AND** a spiritual father. Abraham was their earthly father and He recognized that **BUT** He added that their works showed that their **SPIRITUAL** father was Satan. The Jews then said that they had one Father, even God. Jesus responded: "If God were your Father, ye would love Me: for I proceeded forth and came from God; neither came I of Myself, but He sent Me" (John 8:42). Right after this He said "Ye are of your father the devil, and the lusts of your father ye will do....He that is of God heareth God's words: ye therefore hear them not, because ye are not of God" (John 8:44, 47).

A few verses later Jesus once again recognized their **PHYSICAL** lineage by saying "Your father Abraham" (John 8:56).

This chapter clearly shows us that Jesus recognized that the Jews came from Abraham but because of their sinful deeds, their spiritual father was Satan. He also told them that their father could be God IF they would obey the truth. Romans 2:11 says that "there is no respect of persons with God" (see also Colossians 3:25) and II Peter 3:9 tells us that God is "not willing that any should perish, but that **ALL** should come to repentance." There is NO teaching here of a "serpent seed" lineage whatsoever.

John the Baptist also recognized that the Pharisees' and Sadducees' **EARTHLY** father was Abraham in Matthew 3:7-8 and Luke 3:8. Paul also spoke to the Jews and addressed them as "Men and brethren, children of the stock of Abraham..." (Acts 13:26).

Another verse used for the "serpent seed" is found in I John 3:12 where it says that Cain was of the wicked one.[8] Again we need to read the entire context. John explained that Cain was of the wicked one BECAUSE his works were evil—not because of some genetic factor. Let's read a few verses prior to this starting with verse 8:

> "He that committeth sin is of the devil; for the devil sinneth from the beginning. For this purpose the Son of God was manifested, that He might destroy the works of the devil. Whosoever is born of God doth not commit sin; for his seed remaineth in him: and he cannot sin, because he is born of God. In this the children of God are manifest, and the children of the devil: whosoever doeth not righteousness is not of God, neither he that loveth not his brother. For this is the message that ye heard from the beginning, that we should love one another. Not as Cain, who was of that wicked one, and slew his brother. And wherefore slew he him? Because his own works were evil, and his brother's righteous" (I John 3:8-12).

The context shows that those who are not righteous and those who do not love their brother are children of the devil in a spiritual sense. These people, however, can change their relationship by trusting in Christ as their Saviour. All of us are born in sin but those who trust in Christ pass from death unto life: "We know that we have passed from death unto life, because we love the brethren. He that loveth not his brother abideth in death" (I John 3:14). **Cain, too, had a choice to do right or wrong.** Before he killed his brother, "the Lord said unto Cain, Why art thou wroth? and why is thy countenance fallen? **IF THOU DOEST WELL, SHALT THOU NOT BE ACCEPTED?** and if thou doest not well, sin lieth at the door" (Genesis 4:6-7). It was after this warning that Cain slew Abel (Genesis 4:8).

ALL HAVE SINNED

We are also told in I John 5:19 that the WHOLE WORLD lieth in wickedness—not just a particular lineage or seed. Romans 3:23 states: **"All** have sinned, and come short of the glory of God" and Romans 5:12 says: "By one man sin entered into the world, and death by sin; and so death passed upon **ALL** men, for that **ALL HAVE SINNED."** That man was Adam, not Satan, and because of his sin, **ALL** (not just Cain's lineage) are born in sin. This is why we needed a Savior because without Christ there was no hope and no redemption. John 3:16 says: "For God so loved the world, that He gave His only begotten Son, that WHOSOEVER believeth in Him should not perish, but have everlasting life." There are numerous Scriptures that tell us that there is no respect of persons with God. All are welcomed to come to Christ but it is on the condition of obedience to His Word.

Because all of us are born in sin and Satan is our spiritual father, we need to be ADOPTED into God's family. John 1:12-13 says: "As many as received Him, to them gave He power to become the sons of God, even to them that believe on His name: Which were born, not of blood, nor of the will of the flesh, nor of the will of man, but of God." II Peter 3:9 says that the Lord is not willing that any one should perish but that all should come to repentance.

Another reference to "prove" that the Jews were of the "serpent seed" is where Jesus and John the Baptist called the Pharisees and Sadducees vipers. Again, let's look at the context in Matthew 3. John the Baptist was performing baptisms and people were confessing their sins.

"But when he saw many of the Pharisees and Sadducees come to his baptism, he said unto them, O generation of vipers, who hath warned you to flee from the wrath to come? Bring forth therefore fruits meet for repentance: And think not to say within yourselves, We have Abraham to our father: for I say unto you, that God is able of these stones to raise up children unto Abraham" (Matthew 3:7-9; see also Luke 3:3-9).

Once again we see that these Jews were given a choice. He told these "vipers" that if they would repent they could also be saved. He, too, recognized that Abraham was the LITERAL, PHYSICAL father of these Jews but that if they didn't repent their SPIRITUAL father was Satan.

Likewise Jesus called the Jews a generation of vipers because they had killed His prophets but He also said "how often would I have gathered thy children together, even as a hen gathered her chickens under her wings, and **YE WOULD NOT!**" (Matthew 23:37). Once again we see that the Jews had a choice to do good or evil. It should be obvious that the expression "generation of vipers" is referring to a behavioral characteristic rather than having anything to do with lineage or genetics.

Remember, too, that Jesus came through this SAME lineage. He, too, was from Abraham as we see from Matthew 1:1: "The book of the generation of Jesus Christ, the son of David, the son of Abraham." So, if these Jews were of the "serpent seed" lineage, then we must also believe that Jesus is of the "serpent seed" lineage. Of course, this is blasphemy!

4. IS CAIN MISSING FROM ADAM'S LINEAGE?

People who espouse the "serpent seed" theory say that Cain is missing from Adam's lineage. They claim that the reason is because Cain was not of Adam's lineage but that he was fathered by Satan. Dr. Pugh asserts: "Cain is completely removed from Adam's generation, because he was not his son. Cain was the son of Satan."[1]

Oh, really?! We do find Cain's lineage listed in Genesis 4:17-22. The lineage is as follows:

Cain
Enoch
Irad
Mehujael
Methusael
Lamech
Jabal, Jubal, Tubalcain and sister Naamah

There is no lineage listed for Abel but he was most likely killed before he fathered any children so he would have had no lineage. It certainly does not mean that he was of Satan's seed or that he was unrighteous for the Bible clearly says that he was righteous in Matthew 23:35, I John 3:12, and Hebrews 11:4.

Luke 3 does list the lineage of Jesus' stepfather, Joseph, ending with "Enos, which was the son of Seth, which was the son of Adam, which was the son of God" (Luke 3:38). Of course, neither Abel nor Cain nor **ANY** of Adam's and Eve's other children are listed. Why? The answer is quite simple. The reason why Cain nor the others are listed is because Jesus was not a **DIRECT DESCENDANT** from any of them **EXCEPT** Seth. If I were to trace my ancestry I would list my father and my mother but I would not list my sisters. Does that mean that they had a different father or mother? No! I would also list my grandfathers and my grandmothers but none of my aunts or uncles or cousins. Does that mean that they aren't related to me? Of course not. I wouldn't list them because I would only be tracing a **direct lineage** to me.

Let's turn to the Bible for an illustration. We know that Jacob had 12 sons but when we look at Jesus' lineage from Matthew and Luke we don't see the names of Gad, Asher, Dan, Benjamin, etc. It's not because the other 11 sons were of the serpent seed. It just means that they were not of the direct lineage. Only the son, grandson, great-grandson, etc. are listed but the nephews, nieces, and cousins are not included in a **direct** lineage.

The lineage in Matthew 1 is Joseph's lineage and the list in Luke 3 is Mary's lineage.[2] From David all the way back to Adam, Joseph and Mary shared the same ancestors. It was through David's son Nathan (Luke 3:31) that Mary was born and Joseph was born from David's son Solomon (Matthew 1:6). Nathan, however, **IS NOT** listed in Joseph's ancestry and Solomon **IS NOT** listed in Mary's heritage because only a **SINGLE** line is being traced. We also know that David had many other sons but none of them is listed.

So, Cain is only "missing" from the lineage because Jesus was not a **direct descendant** from Cain. After all, remember that all of Cain's lineage was destroyed in the flood and did not continue— so **NO ONE** (since the time of Noah) is a direct descendant of Cain—and no one is a direct descendant of any of Adam's other children except for Seth.

THE KENITES

Of course, ignoring the clear teaching of Scriptures about Cain's lineage being destroyed in the flood, we find that some people claim: "Cain's offspring in the Bible are called Kenites."[3]

Let's start by noticing that

"...the Kenites mentioned in Jeremiah 35 and 1 Chronicles 2:55 are not the children of the Cain of Genesis 4. First of all,

Scripture does not say that the Kenites are the children of the same Cain who slew Abel. Second, simply because both terms come from the same Hebrew word does not mean that all, some, or any Kenites are the descendents (sic) of the Cain who slew Abel....The Bible records at least 33 men by the name of Zechariah, and not all of them were related (e.g., there is no relationship between these men who were all named Zechariah: 1 Chron. 5:7; 24:25; 2 Chron. 21:2; 2 Kings 14:29). Therefore, individuals can be called the descendents (sic) of Cain, but the Cain they are related to was not the same Cain who slew Abel in Genesis 4 (see for instance, the different Kenites mentioned in Gen. 5:12; Num. 24:21, 22; Judges 1:16; and 1 Sam. 15:6). Third, some Kenites do acts of righteousness, and Johadab the Rechabite could be considered a righteous man of God (1 Sam. 15:6; 2 Kings 10:15, 16, 23, 24; Jer. 35:12-16). It would be impossible for them to be commended for their righteousness by both God and the Israelites if they were 'children of the devil.'"4

Notice, also, that the first mention of the Kenites is found in Genesis 15:19. This was **AFTER** the flood so the Kenites could not have been descendants of Cain but rather of one of Noah's sons (who came from Seth's lineage). As already mentioned, there are different people referred to as Kenites. For instance,

"Hobab, the son of Reuel, was a Kenite and acted as a guide to Israel in the wilderness ([Judges] 1:16; 4:11). Heber, was a Kenite (Judges 4:11 and 5:24 'Most blessed among women is Jael, The wife of Heber the Kenite.') Around the time of Israel's exodus from Egypt, the Kenites showed kindness to Israel (1 Sam 15:6), some Kenites entered the Promised Land along with the Israelites in the conquest led by Joshua (Judg 1:16).

"1 Chron 2:55 'And the families of the scribes who dwelt at Jabez were the Tirathites, the Shimeathites, and the Suchathites. These were the Kenites who came from Hammath, the father of the house of Rechab.' Notice all the families involved. This is there (sic) beginning, Recahab (sic) was the son [of] Rimmon, it does not say they came from Cain. A Kenite is member of the tribe of Kajin. Cain and Kenites are two different names."5

Hobab (mentioned above) was Moses' father-in-law so Moses' wife would have been a Kenite yet we know that Moses himself was a righteous man and God spoke face to face with him (Exodus 33:11). God Himself testified that Moses was a faithful man (Numbers 12:7). Would such a righteous man marry a demonic hybrid? We also know from Numbers 10 that Moses asked his in-laws to come with him and he promised that whatever good the Lord would bestow on Israel would be extended to them (Numbers 10:29-32). Would God bestow His blessings on the so-called "serpent seed"? Exodus tells us that Moses' father-in-law was the priest of Midian and we see that the Midianites were descendants of Abraham and Keturah (Genesis 25:2). Of course, Abraham was a descendant from Shem, Noah's son (Genesis 11:10, 26).

So, regardless of which group of Kenites is being referred to, we know that at least some of them were righteous and **ALL** of them were descendants of Noah and not Cain.

Finally, some people claim that Jesus was talking to the Kenites in John 8:44 when He said "Ye are of your father the devil...."[6] This point was covered in Chapter 3 but we need to remember that Jesus said to these Jews: **"I know that ye are Abraham's seed"** (John 8:37). A few verses later Jesus once again recognized their physical lineage by declaring "Your father Abraham" (John 8:56). There's no proof here that the Kenites were from Cain. In fact, if these were the Kenites that Jesus was talking to in John (and there is **NO** reason to believe that they were), then it would prove that the Kenites were from Abraham. Those trying to twist the Scripture have been caught in their own net.

5. THE NEPHILIM

Belief in the unbiblical theory of Satan producing Cain now results in the idea of the Nephilim. There are slightly varying ideas about the origins of the Nephilim. One popular unbiblical notion is that the Nephilim are space aliens.[1] "Allusions to the fallen angels occur in the Koran."[2] Some Rabbis teach that the sons of God and the Nephilim are the same.[3]

"According to Hebrew and other **LEGENDS** (the Book of Enoch and other non-Biblical writings), they were a race of giants and super-heroes who did acts of great evil. Their great size and power likely came from the mixture of demonic 'DNA' with human genetics."[4]

Many people today claim that the Nephilim "were the offspring of sexual relationships between the sons of God and daughters of men...."[5]

Luciferian Michael Ford agrees:

"As Cain was the embodiment of the fallen angels, who later slept with the daughters of Cain to bear the Nephilim, the race of Daemons and Human, who became devourers of flesh and blood, are by cunning standards our lineage and spiritual fathers. The magicians (sic) earthly symbol or model is Cain the Witchfather, as British Hereditary Witch Nathaniel Harris calls him; the First Satanist and Murderer."[6]

The concept of the Nephilim has been prevalent among New Agers and occultists although the fascination with this idea has been around for a long time. Back in the 15th century Cardinal Bishop of Tusculum claims that the Nephilim population totaled 133,306,668![7] For those who may not be familiar with this idea, here is a small sampling to show how popular this notion is.

☙ The name of a Gothic rock group is Fields of the Nephilim.[8] Their lyrics had mystical themes referencing "Sumerian Mythology, Chaos Magic and Aleister Crowley."[9]

֍ "Nephilim is a role-playing game by Chaosium, in which the players take on the roles of ancient spirits that can move from one human incarnation to another."[10]

֍ "Magic: The Gathering" is a collectible card game which includes creatures such as Glint-Eye Nephilim, Dune-Brood Nephilim, Yore-Tiller Nephilim, Witch-Maw Nephilim, and Ink-Treader Nephilim.[11]

֍ "The Polish heavy metal band Behemoth wrote a song called 'The Nephilim Rising' for their album Demigod."[12]

֍ "The Greek Melodic Death Metal band Septic Flesh have (sic) a song entitled 'Nephilim Sons' on their 5th album, Revolution DNA."[13]

֍ "In the video game Diablo II: Lord of Destruction the Ancients (sic) Ones are referred to as 'Spirits of the Nephilim.' They guard The Worldstone Keep, which leads to the Throne of Destruction, where Baal, the boss of the game resides."[14]

֍ A movie due out in 2009 is called *Nephilim*.[15]

֍ A review for a book entitled *The Last of the Red-Hot Vampires* states:

> "Portia Harding, a no-nonsense physicist, has accompanied her lifelong best friend, romance author Sarah, to England, where she is investigating everything from crop circles to seances. Left at a so-called fairy ring when Sarah runs back to the hotel for her camera, Portia inadvertently summons a spirit named Hope who bestows her gift of weather control and disappears. Swept up into the arms of gorgeous Theo and carried away—or kidnapped, as the pragmatic physicist in her contends—Portia is sure she is hallucinating. She doesn't believe in the paranormal until she discovers that Theo is a soulless nephilim (the offspring of an angel and a human) and that she must pass seven tests to be admitted to the Court of Divine Blood, which is essential since she now controls the weather, which follows her around in the form of a small cloud. MacAlister's fast-paced romp is a delight with all its quirky twists and turns, which even include a murder mystery."[16]

🪶 "In the video game Tomb Raider: The Angel of Darkness the Nephilim are angel-human hybrids that died out. The corpse of the only remaining full-blooded Nephilim is referred to as 'The Sleeper' and is brought to Prague in a sarcophagus by a cult that wishes to resurrect the species in order to bring about a 'New Order.'"[17]

🪶 Frank Black's song "All My Ghosts" contains a reference to the Nephilim in the following lyrics:

"Have you heard about the heavenly angels
How they came to earth and met some ladies
With whom they mated
And their young became giants every one."[18]

These are just a few secular references to the Nephilim but this idea is now overtaking the church world. For instance, Dr. Joye Jeffries Pugh, a Southern Baptist, states that when

"...these spiritual beings mated with earthly women, they produced an interbred race of hybrids called Giants. These mixed offspring were both spiritual and flesh. At death, these entities released evil spirits on the Earth because their spiritual side could not ever reenter Heaven after their flesh perished. These evil spirits, who are known to walk the earth in search of a body that is willing to be opened up to them, are called Demons."[19]

Another evangelical, Terry James, claims: "Nephilim, as they are called in the Bible, are satanic hybrids born of sexual union between fallen angels (demons) and women."[20]

As already mentioned, there is a lot of talk about the return of the Nephilim. Many books, TV programs, and movies are dealing with this. As Christians we need to see what the Bible—not Hollywood or occult literature—teaches about this.

GENESIS 6:4

The verse used to explain the Nephilim theory is found in Genesis 6:4: "There were giants in the earth in those days...." The Hebrew word for "giants" in this passage is "nphil." It is only used here and in Numbers 13:33. "Nphil," however, comes from the Hebrew root word "naphal" (although not all scholars accept this spelling[21]) and means "to fall." From this meaning many people claim that the Nephilim therefore are fallen angels or those who fell from heaven in spaceships.[22] For instance, Zecharia Sitchin alleges that "nephilim" means "those who were cast down" or "those who came down from above" but if the text meant to convey the idea of coming down from heaven, there is another Hebrew word that most likely would have been used. "Yarad" is the Hebrew word that means "to descend (literally, to go downwards; or conventionally to a lower region, as the shore, a boundary, the enemy, etc.; or figuratively, to fall)...." "Yarad" is used in 344 verses in the King James Bible in such places as:

➤ "And the Lord **came down** to see the city and the tower, which the children of men builded" (Genesis 11:5).

➤ "Go to, let us **go down,** and there confound their language, that they may not understand one another's speech" (Genesis 11:7).

➤ "I will **go down** now, and see whether they have done altogether according to the cry of it, which is come unto Me; and if not, I will know" (Genesis 18:21).

➤ "And she made haste, and **let down** her pitcher from her shoulder, and said, Drink, and I will give thy camels drink also..." (Genesis 24:46).

➤ "And he dreamed, and behold a ladder set up on the earth, and the top of it reached to heaven: and behold the angels of God ascending and **descending** on it" (Genesis 28:12).

➤ "And Joseph was **brought down** to Egypt..." (Genesis 39:1).

➤ "And the Lord **came down** upon mount Sinai..." (Exodus 19:20).

➤ "And the Lord **descended** in the cloud..." (Exodus 34:5).

↘ "Then she let them **down** by a cord through the window..." (Joshua 2:15).

↘ "So Michal **let** David **down** through a window..." (I Samuel 19:12).

↘ "Now when Solomon had made an end of praying, the fire **came down** from heaven, and consumed the burnt offering and the sacrifices; and the glory of the Lord filled the house" (II Chronicles 7:1).

↘ "They mount up to the heaven, they **go down** again to the depths..." (Psalm 107:26).

↘ "...I will cause the shower to **come down** in his season; there shall be showers of blessing" (Ezekiel 34:26).

The following references use **BOTH** "naphal" and "yarad" in the same verse: Ezekiel 30:6; 31:12; 32:24; Zechariah 11:2; and I Samuel 25:23. Ezekiel 32:27 has "yarad," "naphal," and "gibbowr" (which will be covered later) all in the same verse. If "to come down" was meant in Genesis 6:4, a different Hebrew word would have been used.

ANGELS DO NOT MARRY

Now, let's look at a few of the over 400 instances where the word "naphal" is used. This word means "to fall," "fugitive," "cease," "die," etc., and is used in passages such as Genesis 2:21 where God caused a deep sleep to **fall** upon Adam and Genesis 15:12 where a deep sleep **fell** on Abraham. The word is also used where Cain's countenance **fell** as well as where different people **fell** on their face. Ezekiel 11:5 says that the "Spirit of the Lord **fell** upon me." Yet another use of this word is where enemies **fell** before the sword, so to read into the Scriptures and try to make this word mean that fallen angels mated with women is a real stretch of the imagination. Besides, according to Matthew 22, Mark 12, and Luke 20 we find that the angels "neither marry, nor are given in marriage," yet Genesis 6:2

clearly reveals that "the sons of God saw the daughters of men that they were fair; and **THEY TOOK THEM WIVES** of all which they chose" so we know that since these "sons of God" married, they were not angels.

Fausset's Bible Dictionary remarks: "'Wives' and 'taking wives,' i.e. marriage, cannot be predicated of angels, fornication and going after strange flesh...."[23]

In about 600 references in the Bible to wife, wives, husband, husbands, marry, and marriage, we find that every single one of them is in reference to a union with a HUMAN man and woman. There is no hint whatsoever in any of these instances of other beings or angels mating with humans. The Bible is very specific that marriage was to be between a man and a woman. In fact, when the Pharisees asked Jesus about divorce, He said that Moses allowed a bill of divorcement because of the hardness of their hearts. He then added: "But **from the beginning of creation God made them male and female.** For this cause shall a man leave his father and mother, and cleave to his wife..." (Mark 10:6-7).

ALIEN ABDUCTION

Of course, there are some who do not want to accept this view. For instance, Thomas Horn writes:

"The familiar Genesis story of Watchers cohabiting with women parallels the modern 'abduction' reports in that the '...sons of God...took them wives of all which they chose.' The implication here is that, as in alien abduction, this was not by mutual agreement or harmony of wills, but that **these women were taken ('took') forcibly at the sole discretion of the powerful beings.** As a result of the abduction-marriages, hybrids were born of the genetic interruption called 'Nephilim.'"[24]

To see if he could be correct in his viewpoint we need to examine the word "took" which in the Hebrew language is "laqach." It is used over 900 times in the Bible. Below are a few verses where this same Hebrew word (in boldface) is used.

✧ "And the Lord God **took** the man, and put him into the garden of Eden to dress it and to keep it" (Genesis 2:15).

✧ "And the Lord God caused a deep sleep to fall upon Adam, and he slept: and He **took** one of his ribs, and closed up the flesh instead thereof" (Genesis 2:21).

✧ "And when the woman saw that the tree was good for food, and that it was pleasant to the eyes, and a tree to be desired to make one wise, she **took** of the fruit thereof, and did eat, and gave also unto her husband with her; and he did eat" (Genesis 3:6).

✧ "And Jacob said, Nay, I pray thee, if now I have found grace in thy sight, then **receive** my present at my hand: for therefore I have seen thy face, as though I had seen the face of God, and thou wast pleased with me. **Take,** I pray thee, my blessing that is brought to thee; because God hath dealt graciously with me, and because I have enough. And he urged him, and he **took** it" (Genesis 33:10-11).

✧ "And their father Israel said unto them, If it must be so now, do this; **take** of the best fruits in the land in your vessels, and carry down to the man a present, a little balm, and a little honey, spices, and myrrh, nuts, and almonds" (Genesis 43:11).

✧ "And I will **take** you to Me for a people, and I will be to you a God: and ye shall know that I am the Lord your God, which bringeth you out from under the burdens of the Egyptians" (Exodus 6:7).

✧ "Thou shalt guide me with Thy counsel, and afterward **receive** me to glory" (Psalm 73:24).

✧ "But thou shalt go unto my country, and to my kindred, and **take** a wife unto my son Isaac."

This Scripture passage shows that Rebekah had a choice in marrying Isaac: "And they called Rebekah and said unto her, Wilt thou go with this man? And she said, I will go" (Genesis 24:4). There was no forced abduction in this passage or any of the above instances.

After seeing a few instances where this same word is used, can one honestly claim that Genesis 6 implies an alien abduction and that **"these women were taken ('took') forcibly at the sole discretion of the powerful beings"?**[25]

Actually, there is a Hebrew word that is used several times in the Scriptures when a woman was "forced" or sexually abused. That word is "`anah." Let's look at some examples given in the Bible. In II Samuel 13 we have the instance where Amnon wanted to have sexual relations with his half-sister Tamar. When he finally got her in a situation where he was alone with her, he said:

> "Come lie with me, my sister. And she answered him, Nay, my brother, do not **force** [Hebrew: `anah] me; for no such thing ought to be done in Israel: do not thou this folly....Howbeit he would not hearken unto her voice: but, being stronger than she, **forced** her, and lay with her" (II Samuel 13:11b-12, 14; see also II Samuel 13:22, 32).

In the book of Judges we find that a stranger passing through the area was lodging with a man when the home was beset by homosexuals demanding that the stranger be brought out to them. The man said:

> "Behold, here is my daughter a maiden, and his concubine; them I will bring out now, and **humble** [Hebrew: `anah] ye them, and do with them what seemeth good unto you: but unto this man do not so vile a thing...so the man took his concubine, and brought her forth unto them and they knew her, and abused her all the night until the morning..." (Judges 19:24-25).

Later on the stranger recounted this story and said: "[T]he men of Gibeah rose against me, and beset the house round about upon me by night, and thought to have slain me: and my concubine have they **forced,** that she is dead" (Judges 20:5).

In Genesis we find this about Jacob's daughter, Dinah: "And when Shechem the son of Hamor the Hivite, prince of the country, saw her [Dinah], he took her, and lay with her, and **defiled** [Hebrew: `anah] her" (Genesis 34:2).

Below are a few more instances with the translation of the Hebrew word boldfaced:

→ "They **ravished** the women in Zion, and the maids in the cities of Judah" (Lamentations 5:11).

→ "In thee have they discovered their fathers' nakedness: in thee have they **humbled** her that was set apart for pollution" (Ezekiel 22:10).

→ "And one hath committed abomination with his neighbour's wife; and another hath lewdly defiled his daughter in law; and another in thee hath **humbled** his sister, his father's daughter" (Ezekiel 22:11).

→ "And it shall be, if thou have no delight in her, then thou shalt let her go whither she will; but thou shalt not sell her at all for money, thou shalt not make merchandise of her, because thou hast **humbled** her" (Deuteronomy 21:14).

→ "Then ye shall bring them both out unto the gate of that city, and ye shall stone them with stones that they die; the damsel, because she cried not, being in the city; and the man, because he hath **humbled** his neighbour's wife: so thou shalt put away evil from among you" (Deuteronomy 22:24).

While there are other meanings to the word "`anah," it is clear that the Hebrew language did have a word that would give the connotation of a forced sexual relationship. This implication, however, IS NOT even suggested in Genesis 6:2. Remember, too, that the Bible says that they took WIVES. A forced sexual relationship does not normally end in marriage.

Supposedly (at least to Horn), as "a result of the abduction-marriages, hybrids were born of the genetic interruption called 'Nephilim.'"[26]

But,

"...there is a very serious objection to the view that Nephilim are offspring of angels. No matter what translation you look at please note that the Nephilim were already on the earth when the sons of God went in to the daughters of men (v. 4). The Nephilim were not a result of the union, since they were already present before the union of 'God's sons' and 'mankind's daughters.'"[27]

Furthermore, we know from II Peter 2:4 that "God spared not the angels that sinned, but cast them down to hell [Greek: tartaroo], and delivered them into chains of darkness, to be reserved unto judgment."

This verse is the only time that the Greek word "tartaroo" is used in Scriptures. This is a special place for these angels to be confined until the day of judgment. In other words, these fallen angels are not walking the earth trying to find bodies to inhabit. They are already confined to hell.

Jude 1:6 also verifies this: "The angels which kept not their first estate, but left their own habitation, he hath reserved in everlasting chains under darkness unto the judgment of the great day." There is no hint that these angels produced children or even mingled with humans.

SONS OF GOD

In reference to the phrase "sons of God," we find that it is mentioned 11 times in Scripture, five of which are in the Old Testament.

Many teach that the "sons of God" as is mentioned in the book of Job is a reference to angels.

"The author of Job was aware of the term used for angel (Kalm mal'ak), as Eliphaz the Temanite used it in Job 4:18. So, if the sons of God were referring to angels, then why not say it?...

"Regardless though, Job 38:7 is an excellent example of angels being termed sons of God. However, this is referring to angels during the Creation Week, before any of them fell (which would have to be after God's declaration that everything was 'very good' in Genesis 1:31). So this doesn't give much support to fallen angels being called sons of God."[28]

We find the phrase "sons of God" six times in the New Testament and each time it refers to the children of God. For instance, John 1:12 says: "As many as received Him, to them gave He power to become the **sons of God,** even to them that believe on His name." Romans 8:14 says: "For as many as are led by the Spirit of God, they are the **sons of God.**"

The other New Testament verses are:

✝ "That ye may be blameless and harmless, the **sons of God,** without rebuke, in the midst of a crooked and perverse nation, among whom ye shine as lights in the world" (Philippians 2:15).

✝ "Behold, what manner of love the Father hath bestowed upon us, that we should be called the **sons of God:** therefore the world knoweth us not, because it knew Him not" (I John 3:1).

✝ "Beloved, now are we the **sons of God,** and it doth not yet appear what we shall be: but we know that, when He shall appear, we shall be like Him; for we shall see Him as He is" (I John 3:2).

✝ "For the earnest expectation of the creature waiteth for the manifestation of the **sons of God**" (Romans 8:19).

It is clear that godly men are referred to as "sons of God" so there is no need to try to interpret this phrase as alluding to the fallen angels.[29] We also see that Adam was called the "son of God" in Luke 3:38 so for Adam's children to be referred to as "sons of God" would not be a problem. Remember, after Seth was born we find that "then began men to call upon the name of the Lord" (Genesis 4:26). In Hosea 1:10 we find that the children of Israel are referred to as "the sons of the living God."

UNEQUAL YOKE

In regards to marriage, the Bible is very specific that the godly should not marry the ungodly. II Corinthians 6:14 warns: "Be ye not unequally yoked together with unbelievers: for what fellowship hath righteousness with unrighteousness? and what communion hath light with darkness?"

We also need to ask a question: Since when are **FALLEN** angels the sons of God? If they are the sons of God, are they redeemed? If they are redeemed, then they are not fallen! If they are fallen, then they are not the sons of God. Righteous angels would not commit this sin and fallen angels are not the sons of God.

With almost 800 references in the Bible to angel, angels, spirit, and spirits, we find that often these words have an identifying expression as well which lets us know if the "spirit" or "angel" being referred to is evil or good. Here are some examples.

✓ evil spirit/s (Acts 19:12, 13, 16; I Samuel 16:14; Judges 9:23; Luke 7:21; 8:2)

✓ familiar spirit/s (Leviticus 19:31; 20:6, 27; I Samuel 28:7, 8; I Chronicles 10:1; II Chronicles 33:6; Isaiah 9:19; 19:3; 29:4; Deuteronomy 18:11; I Samuel 28:3, 9; II Kings 21:6; 23:24)

✓ lying spirit (I Kings 22:22, 23; II Chronicles 18:21, 22)

✓ dumb (mute) spirit (Mark 9:17)

✓ foul spirit (Mark 9:25; Revelation 18:2)

✓ deaf spirit (Mark 9:25)

✓ a spirit of an unclean devil (Luke 4:33)

✓ perverse spirit (Isaiah 19:14)

✓ "spirit that now worketh in the children of disobedience" (Ephesians 2:18)

✓ spirit of fear (II Timothy 1:7)

✓ spirit of infirmity (Luke 13:11)

✓ spirit of divination (Acts 16:16)

✓ spirit of bondage (Romans 8:15)

✓ spirit of slumber (Romans 11:8)

✓ spirit of the world (I Corinthians 2:12)

✓ spirit that confesseth not Jesus (I John 4:3)

✓ spirit of antichrist (I John 4:3)

✓ spirit of error (I John 4:6)

✓ unclean spirit/s (Matthew 10:1; 12:43; Zechariah 13:2; Mark 1:23, 26, 27; 3:11, 30; 5:2, 8, 13; 6:7; 7:25; Luke 4:26; 6:18; 8:28; 9:42; 11:24; Acts 5:16; 8:7; Revelation 16:13)

✓ spirit of whoredoms (Hosea 4:12)

✓ "...possessed with devils: and He cast out the spirits..." (Matthew 8:16)

✓ spirits more wicked than himself (Matthew 12:45)

✓ spirits of devils (Revelation 16:14)

✓ seducing spirits (I Timothy 4:1)

✓ angel of the bottomless pit (Revelation 9:11)

✓ angels that sinned (II Peter 2:4)

✓ the devil and his angels (Matthew 25:41)

✓ evil angels (Psalm 78:49)

✓ angels which kept not their first estate (Jude 1:6)

✓ the dragon and his angels (Revelation 12:7)

✓ good spirit (Nehemiah 9:20)

✓ holy Spirit (Psalm 5:11; Isaiah 63:10, 11; Luke 11:13; Ephesians 1:13; 4:30, I Thessalonians 4:8)

✓ eternal Spirit (Hebrew 9:14)

✔ Spirit of truth (John 14:7)

✔ Spirit of the Lord (Judges 3:10; 6:34; 11:29; 13:25; 14:6, 19; 15:14; I Samuel 10:6; 16:13, 14; II Samuel 23:2; I Kings 18:12; 22:24; II Kings 2:16; II Chronicles 18:23; 20:14; Isaiah 11:2; 40:7, 13; 59:19; 61:1; 63:14; Ezekiel 11:5; 37:1; Micah 2:7; 3:8; Luke 4:18; Acts 5:9; 8:39; II Corinthians 3:17, 18)

✔ spirit of prophecy (Revelation 19:10)

✔ God says: "My spirit" (Genesis 6:3; Isaiah 30:1; 59:21; Joel 2:29)

✔ Spirit of your Father (God) (Matthew 10:20)

✔ Spirit of Christ (I Peter 1:11; Romans 8:9)

✔ Spirit of His Son (Jesus) (Galatians 4:6)

✔ spirit of wisdom (Ephesians 1:17; Isaiah 11:2; Deuteronomy 34:9; Exodus 28:3)

✔ holy Spirit of God (Ephesians 4:30)

✔ Spirit of Jesus Christ (Philippians 1:19)

✔ Spirit of God (Genesis 1:2; 41:38; Exodus 31:3; 35:31; Numbers 24:2; I Samuel 10:10; 11:6; 19:20, 23; II Chronicles 15:1; 24:20; Job 27:3; 33:4; Ezekiel 11:24; Matthew 3:16; 12:28; Romans 8:9, 14; 15:19; I Corinthians 2:11, 14; 3:16; 7:40; 12:3; Ephesians 4:30; I John 4:2; Revelation 3:1; 4:5; 5:6)

✔ spirit of holiness (Romans 1:4)

✔ Spirit of life (Romans 8:2; Revelation 11:11)

✔ Spirit of adoption (Romans 8:15)

✔ Spirit of the living God (II Corinthians 3:3)

✔ spirit that confesseth Jesus (I John 4:2)

✔ spirit of grace (Hebrews 10:29; Zechariah 12:10)

✓ ministering spirits (Hebrews 1:14)

✓ holy angel (Acts 10:22)

✓ the angel Gabriel was sent from God (Luke 1:26)

✓ angel of His presence (Isaiah 63:9)

✓ God said: "I send an Angel" (Exodus 23:20)

✓ angel of light (II Corinthians 11:14)

✓ angel from heaven (Galatians 1:8)

✓ God said: "Mine Angel" (Exodus 23:23; 32:24; Revelation 22:16)

✓ angel of the Lord (Genesis 16:7, 9, 10, 11; 22:11, 15; Exodus 3:2; Numbers 22:22, 23, 24, 25, 26, 27, 31, 32, 34, 35; Judges 2:1, 4; 5:23; 6:11, 12, 21, 22; 13:3, 13, 15, 16, 17, 18, 20, 21; II Samuel 24:16; I Kings 19:7; II Kings 1:3, 15; 19:35; I Chronicles 21:12, 15, 16, 18, 30; Psalm 34:7; 35:5, 6; Isaiah 37:36; Zechariah 1:11, 12; 3:1, 5, 6, 12:8; Matthew 1:20, 24; 2:13, 19; 28:2; Luke 1:11, 2:9; Acts 5:19; 7:30; 8:26; 12:7; 12:23)

✓ The Lord "will send His angel" (Genesis 24:40)

✓ Abraham said: "The Angel which redeemed me from all evil" (Genesis 48:16)

✓ angel of the church (Revelation 2:8)

✓ angel/s of God (Judges 6:20; Genesis 28:12; 32:1; Matthew 22:30; Luke 12:8, 9; 15:10; John 1:51; Hebrews 1:6)

✓ Michael and his angels (Revelation 12:7)

✓ holy angels (Matthew 25:31)

✓ angels which are in heaven (Mark 12:25)

✓ angels of heaven (Matthew 24:36)

✓ elect angels (I Timothy 5:21)

If the text was intended to convey the message that the "sons of God" were good angels or the fallen angels, one of the above expressions would most likely have been used so that we would have had no doubt as to what was meant.

"THERE WERE GIANTS IN THE EARTH"

Let's return to Genesis 6:4: "There **WERE** giants in the earth in those days; **AND ALSO AFTER THAT,** when the sons of God came in unto the daughters of men, and they bare children to them, the same became mighty men which were of old, men of renown."

Notice that the giants were in the land **BEFORE** the sons of God mated with the daughters of men so this mating (whether human, demonic, angelic, or alien) **WAS NOT** the cause of the giants.[30]

We will now look at the phrase "the same became mighty men." Patrick Heron, author of *The Nephilim and the Pyramid of the Apocalypse,* writes:

> "The offspring of the Nephilim were the gibbor, or giants; Hybrids of humans with the Fallen Angels. Enoch contends that the demons that inhabit the world today are the dispossessed spirits of these offspring of angels with humans."[31]

Thomas Horn states:

> "Don't be quick to bypass this question, as the 'Mighty ones' of the King James and other Bible versions is **Gibborim**—the same Hebrew term **used elsewhere in ancient literature to describe the Nephilim** which are correctly translated here in the Greek [Septuagint] as 'giants.'"[32]

Stephanie Michelle Whitaker, a graduate of the Institute of Jewish Studies, believes that the "Gibborim were the Demonic Offspring of the Nefilim and the human women."[33]

Clyde Lewis claims:

> "They are half fallen angel and half human being. They are the Gibborim, mighty men of renown like Hercules the Titan.

They are the stock that the antichrist will come from. They are fully fallen hosts and fully man. They were here before the flood and AFTER.

"They are the alien hybrids, greys, and UFOs of modern times.

"They are the seed of Satan."[34] [Emphasis in the original.]

Although there are slight variances, the basic idea presented from the above quotes is that the gibborim were either the Nephilim or the offspring of the Nephilim. Are either of these views correct according to the Bible? Let's go to the Bible and find out!

The Hebrew word for "mighty" is "gibbowr" and means champion, chief, strong man, valiant man, giant, warrior, or tyrant. In fact, the modern Hebrew meaning of this word is simply "Hero."[35]

BUNGLING OAFS

The Hebrew sure gives a different meaning to this word than Patrick Heron does. He states:

"The giants were probably **BUNGLING OAFS.** That's why a 17 year old youth called David could skip around Goliath and sink a stone in his head before he had time to draw his sword.

"And why the Israelites under Joshua could conquer the Promised Land and capture '60 of the giant cities of Bashan.'"[36]

Heron is saying that these giants (or gibborim, gibbor, gibbowr) were basically clumsy or stupid since that is the meaning of "oaf."[37] He thinks that Goliath (a gibborim) was so inept that it was no big deal for David to be able to kill him. The Bible, however, presents a completely different picture. For forty days Goliath taunted the Israelites and dared them to send a man to fight him (Samuel 17:16). He

"...had an helmet of brass upon his head, and he was armed with a coat of mail; and the weight of the coat was five thousand shekels of brass. And he had greaves of brass upon his legs, and a target of brass between his shoulders. And the staff of his spear was like a weaver's beam; and his spear's head weighed six hundred shekels of iron: and one bearing a shield went before him. And he stood and cried unto the armies of Israel, and said unto them, Why are ye come out to set your battle in array? am not I a Philistine, and ye servants to Saul? choose you a man for you, and let him come down to me. If he be able to fight with me, and to kill me, then will we be your servants: but if I prevail against him, and kill him, then shall ye be our servants, and serve us....And all the men of Israel, when they saw the man, fled from him, and were sore afraid" (I Samuel 17:5-9, 24).

When David heard the giant's dare, he told Saul: "Let no man's heart fail because of him; thy servant will go and fight with this Philistine" (I Samuel 17:32). Saul's response was: "Thou art not able to go against this Philistine to fight with him: for thou art but a youth, and he a MAN OF WAR FROM HIS YOUTH" (I Samuel 17:33). Goliath was not a "bungling oaf." He was a warrior and a man of war. Had the Israelites thought he was a bungling oaf, they would not have feared him. Furthermore, David didn't kill Goliath in his own strength or because of his own ability. He said that the "battle is the Lord's" (I Samuel 17:47) and that the Lord would be the one who would deliver the Israelites.

Heron also mentioned that Joshua could conquer the Promised Land because these giants were "bungling oafs."[38] He makes these conquests seem simple but they were not simple—they were miraculous feats because of the Lord's help. Moses told the Israelites: "Hear, O Israel: Thou art to pass over Jordan this day, to go in to possess nations **GREATER AND MIGHTIER** than thyself, cities great and fenced up to heaven" (Deuteronomy 9:1). Other such verses are found in Deuteronomy 4:38; 7:1; 11:23 and Numbers 13:28. Without the Lord fighting for the Israelites, the conquests would not have been accomplished. We also know that when the Israelites had spied out the land they came back with the report that the inhabitants were stronger than they were. Only Joshua and Caleb thought that they were able to conquer the land. Because of the Israelites' reluctance to conquer the Promised Land, the Lord told them that they would not be able to enter the land. After hearing this verdict, the people mourned and

> "...they rose up early in the morning, and gat them up into the top of the mountain, saying, Lo, we be here, and will go up unto the place which the Lord hath promised: for we have sinned. And Moses said, Wherefore now do ye transgress the commandment of the Lord? but it shall not prosper. Go not up, for the Lord is not among you; that ye be not smitten before your enemies. For the Amalekites and the Canaanites are there before you, and ye shall fall by the sword: because ye are turned away from the Lord, therefore the Lord will not be with you. But they presumed to go up unto the hill top: nevertheless the ark of the covenant of the Lord, and Moses, departed not out of the camp. Then the Amalekites came down, and the Canaanites which dwelt in that hill, and smote them, and discomfited them, even unto Hormah" (Numbers 14:40-45).

In other words, these inept "bungling oafs" overcame the Israelites and killed them when the Lord was not with Israel. In fact, as already mentioned, the word "gibbowr" means champion, strong man, valiant man, warrior, etc., so the giants couldn't have been so inept. (As an extra note, it should be noticed that Amalek was from Abraham's lineage. He was his great-great-grandson [Genesis 36:12]. He was not from Cain's or even Ham's lineage.)

ARE GIBBORIM HYBRIDS?

Thomas Horn claims that the word "gibborim" is "the same Hebrew term **used elsewhere in ancient literature to describe the Nephilim....**"[39] To see if this is true, we need to look at several Bible references where the word "gibbowr" is mentioned. This will help us see if the gibborim are actually hybrids or half-demon, half-human offspring.

In Joshua 8, when the children of Israel were ready to conquer Ai, Joshua chose 30,000 **mighty** [Hebrew: gibbowr] men of valour" to go to war. These weren't giants. They were heroic men from among the Israelites who were able to fight a battle. Jephthah, who became a judge of Israel, was called a "**mighty** man of valour." King David was called "a **mighty** valiant man, and a man of war." David certainly wasn't a giant or there wouldn't have been any concern about his safety when he fought Goliath. David himself had a group of **mighty** men, one of whom was Uriah, the husband of Bathsheba. In II Chronicles 17 we find that at least 700,000 "**mighty** men" waited on King Jehoshaphat. If it were true that the gibborim (or mighty men) were giants, that would be a lot of giants in Israel but we need to remember that Jehoshaphat was a good king and God was with him so it would be hard to believe that he had that many half-demon attendants. In II Chronicles 13 we see that there was a war between the king of Israel and the king of Judah and there were 400,000 **mighty** men on one side and 800,000 on the other side. This would be over 1 million so-called "giants" or gibborim involved in just this one war between Israel and Judah!! Remember, too, these "gibborim" are ISRAELITES. There were not of some surrounding pagan nation. Even God is referred to as **"mighty"** [Hebrew: gibbowr]. Obviously, God was not half-demon or the offspring of the Nephilim.

If we would get back to the Bible and study it, we would not be so apt to fall for "Jewish fables" (Titus 1:14).

Below are a few more references (in boldface) where the Hebrew word "gibbowr" is used.

❊ "For the Lord your God is God of gods, and Lord of lords, a great God, a **mighty,** and a terrible, which regardeth not persons, nor taketh reward" (Deuteronomy 10:17).

❊ "And their brethren among all the families of Issachar were valiant men of **might,** reckoned in all by their genealogies fourscore and seven thousand" (I Chronicles 7:5). (Notice the number of these mighty men: 87,000—and that's just the families of Issachar!)

❊ "Now therefore, our God, the great, the **mighty,** and the terrible God, who keepest covenant and mercy..." (Nehemiah 9:32).

❊ "Which is as a bridegroom coming out of his chamber, and rejoiceth as a **strong man** to run a race" (Psalm 19:5).

❊ "Who is this King of glory? The Lord strong and **mighty,** the Lord **mighty** in battle" (Psalm 24:8).

❊ "Bless the Lord, ye His angels, that **excel** in strength, that do His commandments, hearkening unto the voice of His word" (Psalm 103:20).

❊ "His seed shall be **mighty** upon earth: the generation of the upright shall be blessed" (Psalm 112:2).

❊ "...Naomi had a kinsman of her husband's, a **mighty** man of wealth...."

❊ "A lion which is **strongest** among beasts, and turneth not away for any" (Proverbs 30:30).

❊ "For unto us a child is born, unto us a son is given: and the government shall be upon His shoulder: and *His name shall be called Wonderful, Counsellor, The* ***mighty*** *God, The everlasting Father, The Prince of Peace"* (Isaiah 9:6).

❊ "The remnant shall return, even the remnant of Jacob, unto the **mighty** God" (Isaiah 10:21).

❊ "The Lord thy God in the midst of thee is **mighty...**" (Zephaniah 3:17).

> "The word gibborim is used in the Tanakh [the Old Testament] in excess of 150 times and applied to men as well as lions (Book of Proverbs 30:30), hunters (Genesis 10:9), soldiers (Book of Jeremiah 51:30) and leaders (Book of Daniel 11:3)."[40]

NEPHILIM ARE NOT THE FALLEN ANGELS

Hopefully you will be able to see **FROM THE BIBLE** that the Nephilim and the gibborim **ARE NOT** the fallen angels nor the offspring of the fallen angels.

Let's once again return to Genesis 6:4: "There were giants in the earth in those days; and also after that, when the sons of God came in unto the daughters of men, and they bare children to them, the same became mighty men which were of old, men of renown." We will now look at the phrase "men of renown."

The word "renown" (Hebrew: shame) means honor or authority. It is usually translated simply as "name" as in Genesis when Adam gave **names** to all the cattle or where Adam called his son's **name** Seth or in Genesis 4 where men began to call "upon the **name** of the Lord." We need to be careful that we don't read more into this verse than is there.

We also notice that Genesis 6:4 uses the Hebrew word "iysh" as in "men [iysh] of renown." "Iysh" is used over 1400 times in the Hebrew and means "a man as an individual or a male person."

"This term is used consistently as 'man' or descendants of Adam—even Adam used it of himself in Genesis 2:23, yet it is never used of fallen angel (sic), demons, or of Satan. It was used for some unfallen angels when they took the form of a man, though. If the Nephilim were crossbreeds between men and fallen angels, then why did the Bible use the term men (iysh) as opposed to something that would lead us to believe they were not fully men?

"If we follow the context of **iysh** into the following verses in Genesis 6, we find:

"Verse 4: Nephilim are **men** of renown

"Verse 5: wickedness of **man** great

"Verse 6: God sorry He made **man** on earth

"Verse 7: Blot out **man** from earth

"Verse 8/9: Noah found favor with God and was a righteous **man**

"The context reveals that Noah was compared with and amongst the men being discussed in Genesis 6, yet unlike them he was righteous (Genesis 6:9). There is no mention of Noah being fully human and other men being half-breeds, but merely that he was righteous among them. Having Noah be righteous among his generations is slight support for the view that sees the sons of God as human."[41]

With this in mind, we also find in Genesis 4:1 that Cain was likewise a man: "And Adam knew Eve his wife; and she conceived, and bare Cain, and said, I have gotten a **MAN** [Hebrew: iysh] from the Lord." He was not a half-demon, half-human hybrid. Goliath was also called a man:

> "...behold, there came up the **champion** [iysh], the Philistine of Gath, Goliath by name, out of the armies of the Philistines...And all the **men** [iysh] of Israel when they saw the **man** [iysh], fled from him, and were sore afraid. And the **men** [iysh] of Israel said, Have ye seen this **man** [iysh] that is come up? surely to defy Israel is he come up: and it shall be, that the **man** [iysh] who killeth him, the king will enrich him with great riches..." (I Samuel 17:23-25, in part).

Did you notice that the same word "iysh" is used for Goliath as well as the Israelites? There is no differentiation that one is fully human and the other is a hybrid consisting of half-demon.

The Scripture also plainly tells us in Numbers 23:19: "God is NOT a man [iysh]...." "I am God and not man [iysh]..." (Hosea 11:9).

Clearly, there is **NO** Biblical support for the idea that the Nephilim are the fallen angels or the offspring of the fallen angels. Remember, Jesus Himself told us that that angels "neither marry, nor are given in marriage" (Matthew 22:30; Mark 12:25; Luke 20:34-36).

In the next chapter we will consider the reason why God sent the Flood.

6. WHY WAS THE FLOOD SENT?

Genesis 6 tells us that "it repented the Lord that He had made man on the earth, and it grieved Him at His heart. And the Lord said, I will destroy man whom I have created from the face of the earth...for it repenteth Me that I have made them" (Genesis 6:5-7).

Some people, basing their beliefs on a statement found in some Apocryphal books such as the *Book of Enoch,* the *Book of Jasher,* the *Book of Jubilees,* etc., have purported that God sent the flood to destroy the animals (as well as humans) because the animals had had genetic modification and cross-species experiments performed on them.[1] For instance, the *Book of Jasher* says that men "taught the mixture of animals of one species with the other, in order therewith to provoke the Lord....And the Lord said, I will blot out man that I created from the face of the earth... (Jasher 4:18-19).

Talk show host, Steve Quayle, believes that Adam and Eve were not the first people on earth. He believes that that discinction "belonged to an **EVOLVED** people called the Nephilim (i.e., the fallen ones)" and that the Nephilim were here thousands of years before Adam and Eve appeared on the scene. He alleges that when Adam and Eve left the Garden of Eden they took up residence with the already-existing Nephilim and they started mating with each other and from these unions, the giants were born.[2]

He further speculates that the fallen angels wanted to clothe

"...themselves with flesh that already existed. That which already existed included the fish of the sea, the fowl of the air, the beasts of the field. Of course, they found that the beasts best suited their purpose. But how did they eventually **EVOLVE** out of them a people bearing their image? In this fashion: when they abandoned their natural abode, Lucifer and the many angels loyal to him made their way into this material world and started playing around in the animals. As spirits, they entered the beasts at will.

And as beings of a higher order, they quickly gained complete control over them. Their play with the animals no doubt took many forms, but they probably derived their greatest fun and pleasure in matings. Naturally, the more these spirits played around the more they got themselves entangled in the flesh and its lusts. In time, the world of the flesh began to exert such an irresistible pull upon them that they became permanent incarnations in the beasts. From these incarnations sprang the Nephilim who—millenniums later—fathered the giants.

"Of course, even while they lived in Nephilim bodies these fallen angels still bore God's image. So it happened that after a long period of **EVOLUTION** the outward appearances of the animals, particularly the two-footed ones, began to undergo changes that brought their facial and bodily features into a closer resemblance to the images of the rebellious spirits with them. Thus, by the year 4004 B.C., they looked strikingly similar to Adam."[3]

Dr. Yulish claims that the sons of Elohim

"...merge[d] their DNA with a range of earth animals in an attempt to physically replenish their numbers. The result of this action sees the conception of a collection of beasts now relegated to human mythology. Some of which include 'centures' (sic), 'satyrs,' 'elephant headed gods' and 'multiple limbed humanoids.'"[4]

NEPHILIM INCLUDED THE PEGASUS

Another source states that God "destroyed the seed of the Nephilim which included the Pegasus, Minotaur, Cyclops, Centaur, etc."[5]

Did God REALLY send the flood to get rid of such creatures? Let's consider what the Bible reveals about this. At the beginning of creation we find that

"...God created great whales, and every living creature that moveth, which the waters brought forth abundantly, **after their kind,** and every winged fowl **after his kind:** and God saw that it was good....And God said, Let the earth bring forth the living creature **after his kind,** cattle, and creeping thing, and beast of the earth **after his kind:** and it was so. And God made the beast of the earth **after his kind,** and cattle **after their kind,** and every thing that creepeth upon the earth **after his kind:** and God saw that it was good" (Genesis 1:21, 24-25).

The word "kind" in Hebrew means "species," "sort," or "form."

God had pronounced that His creation was good but did fallen angels or the Nephilim tamper with the animals' and birds' DNA and create hybrid creatures such as centaurs, satyrs, chimeras, etc.? Was this why God sent the flood? Did He want to rid the earth of such monstrosities? The simple answer is: **NO!** If God wanted to wipe out these creatures, why did He tell Noah to spare two of each of them? He said:

"...of **EVERY** living thing of **ALL** flesh, two of **EVERY SORT** shalt thou bring into the ark, to *keep them alive* with thee; they shall be male and female. Of fowls after their kind, and of cattle after their kind, of **EVERY** creeping thing of the earth after his kind, two of **EVERY SORT** shall come unto thee, to *keep them alive*" (Genesis 6:19-20; see also Genesis 7:2-3).

When the flood was over, God said: "Bring forth with thee every living thing that is with thee, of all flesh, both of fowl, and of cattle, and of every creeping thing that creepeth upon the earth; **that they may breed abundantly in the earth, and be fruitful, and multiply upon the earth**" (Genesis 8:17). Why would God destroy the earth because of genetic manipulation yet tell Noah to spare some of the hybrids, and then turn around and command that they breed **ABUNDANTLY** and **MULTIPLY** on the earth? Wouldn't such a theory suggest that God was fickle, irrational, confused, and inconsistent?

Also, if Noah had taken these monstrosities into the ark, then we would **still** see such creatures today as the minotaur, satyr, centaur, etc., as they were told multiply.

You may wonder why the animals were destroyed if they weren't misfits. Well, one possible reason is that God didn't want the animal kingdom to increase and overpower mankind. The animals had already multiplied for about 1500 years when the flood came. Since life and vegetation was destroyed with the flood, the animals would not have been able to survive. Their vast quantities would have outnumbered mankind and mankind would not have been able to survive. The animals would have contended for any surviving food source—including humans.

When the Israelites were to conquer the Canaan land, the Lord told them that He would put out the nations little by little. They were not to "consume them at once, lest the beasts of the field increase upon thee" (Deuteronomy 7:22). The same thing most likely applied to the animals when the flood came.

Another theory put forth about why God sent the flood was to rid the earth of the Nephilim.

WAS CAIN SATAN'S SEED?

Dr. Pugh alleges:

"Through Cain, **Satan had created a human from his own seed.** Cain was the first offspring produced as a result of the Sons of God mating with a woman. Cain's birth and his choice to remain possessed by Satan produced the mixed blood line—first of the Nephilim and then that of the Dragon Kings. This mixed lineage is how Satan, the guardian of sacred knowledge, came to live and reign among man in the world."[6]

What caused God to destroy mankind? Some evangelicals (as well as occultists) teach that the flood came because of the Nephilim and their offspring. Pugh states: "The Bible states forthright that God brought the Great Flood in Noah's day to destroy the Nephilim (Giants) and the wicked flesh of Satan's lineage through Cain."[7] "This union produced the Giants, and was the reason given as to why the Flood was brought upon the Earth."[8]

She claims that the Bible states this—but she failed to provide a verse. Perhaps the reason a verse is not supplied is because **THERE IS NO SUCH VERSE!**

Please notice that Pugh believes that **"Satan had created a human from his own seed"**[9] and that the flood came to destroy this seed. The Bible, however, states: "And the Lord said, **I** will destroy **MAN WHOM I HAVE CREATED** from the face of the earth; both man, and beast, and the creeping thing, and the fowls of the air; for it repenteth Me that **I HAVE MADE THEM**" (Genesis 6:7). "For yet seven days, and I will cause it to rain upon the earth forty days and forty nights; and **every living substance THAT I HAVE MADE will I destroy** from off the face of the earth." In other words, all that was destroyed came from God's hands—not Satan's, the fallen angels', or men's hands (Genesis 7:4). In Jeremiah God says: "I have made the earth, the man and the beast that are upon the ground, by My great power and by My outstretched arm, and have given it unto whom it seemed meet unto Me" (Jeremiah 27:5). "I have made the earth, and created man upon it..." (Isaiah 45:12).

The Hebrew word for man in the above reference is "adam" and is used in 527 verses such as:

➤ "And God said, Let us make **man** in our image..." (Genesis 1:26).

➤ "So God created **man** in His own image, in the image of God created He him; male and female created he them" (Genesis 1:27).

➤ "And the Lord God formed **man** of the dust of the ground, and breathed into his nostrils the breath of life; and **man** became a living soul" (Genesis 2:7).

➤ "And the Lord God planted a garden eastward in Eden; and there He put the **man** whom He had formed" (Genesis 2:8).

If the "Nephilim" were from Satan and not from God, why did God say that **HE** made them? Also, if the Nephilim were from

Satan, then the flood wasn't sent to destroy them because the flood only destroyed the creatures that God made. If the flood was only sent to destroy the Nephilim, then why were those from Seth's lineage also destroyed? Neither of these ideas is consistent with the Scriptures. When people go outside of Scripture, the theories they put forth just don't line up with God's Word.

Notice, too, that Genesis 5 gives us the lineage of Seth. It **SPECIFICALLY** tells us that Adam begat Seth who begat Enos all the way down to Lamech who begat Noah. If the so-called Nephilim had interbred with Seth's lineage, when did it take place since each male listed here in Genesis 5 was directly begotten from a **human** father starting with Adam? These are human men begetting children. Where do the "fallen angels" enter into this picture? Even in Genesis 4 where we find Cain's lineage, we only see a human father begetting a human child. Even if Cain had been Satan's son (and he definitely was not), each succeeding generation would contain less and less of the so-called serpent seed. For instance, his grandson would only be 1/8th serpent seed and his great-great grandson would only have 1/32nd or about 3% of the tainted seed. By the time of the flood, there wouldn't have been much "serpent seed" left—and the flood destroyed **ALL** of Cain's remaining lineage.

FLOOD WAS BECAUSE OF WICKEDNESS

We know from the Bible that the flood came because of man's wickedness: "God saw that the wickedness of man was great in the earth, and that every imagination of the thoughts of his heart was only evil continually....The earth also was corrupt before God, and the earth was filled with violence" (Genesis 6:5, 11).

Since we have already shown from the Scriptures that the Nephilim were not the fallen angels nor their offspring, statements such as those given by Pugh cannot be true. Furthermore, if the Nephilim came from Cain's lineage and God sent the flood to destroy them, why was Seth's lineage also destroyed? In fact, Genesis 5:4

tells us that after Adam had Cain, Abel, and Seth, he also had other sons and daughters. **ALL** of their lineages were destroyed in the flood along with all the animals. Genesis 7:21-23 clearly states:

> "And **ALL** flesh died that moved upon the earth, both of fowl, and of cattle, and of beast, and of every creeping thing that creepeth upon the earth, and **EVERY MAN:** All in whose nostrils was the breath of life, of all that was in the dry land, died. And every living substance was destroyed which was upon the face of the ground, both man, and cattle, and the creeping things, and the fowl of the heaven; and they were destroyed from the earth: and **NOAH ONLY REMAINED ALIVE, AND THEY THAT WERE WITH HIM IN THE ARK.**"

Considering that **ALL** of Cain's lineage (as well as the other lineages) were destroyed in the flood, there remained **NONE** of his bloodline. Even if Cain had been Satan's seed, **ALL** of this bloodline perished and, therefore, could no longer produce any further "serpent seed" lineage. As already mentioned, we know **FROM THE SCRIPTURES** that Cain **WAS NOT** from Satan's seed but even if he had been, the flood **ENDED** all reproduction from this heritage.

To try to get around the clear teaching of the Scriptures, several more theories are suggested. One idea is that Noah's wife was from Cain's lineage. According to the *Sefer haYashar (midrash)* Noah's wife was the sister of Tubal-Cain (from Cain's lineage) but she was not the mother of Shem, Ham, and Japheth.[10] Just supposing this is true (and there is **NO** Scriptural basis to suggest that it is), when Noah's wife died, then Cain's lineage ceased forever since she was supposedly the last person surviving from his line. Since it is claimed that she was not the mother of Noah's sons, the "serpent seed" lineage could not have continued through them.

DID GOD "FORGET"?

Of course, if God had sent the flood to destroy the "serpent seed," do you think He would have "forgotten" that Noah's wife was of the serpent seed? Do you think God would have destroyed **ALL** of the other people but just happened to "miss" Noah's wife? God wouldn't be that foolish!

DID OG SURVIVE THE FLOOD?

Another idea put forth is that the giant Og survived the flood. According to the *Jewish Encyclopedia* there are several legends about this.

> "Og was not destroyed at the time of the Flood (Niddah 61a), for, according to one legend, the waters reached only to his ankles....Another tradition states that he fled to Palestine, where there was no flood (Rashi to Niddah, *ad loc.*); while, according to a third legend, he sat on a rung of the ladder outside the ark, and, after he had sworn to be a slave to Noah and his children, received his food each day through a hole made in the side of the ark...."[11]

Og's age is given as 3600 years and his height, according to Kazwini, is 23,330 ells.[12] An ell varies from 27-45 inches so that would make Og somewhere between approximately 52,492 and 87,487 feet tall or about 10 to 16 **MILES** tall! (Now that's a really **TALL** tale!) Mount Everest is the highest mountain and it is only 29,035 feet high.[13]

At the height of Mount Everest, we find that the sky is dark. "The sky is black for a simple reason. There is not enough air up there to scatter light. There is not enough air up there to sustain human life for more than a few hours."[14]

> "'Very few people can stay indefinitely at altitudes above 5,500 m (18,000 ft), and thrive,' says Robert Schoene, a high-altitude physiologist at the University of Washington. The main obstacle: the amount of oxygen available for breathing. Oxygen is the gas nearly all organisms depend on to survive. Living things use oxygen to metabolize, or burn food for fuel and energy."[15]

Now, if Og were about 2-3 times taller than Mount Everest, and most people couldn't survive on Mt. Everest because of the low level of oxygen, how could have Og lived at a much higher altitude and survived for 3600 years? Even more amazing is how he could sit on a rung of a ladder outside the ark. How much would have Og weighed at his height? I didn't know ladder rungs (or the ark) could withstand such weight or that the ark was that large. According to the Bible the ark was thirty cubits or about 45 feet high (Genesis 6:15).

Of course, these aren't the only problems with this "tall tale."

Wouldn't each step he took cause an earthquake? Yet the first earthquake did not occur until the days of Moses when the children of Israel were in the wilderness (see Number 16:30).

How much food would he need to consume each day to stay alive? How or where would he sit down? (A ladder rung would never suffice!) Where did he live? The Egyptian Pyramid was the tallest building in the world for 4,500 years (until the 19th century) and that was only about 450 feet high.[16] The tallest building now (as of November 2008) is only 1,670.6 feet high[17] (although in 2009 a new structure should reach 2,684 feet high[18]). Even the new structure is only 1/2 mile high yet Og was supposed to be 10 to 16 miles tall. If such a building did exist at that time there would have to be some evidence of its remains but none survive.

Where would Og sleep? According to the Bible, Og's bedstead was nine cubits long and four cubits wide (Deuteronomy 3:11). A cubit is approximately 18 inches so his bed was about 13.5 feet by 6 feet. Normally, a bed would be LONGER than the person occupying it. If so, then Og was less than 13.5 feet. He may have even had a bed much larger than necessary such "as Alexander the Great did for each of his foot soldiers, to impress the Indians with an idea of the extraordinary strength and stature of his men...."[19] At any rate, the "Jewish fable" and the Bible are in conflict but the Bible account is far more realistic.

We also know from the Bible that Og was the king of Bashan (Numbers 21:33; 32:33; Deuteronomy 1:4; 3:1, 3, 11; 4:47; 29:7;

Joshua 9:10; 12:4; 13:30; I Kings 4:19; Nehemiah 9:22; Psalm 135:11; 136:20) and that the Israelites killed him in one of the battles (Numbers 21:32-35).

Here is the **LEGEND** (not the Biblical account) of how Og was killed:

"During the battle of Edrei (Num 21.33) Og sat on the city wall, his legs, which were eighteen ells long, reaching down to the ground; Moses did not know what monster he had before him until God told him that it was Og. Og hurled an entire mountain against the Israelites, but Moses intercepted it (Deut. R. l.c.). According to another legend, Og uprooted a mountain three miles long, intending to destroy all Israel at once by hurling it upon their camp, which was also three miles in length; but while he was carrying it upon his head a swarm of locusts burrowed through it, so that it fell round his neck. When he attempted to throw off this unwieldy necklace long teeth grew from both sides of his mouth and kept the mountain in place. Thereupon Moses, who was himself ten ells tall, took an ax of equal length, jumped upward ten ells, so that he could reach Og's ankles, and thus killed him (Ber. 54b).

"Shabbat (151b) and 'Erubin (48a) also indicate that Og was regarded as an unusually large giant. A legend says that a grave-digger pursued a stag three miles inside of one of Og's bones without reaching the other end (Niddah 24b)."[20]

This legend claims that Moses himself was ten ells tall which would make him about 22.5 feet to 37.5 feet tall. Wouldn't this make Moses one of the Nephilim giants if this tale were true? Why would God call a Nephilim to lead His people into the promised land after He destroyed them in the flood? (A slightly different, yet similar, story appears in the *Book of Jasher*. See Jasher 85:24-27.[21]) No wonder Paul warned Titus not to give "heed to **JEWISH FABLES,** and commandments of men, that TURN FROM THE TRUTH" (Titus 1:13b-14).

The fable has Og living long before the Flood until many centuries later when he was killed by the Israelites but, again, we find a conflict with the Scriptures for we see that Og was an Amorite (Deuteronomy 4:47; 31:4; Joshua 9:10). The race of the Amorites did not begin **UNTIL AFTER** the flood as it was Noah's great-grandson who fathered the Amorites (see Genesis 10:6, 15-20). So Og could have only been born quite a while **AFTER** the flood. Remember, too, that this giant was not from Cain's lineage nor from the so-called Nephilim but from Seth's and Noah's lineage!

There are various flood stories in different cultures.

> "Since all nations have descended from the family then preserved in the ark, it is natural that the memory of such an event should be perpetuated in various national traditions. Such is indeed the fact. These traditions have been found among the Egyptians, Chaldeans, Phoenicians, Greeks, Hindoos, Chinese, Japanese, Scythians, and Celts, and in the western hemisphere among the Mexicans, Peruvians, and South sea islanders."[22]

The memory of this event was passed down from generation to generation but the stories from most cultures were embellished until the true story (as recorded in the Bible) has been tainted and distorted. Surprisingly, and disappointingly, even so-called Christians are now promoting other viewpoints.

WERE THERE OTHER SURVIVORS?

One such theory put forth by some people (including so-called evangelicals) to "prove" that the Nephilim survived the flood is that there were other survivors in addition to Noah, his wife, his three sons, and their three wives. For example, Sherry Shriner falsely claims:

> "Some argue that these creatures were all destroyed at the time of the flood, yet there are oral and written records of different tribes of people that hid in the bowels of the earth to protect themselves from the coming flood."[23]

Dr. Pugh mentions a work entitled *The Deluge* which

> "...tells the story of Satan, whom the Sumerians called ENKI, devising a plan to save King Ziusudra from the Flood. The poem

depicts Ziusudra as the savior of the seeds of ENKI (Satan). His ship/Ark contained only the seeds of living things, like a biogenetic laboratory with only enough animals to feed the survivors chosen for the ride. This explains why there have been two Arks discovered in recent years."[24] [Emphasis in the original.]

She continues:

"The Bible explains that God told Noah every detail in constructing his Ark. There is no mention of God ever telling him to use metal. Metallurgy was a science used by Cain's lineage. They had extensive knowledge of that skill, but Noah did not. The Ark that rests at the peak of Ararat is reminiscent of a large box in the shape of a rectangle. This design, without the use of metal, would be more in line with God's instructions. Even still, two Arks may have survived the Flood. If that is the case, then **the history of Noah and King Ziusudra may *both* be true.** From the biblical record, we know Noah survived the Flood; but did Ziusudra? Ziusudra's boat may have sunk and is where Ham found the 'Tablets of Destiny' (sic). The wreckage would have been located near Ham's descent from Mount Ararat after the Flood."[25]

Can **BOTH** stories be true? Of course not!! The Bible very specifically states: "...wherein few, that is, **eight souls** were saved by water" (I Peter 3:20). There is no room Scripturally for King Ziusudra or Og—or anyone else—to have escaped the flood. Pugh is free to believe the legend of King Ziusudra but then she can't **HONESTLY** claim to believe the Bible. To suggest that **BOTH** stories could be true shows her unbelief in God's Word.

SUMERIAN CLAY TABLETS

Later in her book she adds:

"These hybrids died, just like their mixed descendants the Giants, who perished in the Flood. The fathers of both the hybrids and Giants are the same. They are the 'Watchers' (Fallen Angels) who are totally spiritual beings and who, **according to Sumerian Clay Tablets, escaped the Flood in their heavenly boats.**

Apparently, they have taught their hybrids how to fly those heavenly boats in order to escape any future disasters."[26]

Pugh is once again making an assumption that hybrids exist and are the descendants from the fallen angels. As already proven, this is unscriptural. She then resorts to the Sumerian Clay Tablets and then makes that so-called "truth." If the Bible is true (and we know that it is), then the Sumerian Clay Tablets are wrong about beings escaping the flood.

The Bible clearly reveals that God warned: "I, even I, do bring a flood of waters upon the earth, to destroy **ALL FLESH,** wherein is the breath of life, from under heaven; and **EVERY THING** that is in the earth" (Genesis 6:6).

"And **ALL** flesh died that moved upon the earth, both of fowl, and of cattle, and of beast, and of every creeping thing that creepeth upon the earth, AND EVERY MAN: ALL in whose nostrils was the breath of life, of ALL that was in the dry land, DIED. And every living substance was destroyed which was upon the face of the ground, both man, and cattle, and the creeping things, and the fowl of the heaven; and they were destroyed from the earth: and NOAH **ONLY** remained alive, *and they that were with him in the ark"* (Genesis 7:21-23).

Were the "hybrids" with Noah? Of course not. Was ANY ONE else spared or did any one escape? Not according to the Bible. Are you going to believe God's Word or the Sumerian Clay Tablets? Joye certainly has made her choice—and it isn't the Bible that she has chosen to believe.

Besides, if these so-called hybrids can live in the spiritual world as well as the physical world, why would they even need a boat to escape?

ONLY A LOCAL FLOOD?

Another theory not only promoted by many liberals but also by a growing number of evangelicals such as Arnold Murray of

Shepherd's Chapel is that the flood was only a local flood and only destroyed the surrounding area.[27] This theory would allow some other people to survive which could allow the so-called Nephilim race to continue. One question that needs to be asked, however, is if God sent the flood to destroy the Nephilim race why would He intentionally allow some of them to survive? Wouldn't that defeat His purpose? Why was it essential for Noah to preserve life on the ark if surrounding areas were unaffected by the flood? Wasn't this an unnecessary task? Why couldn't Noah and his family just move to the unflooded area? The ark wouldn't have even been needed to preserve the animals as they could have survived in the unflooded areas.

The Bible is very clear in Genesis 9:18-19: "And the sons of Noah, that went forth of the ark, were Shem, and Ham, and Japheth.... These are the three sons of Noah: and OF THEM was the WHOLE EARTH OVERSPREAD." Every living person on earth today has come from one of these three sons. Since **ALL** the earth was populated from just these three children, we know that there were no other survivors who produced offspring. Do you want to believe God's Word or a false theory?

We also know that God promised that He would never destroy the entire earth with another flood:

> "I will establish My covenant with you; neither shall **ALL FLESH** be cut off any more by the waters of a flood; neither shall there any more be a flood to destroy the earth....And I will remember My covenant, which is between Me and you and every living creature of all flesh; and the waters shall no more become a flood to destroy **ALL FLESH**" (Genesis 9:11, 15).

In Isaiah 54:9 God says that He has "sworn that the waters of Noah should no more go over the earth." Had God meant a local flood, He would not have kept His promise since there have been many local, destructive floods throughout the centuries. Peter also explains that "the world that then was, being overflowed with water, perished" (II Peter 3:6). He goes on to explain that next time God will destroy the entire earth with fire:

"But the heavens and the earth, which are now, by the same word are kept in store, reserved unto fire against the day of judgment and perdition of ungodly men....But the day of the Lord will come as a thief in the night; in the which the heavens shall pass away with a great noise, and the elements shall melt with fervent heart, the earth also and the works that are therein shall be burned up....wherein the heavens being on fire shall be dissolved, and the elements shall melt with fervent heat? Nevertheless we, according to His promise, look for new heavens and a new earth, wherein dwelleth righteousness" (II Peter 3:7, 10, 12-13).

In the midst of this dire warning, we see God's mercy: "The Lord is not slack concerning His promise, as some men count slackness; but is longsuffering to us-ward, **NOT WILLING THAT ANY SHOULD PERISH, but that ALL should come to repentance**" (II Peter 3:9).

"For God so loved the world, that He gave His only begotten Son, that whosoever believeth in Him should not perish, but have everlasting life. For God sent not His Son into the world to condemn the world; but that the world through Him might be saved" (John 3:16-17).

Have you made your choice to follow Jesus and be saved?

WAS HAM A NEPHILIM?

Some people suggest that one way the "Nephilim" lineage passed through the flood was through Ham.[28] Pugh writes:

"The goats nor their father, Satan, will never (sic) inherit Heaven as their abode for eternal life, but are damned for all eternity to a Lake of Fire. Ham became the evil seed who re-fathered the nation of goats after the Flood. Because of his allegiance to Satan, Masonic history declares that Ham was not the true son of Noah. Their account teaches that Ham was really the son of a pharaoh (sic) from Cain's lineage, who perished in the Flood....

"According to the oldest Masonic Manuscripts, like the *Edinburgh Script,* the 'Founders of the Craft' were recorded as being from the lineage of Cain through his descendent, Lamech. Lamech's children were Jabal, Jubal, Tubalcain, and Naamah. These children, according to Masonic history, recorded all sacred mysteries and pre-flood knowledge on 'Pillars' that survived the Flood. The information on the 'Two Pillars' was found and then inscribed on 'Emerald Tablets' by Tubalcain's grandson, Ham, after the Flood. The *Edinburgh Script* maintains that the founder of these precious 'Pillars of Knowledge' was the biblical Ham. The fact that Ham was led to rediscover this knowledge, according to this secret script, hinges on their records that he was really Noah's stepson and that his true father was a Pharaoh from the lineage of Cain. Their historic record maintains that Ham came from the lineage of Cain and not from the lineage of Seth. This old manuscript makes it very clear that Ham was the grandson of Tubalcain and his father was a Pharaoh."[29]

Could this possibly be true? Could Ham be the son of a Pharaoh instead of the son of Noah? Could the Masonic **LEGEND** be correct? Let's once again turn to the Bible. Genesis 5:32 states: "Noah **BEGAT** Shem, Ham, and Japheth." Also, Genesis 6:10 clearly says: "Noah **BEGAT** three sons, Shem, Ham, and Japheth."

WAS HAM NOAH'S STEPSON?

Pugh knows that the Bible clearly states that Ham was Noah's son so she tries to find another way around this by asking:

"Could it be possible that Noah was not really Ham's biological father, just as Adam was not Cain's?

"We know the Bible does give credit to one's stepfather being titled as father within a lineage. For example, Jesus is genealogically linked in *Matthew 1:1-16* through his stepfather, Joseph, to King David....

"Ham's single rebellion re-introduced the post-Flood world back to the alchemical knowledge of mixing, which is the foundation stone for the sacred mysteries. His lineage renewed Satan's agenda against God and mankind. Jehovah commanded, time and time again, that 'His Chosen People' refrain from sexual involvement with Ham's descendents (sic), the Canaanites. God made this clear when He blessed the lineage of Noah's son, Shem, to receive the Promised Land. It was Shem's lineage who eventually removed the Canaanites from this land. Shem's descendents (sic), known to us as the Hebrew Children whom Moses led out of Egypt, took over that sacred land just as God had promised. What Jehovah wanted utmost was to keep the good seed separated from the evil—His sheep from Satan's goats."[30]

The above quotation is permeated with errors. We know that Joseph was not Jesus' literal father but we also find that the Bible **NEVER** says that Joseph **BEGAT** Jesus. An adopted person is referred to as a son or daughter of his or her adopted parents but those parents cannot say that the child was **BEGOTTEN** by them. There is a big difference. In reference to Christ, Matthew 1:16 says: "And Jacob begat Joseph the husband of Mary, of whom was born Jesus, who is called Christ." Notice that Christ was born of Mary but **WAS NOT** begotten from Joseph. Genesis, however, specifically states that Noah **BEGAT** Ham.

Pugh also only states part of the truth. She said that God blessed Shem's lineage **BUT** the Bible says that God blessed **ALL** the sons of Noah which would include Ham: "And God blessed Noah **AND HIS SONS,** and said unto them, Be fruitful and **MULTIPLY, AND REPLENISH** the earth" (Genesis 9:1). A few verses later God reiterates: "And you, be ye fruitful, and multiply; bring forth abundantly in the earth, and multiply therein" (Genesis 9:7). Do you see a problem here? Why would God destroy the earth because of the "serpent seed" but allow Ham (who is claimed to be of the "serpent seed") to survive and then **BLESS** Ham (along with the other sons) and instruct him to be fruitful and multiply seed abundantly? Wouldn't this be a very foolish move on God's part—if it were true? Why would God go to the bother of destroying all but one of the Nephilim and then tell him to "bring forth abundantly"?

Moreover, Genesis 6:9 tells us that "Noah was a just man and perfect in his generations...." The word "perfect" means entire or without blemish, without spot, undefiled, and upright but other than Noah and his family, we find that the "wickedness of man was great...and that every imagination of the thoughts of his heart was only evil continually." Noah was separate from this evil. Many teach Noah's "perfection" means that his bloodline was not tainted with the serpent seed.

"So we see that the integrity of Noah's family history was without blemish in stark contrast to all of the creation that surrounded him. Noah's bloodline was not defiled. Said in a more modern way, Noah's DNA was unaltered. It was still as God had originally created it. This is probably the most important aspect that differentiated Noah from his contemporaries, (besides being righteous). He was still genetically pure! Conversely, this is why all other flesh, including animals, had to be destroyed! Their DNA was altered in some way. By having altered DNA they were impure, defiled, and worthy of total destruction."[31]

"When God said that He found Noah and his sons and wives righteous, it wasn't JUST tied to their obedience to God, but to the fact that they were the LAST and ONLY ones on the earth who did NOT have a hint of Nephalim (sic) DNA in their bodies and blood."[32] [Emphasis in the original.]

WAS NOAH THE ONLY ONE WITH PURE DNA?

Is this true? Were Noah and his 3 sons the ONLY ones with pure DNA? If an uncontaminated bloodline were the only criteria for surviving the flood, then Noah's brothers and sisters would also have been spared as they came from the same bloodline. Genesis 5:28-30 states:

"And Lamech lived an hundred eighty and two years, and begat a son: And he called his name Noah, saying, This same shall comfort us concerning our work and toil of our hands, because of the ground which the Lord hath cursed. And **Lamech** lived after he begat Noah five hundred ninety and five years, and **BEGAT SONS AND DAUGHTERS.**"

Noah was not an only child. By this account he had brothers and sisters. **NONE** of these siblings were spared from the flood so an untainted bloodline wasn't what set Noah apart from the others.

We are further told that Noah was perfect "in his generations" and this word means "posterity" which would mean his descendants were also perfect or righteous. This would, of course, include Ham.

Remember, too, the Canaanites WERE NOT descendants of Cain (as Pugh claims). They were descendants from the lineage of Seth (Genesis 9:18; 10:6). Also, Ham was not the grandson of Tubalcain (who was from Cain's lineage). He was the grandson of Lamech (from Seth's lineage) according to Genesis 5:28-29, 32.

Furthermore, the *Edinburgh Manuscript* **DOES NOT** state that Ham was the step-son of a Pharaoh nor does it state that Ham came from Cain's lineage as Pugh claims. Remember, she wrote: "The *Edinburgh Script* maintains that the founder of these precious 'Pillars of Knowledge' was the biblical Ham....This old manuscript makes it very clear that Ham was the grandson of Tubalcain and his father was a Pharaoh."[33] I read this document and could not find the word "Pharaoh," "stepson," or even "Ham" in the manuscript nor did it mention that Ham was the son or grandson of Tubalcain. The truth is that this manuscript claims that the person who found one of the pillars of wisdom was from **Shem's** lineage.[34]

Of course, the *Edinburgh Manuscript* does not agree with the Bible so why would any Bible-believing Christian go to it in the first place in order to establish a Biblical fact? Pugh seems to be a master of deception. First, she ignores the clear teaching of the Bible. Second, she goes to a document that does not agree with the Bible and then she even changes that and claims that it states something it does not say. Third, she tries to fit these distortions back into the Bible to "prove" something that was never there in the first place.

One unique theory about how the Nephilim survived the flood comes from a Gothic website. Philip Faith claims that the giant Og had relations with Ham's wife. Because of this, she was pregnant when she entered the ark. The baby that was born would have carried the Nephilim lineage thus preserving the Nephilim bloodline. Could this be a possibility?

We need to ask why God would send the flood to destroy all the Nephilim but "forget" that Ham's wife was pregnant and carrying the Nephilim seed.

If we turn to the Bible we can find our answer. Genesis 7:11 tells us: "In the six hundredth year of Noah's life, in the second month, the seventeenth day of the month, the same day were all the fountains of the great deep broken up, and the windows of heaven were opened." Genesis 8:13-16 tells us that Noah left the ark in his 601st year, the second month, and the twenty seventh day. That would be a total of 370 days if a lunar calendar were used. The typical gestation period for a baby is 280 days.[35] Remember, that Ham's wife was supposedly already pregnant when she entered the ark plus she was inside for another 370 or more days. How many people came out of the ark? "Noah went forth, and his sons, and his wife, and his son's wives with him" (Genesis 8:18). That makes 8 people—not 9. Furthermore, Genesis 10:1 clearly states: "Now these are the generations of the sons of Noah, Shem, Ham, and Japheth: and unto them were sons born **AFTER** the flood." I Peter 3:20 adds that "few, that is, **EIGHT** souls were saved by water." Eight people went in and eight people came out. No, Ham's wife was not pregnant when she entered the ark, she did not give birth while she was in the ark, and the so-called Nephilim bloodline did not survive the flood.

DID HAM COMMIT A HOMOSEXUAL ACT?

Yet another explanation used to try to show how Cain's "serpent seed" lineage survived the flood is that it is claimed that Ham had a homosexual relationship with Noah and that supposedly caused the serpent lineage to continue.[36]

Martin Luther Hyles alleges:

"Noah was not cultivating grapes to get drunk. Noah was operating a sophisticated scientific operation designed to reconstitute animals from the DNA samples he possessed. Ham was a necessary participant. Through an ingenious scientific process lost to history. Ham would seed the DNA into Noah's body. Noah acted as an incubator for the animal zygotes until they reached a certain level of development. At that point they would be transferred to the uterus of a cow or antelope.

"At any one time, a hundred or more zygotes were living free in Noah's abdomen. It was Ham's job to 'impregnate' Noah with the cloned embryos as each batch was ready. What was unknown to Noah however was that Ham had saved DNA from a dubious source prior to the flood.

"Prior to the flood, Ham had been in a homosexual relationship with a member of the Nephilim, the giants in the land for which God sent the flood in the first place. The Nephilim were fallen from heaven along with their leader Satan. Ham combined the DNA from himself and this Nephilim and produced a clone. This clone he introduced into the body of Noah. This is the sin of Ham."[37]

Romans 1 seems very applicable:

"Professing themselves to be wise, They became fools, And changed the glory of the uncorruptible God into an image made like to corruptible man, and to birds, and fourfooted beasts, and creeping things....Who changed the truth of God into a lie, and worshipped and served the creature more than the Creator, who is blessed for ever" (Romans 1:22-23, 25).

This theory about "the sin of Ham" might be regarded as ludicrous by many people, but the website where this statement occurred was ranked #2 for the "Fundamental Top 500" sites. It also ranked #5 in the "Baptist Top 1000" and was listed in the "Christian Top 1000" as well as holding rank #3 in "The Best Baptist Websites at Baptist411.com." In other words, this is a site that is visited frequently.

To see if such a theory could possibly be true, we need to once again consult the Bible. Genesis 9 tells us that after the flood Noah began to be an husbandman and he planted a vineyard and drank of the wine and became drunken. In this drunken state he was uncovered within his tent. Before saying Noah was wicked and evil, we need to realize that when the flood took place there were changes in the atmosphere and this reduction of atmospheric pressure would have an effect on the process of fermentation. Dr. Jobe Martin explains:

> "Because the water came down as rain, the atmospheric pressure was reduced by at least one half. Alcohol fermentation rates are doubled when the pressure is cut in half. Therefore, because alcohol ferments faster and gets into your blood and brain more quickly in system #2 [the present heaven and earth] than it did in system #1 [the heaven and earth of Adam and Noah], Noah likely was caught by surprise. He was God's righteous man. He had not forgotten to make an altar and sacrifice in worship of his Lord and Savior."[38]

So, Noah very likely was unaware of the reaction that the wine would have on him. We do know that Noah was a righteous man before the flood and after seeing God destroy wicked mankind, do you think he would be so foolish or feel safe about committing wilful sin against God? We also know from Genesis 9:1 that God **BLESSED** Noah and his sons so they all had been under God's blessing after the flood and verse 8 says that God established his covenant with Noah and his sons. Regardless of what did happen, he was in a drunken state when Ham entered his tent and saw that he was uncovered. One variation of the "serpent seed" belief is that Ham engaged in a homosexual act with Noah at this time. Of course, there is no indication of such a thing in these verses. As just mentioned, Noah, as well as Ham, had seen the entire world destroyed for wickedness. We also know that Ham had at least 4 children already (Genesis 10:6).

The Bible simply says that Ham saw his father uncovered and he told his brothers. His brothers, knowing that their father was naked, took a garment and walked backward so that they would not see him in this condition and they covered him. Now, if the word "nakedness" in Genesis 9:22 means "a homosexual act," then the word must mean the same thing in verse 23—but it doesn't fit the context. It's just that simple.

> "And Ham, the father of Canaan, saw the **nakedness** of his father, and told his two brethren without. And Shem and Japheth took a garment, and laid it upon both their shoulders, and went backward, and covered the **nakedness** of their father; and their faces were backward, and they saw not their father's **nakedness**" (Genesis 9:22-23).

Why was a garment needed if "nakedness" meant a homosexual act? Are we to also assume that the word "nakedness" in Genesis 42:12 means a homosexual act? "And he said unto them, Nay, but to see the **nakedness** of the land ye are come." When we try to reinterpret the Scriptures with our own ideas, we end up with absurd, irrational, and preposterous concepts.

DID NOAH'S WIFE COMMIT INCEST?

One final theory given about the "serpent seed" surviving the flood states: "Noah had three sons in the righteous line but Ham was evil. His incest with his father's wife reproduced the Serpent seed on this side of the Flood."[39]

> "Cain's race is not on the Book of Life. It came through the Flood in the person of Noah's wife, Naamah, who was not the mother of his three sons. It was reproduced by her incest with Ham."[40]

There is no hint whatsoever that anything of this nature happened. Even if it did occur there is no record that any children were produced from this act and unless a child was born, there is no way that this lineage could continue. Even if a child were produced, no name (or lineage) is listed, so there is no way to be able to trace the lineage of those carrying this supposed "serpent seed" trait.

Briefly, let's return to Quayle's comment about how the fallen angels played around with the **fish,** the fowls, and the beasts until they became entangled in the flesh themselves. From this manipulation the Nephilim were presumedly born. The flood was supposed to destroy all the Nephilim--but Quayle evidently doesn't know the Bible well enough because we see that the **fish** were not destroyed in the flood. Only "all that was in the **DRY LAND**, died" (Genesis 7:22). Once again we find the theories proposed by such individuals make God look inept. He supposedly sent the flood to destroy the Nephilim but He "forgot" that the fallen angels had tampered with the fish so He didn't destroy the fish. This means that when God sent the flood He didn't destroy **ALL** the creatures that had genetic manipulation and altered DNA.

NONE of these theories presented here can be verified by Scripture. In fact, if we would just check the Scriptures out, we should easily be kept from falling for such false doctrines, fables, and outright lies.

Sadly, more time seems to be spent in twisting the Scriptures to one's own destruction than accepting the untainted truth of God's Word. We need to search the Scriptures rather than explore occult theories or concoct ideas that contradict the Bible.

7. "AS IN THE DAYS OF NOAH"

There is an increased interest in alien abductions, UFOs, cloning, Nephilim, etc. Some people are trying to correlate today's fascination with these issues to what supposedly occurred in the "days of Noah." Dr. Joye Pugh writes:

> "The Bible records the increase in the pagan worship of nature, as well as the powers of Demons and strange occurrences in the skies near the 'End of the Age.' Scripture also says that the increase of evil during these last days will be *'like unto the days of Noah.'* Remember, the Great Flood was brought about by Jehovah to rid the Earth of the evil half-breed race called the Giants, who were born through the wicked lineage of Cain and the Fallen Angels. Jehovah wanted the Spirit of Cain, which is the 'Spirit of Selfishness,' to be removed from the earth. Because we are witnessing the Alien's promotion of nature worship with abductees, there can be no doubt that we are living in the last days spoken of in the Bible."[1]

We have just covered the reason why God sent the flood—and it wasn't to remove aliens and hybrids. Nonetheless, one notion that is gaining popularity is that of the so-called Star Children. In 1995 Jenny Randles wrote a book entitled *Star Children: The True Story of Alien Offspring Among Us.*[2] In the editorial review for this book we find: "Some star children believe that they are the hybrid offspring of aliens and humans, conceived during space abductions. Others may have extraterrestrial spirits living within their human bodies."[3]

INDIGO CHILDREN

Another term for the Star Children is Indigo Children. This concept first gained popularity in a book entitled *The Indigo Child* written by Lee Carroll and Jan Tober in 1998.[4]

"Lee Carroll is an American New Age channeller, speaker and author.

"Originally an audio engineer, Carroll began to channel communications which he claimed originated from a being from a higher dimension called Kryon in 1989. He describes Kryon as a disembodied entity of a different order than human, who has 'been with the Earth since the beginning.'"[5]

Carroll claims he "learned about the concept of Indigo children while channeling a being known as Kryon, Master angelic energy."[6]

"The term Indigo children originates from the 1982 book 'Understanding Your Life Through Color,' by Nancy Ann Tappe, a self-styled synesthete and psychic, who claimed to possess the ability to perceive human auras. She wrote that during the mid 1960's she began noticing that many children were being born with indigo auras. Today she estimates that 60% of people age 14 to 25 and 97% of children under ten are 'Indigo.'"[7]

The Indigo Children (also called Crystal Children, Children of the New Times, Metagifted Children, Ascending Children, Children of the New Dream, Millennium Children, Crystalline Children, The Mystic Children, Star Kids, Children of Aids, Angels on Earth, Children of Now, Children of the Stars, The Masters, Children of Winter, Super Psychic Children, Star People, Psychic Children, Star Children, Children of Oz, Star Seed, Children of Oneness, The New Children, etc.)[8] are children who supposedly exhibit psychic powers[9] "such as clairvoyance, clairaudience, clairsentience, healing powers, pre-birth and previous life recall, etc."[10] They are also presumed to be alien hybrids.

One movie was called simply *Indigo*.[11] Also, Steven Spielberg had a TV Mini Series called *Taken* in which "he portrays the evolution of a perfect hybrid being, a blend of Extraterrestrial and Human DNA. Her name is 'Allie,' and she is a media foreshadow of what is yet to come."[12]

Actually, this idea is not really all that new. A book written almost sixty years ago by Arthur C. Clarke was entitled *Childhood's*

End and was about "all children on earth evolving to starchildren or little gods."[13]

Connecting the idea of the Indigo and Star Children to Noah's day, Sherry Shriner claims:

"'As in the Days of Noah'...Noah and his sons were the only humans left alive with pure human DNA....

"Today we have Indigo and Star children that are blatantly hybrid children of the aliens and not hiding it. The hybrids are coming out of the closet....

"Over the past thousands of years contaminated DNA has engulfed mankind and their genealogical lines. The Serpent Seed dominates earth through it's (sic) offspring and technology that controls whole governments and militaries."[14]

Matthew 24 and Luke 17 explain that "as it was in the days of Noe [Noah], so shall it be also in the days of the Son of Man" when Christ returns again. Proponents of the Nephilim theory point to these verses and say: "See, this proves that there were hybrids in Noah's day and there will be fallen angels once again mating with mankind and producing more hybrids in the end times."

MANKIND WAS WICKED

Of course, these verses say no such thing! How were the days of Noah? Genesis 6 says: "God saw that the wickedness of man was great in the earth, and that every imagination of the thoughts of his heart was only evil continually...for all flesh had corrupted his way upon the earth" (Genesis 6:5).

What will it be like in the last days?

"This know also, that in the last days perilous times shall come. For men shall be lovers of their own selves, covetous, boasters, proud, blasphemers, disobedient to parents, unthankful, unholy, Without natural affection, trucebreakers, false accusers, incontinent, fierce, despisers of those that are good, Traitors, heady, highminded, lovers of pleasures more than lovers of God; Having a form of godliness, but denying the power thereof: from such turn away....But evil men and seducers shall wax worse and worse, deceiving, and being deceived" (II Timothy 3:1-5, 13).

"...there should be mockers in the last time, who should walk after their own ungodly lusts" (Jude 1:18).

"Now the Spirit speaketh expressly, that in the latter times some shall depart from the faith, giving heed to seducing spirits, and doctrines of devil; Speaking lies in hypocrisy; having their conscience seared with a hot iron....But refuse profane and old wives fables, and exercise thyself rather unto godliness" (I Timothy 4:1-2, 7).

Certainly the last days will be days of wickedness, perversion, pleasure, deception, and a false spirituality. There will be a "form of godliness" but "the way of truth shall be evil spoken of" (II Peter 2:2). "For the time will come when they will not endure sound doctrine; but after their own lusts shall they heap to themselves teachers, having itching ears; And they shall turn away their ears from the truth, and shall be turned unto fables" (II Timothy 4:3-4). Amos tells us: "Behold the days come, saith the Lord God, that I will send a famine in the land, not a famine of bread, nor a thirst for water, but of hearing the words of the Lord" (Amos 8:11).

EATING, DRINKING, AND MARRYING

In addition to the excessive corruption and depravity of Noah's day we notice something else from Matthew: "In the days that were before the flood they were eating and drinking, marrying and giving in marriage, until the day that Noe entered into the ark" and "the flood came, and destroyed them all" (Matthew 24:38-39). These activities, in themselves, were not necessarily wrong. The problem is that people were living their lives normally and were not expecting any thing different to take place. They were more concerned about their daily business than they were about where they would spend eternity. As Psalm 10:4 says: "The wicked...will not seek after God: God is not in all his thoughts."

Noah's day was not the only time when wickedness proliferated. Most people only mention Noah's day because they are trying to "prove" that the Nephilim were the offspring of fallen angels but the Bible also refers to the days of Lot in connection with the end times. Luke states: "Likewise also as it was in the days of Lot; they did eat, they drank, they bought, they sold, they planted, they builded" (Luke 17:28).

There was great transgression and depravity in the days of Lot as well. Genesis 19 says that Lot went to his daughters and his sons in law and told them to get out of Sodom because God was going to destroy it but "he seemed as one that mocked unto his sons in law." We see the same unconcern about the last days in II Peter 3 which says:

> "There shall come in the last days scoffers, walking after their own lusts, And saying, Where is the promise of His coming? for since the fathers fell asleep, all things continue as they were from the beginning of the creation. For this they willingly are ignorant of....But the day of the Lord will come as a thief in the night; in the which the heavens shall pass away with a great noise, and the elements shall melt with fervent heat, the earth also and the works that are therein shall be burned up. Seeing then that all these things shall be dissolved, what manner of persons ought ye to be in all holy conversation and godliness....Wherefore, beloved, seeing that ye look for such things, be diligent that ye may be found of Him in peace, without spot, and blameless" (II Peter 3:3-5a, 10-11, 14).

BIBLE COMPARISONS

Let's notice **FROM THE BIBLE** several correlations about Noah's day, Lot's day, and the end times. First (as already mentioned), there was great wickedness.

Noah's day: "And God saw that the wickedness of man was great in the earth..." (Genesis 6:5).

Lot's day: "...the cry of Sodom and Gomorrah is great, and because their sin is very grievous" (Genesis 18:20). "...Lot, vexed with the filthy conversation of the wicked" (II Peter 2:7).

End times: "...because iniquity shall abound, the love of many shall wax cold" (Matthew 24:12).

Second, everyone was going about their business in the usual manner. The destruction came suddenly even though warnings had been issued before time.

Noah's day: "...as in the days that were before the flood they were eating and drinking, marrying and giving in marriage, **UNTIL** the day that Noe entered into the ark, And knew not until the flood came, and took them all away; so shall also the coming of the Son of man be" (Matthew 24:38-39; see also Luke 17:27).

Lot's day: "...they did eat, they drank, they bought, they sold, they planted, they builded" (Luke 17:28).

End times: "...take heed to yourselves, lest at any time your hearts be overcharged with surfeiting, and drunkenness, and cares of this life, and so that day come upon you unawares. For as a snare shall it come on all them that dwell on the face of the whole earth" (Luke 21:34-35). "Where is the promise of His coming?...**all things continue as they were from the beginning of the creation**" (II Peter 3:4).

NORMAL ACTIVITIES BUT IGNORING GOD

Notice that the activities were nothing unusual or even sinful. People were eating, drinking, buying, selling, planting, building, and marrying. In other words, they were just living life—but they were only concerned about the physical realm and there was no concern for their spiritual welfare.

Third, we realize that only a **FEW** were saved.

Noah's day: "...in the days of Noah...eight souls were saved..." (I Peter 3:20).

Lot's day: Only Lot and his two daughters were spared (Genesis 19:16, 26).

End times: "...strait is the gate, and narrow is the way, which leadeth unto life, and few there be that find it" (Matthew 7:14). "...when the Son of man cometh, shall He find faith on the earth?" (Luke 18:8). "And except those days should be shortened, there should no flesh be saved: but for the elect's sake those days shall be shortened" (Matthew 24:22; see also Mark 13:20). "...if the righteous scarcely be saved, where shall the ungodly and the sinner appear?" (I Peter 4:18).

The people of Noah's day were warned that a flood was coming. II Peter 2:5 tells us that Noah was a "preacher of righteousness" but even though the warning was given, it was ignored until it was too late. "How shall we escape, if we neglect so great salvation?" (Hebrews 2:3).

God said:

"Because I have called, and ye refused; I have stretched out My hand, and no man regarded; But ye have set at nought all My counsel, and would none of My reproof: I also will laugh at your calamity; **I will mock when your fear cometh....**For that they hated knowledge, and did not choose the fear of the Lord. They would none of My counsel: they despised all My reproof. Therefore shall they eat of the fruit of their own way, and be filled with their own devices....But whoso hearkeneth unto Me shall dwell safely, and shall be quiet from fear of evil" (Proverbs 1:25-26, 29-31, 33).

"He, that being often reproved hardeneth his neck, shall suddenly be destroyed, and that without remedy" (Proverbs 29:1).

God has provided the way of escape through Jesus Christ but if we refuse His provision, there is no other way. Noah's ark was opened—**UNTIL** God shut the door. Lot tried to get some other family members to go to safety with him, but they refused. In reference to Christ's coming we have the illustration about the ten virgins. When the bridegroom came, "they that were ready went in with him to the marriage: and the door was shut" (Matthew 25:10). After the door was shut others tried to get in—but it was **TOO LATE.**

RIGHTEOUS RIDICULED

Another comparison we find in reference to Lot's day and the end times is that the righteous were ridiculed. Lot tried to warn his family members but he was rebuffed. "And Lot went out and spake unto his sons in law, which married his daughters, and said, Up, get you out of this place; for the Lord will destroy this city. But he seemed as one that mocked unto his sons in law" (Genesis 19:14).

There will also be mockers in the end times. Peter warns: "Knowing this first, that there shall come in the last days scoffers, walking after their own lusts" (II Peter 3:3). Jude also tells us that "there should be mockers in the last time" (Jude 1:18).

We also need to notice that both Noah and Lot had family members who were not spared. In fact, it was Lot's own family who ignored his warning. Noah also had brothers and sisters (and most likely aunts, uncles, cousins, nieces, and nephews) who perished in the flood (see Genesis 5:28-30). Many of us today will also have unsaved family members who will be lost.

Continuing with the context of "as in the days of Noah," we find the following illustration:

"But know this, that if the goodman of the house had known in what watch the thief would come, he would have watched, and would not have suffered his house to be broken up. Therefore be ye also ready: for in such an hour as ye think not the Son of man cometh....Blessed is that servant, whom his lord when he cometh shall find so doing. Verily I say unto you, That he shall make him ruler over all his goods. But and if that evil servant shall say in his heart, My lord delayeth his coming; And shall begin to smite his fellowservants, and to eat and drink with the drunken; The lord of that servant shall come in a day when he looketh not for him, and in an hour that he is not aware of, And shall cut him asunder, and appoint him his portion with the hypocrites: there shall be weeping and gnashing of teeth" (Matthew 24:43-44, 46-51; see also Luke 12:36-48).

If you knew a thief was planning to break into your home tonight, wouldn't you do all you could to protect your home, yourself, and your family? The Scriptures tell us that the Lord's coming will be like a thief in the night—but only to those who are not watching. Are **YOU** watching?

"Remember therefore how thou hast received and heard, and hold fast, and repent. If therefore thou shalt not watch, I will come on thee as a thief, and thou shalt not know what hour I will come upon thee" (Revelation 3:3).

"For yourselves know perfectly that the day of the Lord so cometh as a thief in the night....But ye, brethren, are not in darkness, that that day should overtake you as a thief" (I Thessalonians 5:2, 4).

It should be clear that the references to "as in the days of Noah" and "in the days of Lot" are not referring to the Nephilim or hybrids but about being ready for when the Lord returns.

"Watch therefore, for ye know neither the day nor the hour wherein the Son of man cometh" (Matthew 25:13).

"Watch ye therefore, and pray always, that ye may be accounted worthy to escape all these things that shall come to pass, and to stand before the Son of man" (Luke 21:36).

"Therefore be ye also ready: for in such an hour as ye think not the Son of man cometh" (Matthew 24:44; see also Luke 12:40).

"And what I say unto you I say unto all, **Watch**" (Mark 13:37).

8. WHAT IS THE "NESHAMA"?

In the unscriptural *Book of Enoch* we are told that when the hybrid beings died, a demon was released. It is understandable that occultists and other non-Christians believe unscriptural doctrines but, sadly, some evangelicals are also echoing this idea. Dr. Pugh writes:

> "Unfortunately, Satan and his Fallen Angels were jealous of the beauty of humans, thereby tempting Eve and the daughters of man in their retaliation. Because these spiritual beings mated with earthly women, they produced an interbred race of hybrids called Giants. These mixed offspring were both spiritual and flesh. At death, these entities released evil spirits on the Earth because their spiritual side could not ever reenter Heaven after their flesh perished. These evil spirits, who are known to walk the earth in search of a body that is willing to be opened up to them, are called Demons."[1]

Patrick Heron proclaims the same thing:

> "Before leaving the Book of Enoch, there are two other points I would like to bring to your attention which are in this book. The first is concerning the evil spirits which inhabit the earth, who, according to Enoch, are the spirits that remain after the death of the giants which are the product of flesh and spirit.

> "That is, the angels who are spirit, left their first estate and came to earth and lay with flesh and blood women. The product of this union of spirit and blood were the giants. But when the giants died, their spirits remain (sic) on this earth and are responsible for much of the pain and oppression which humans suffer today....

> "When the giants were destroyed in the Flood, their spirits exited from the body and remained at large. And, according to Enoch, it is these spirits that inhabit the earth today and cause the mayhem that humankind has to endure today and all through the ages."[2]

Let's stop to notice several ideas presented in these few paragraphs.

WAS SATAN JEALOUS OF MANKIND'S BEAUTY?

Pugh said that Satan and his angels were jealous of mankind's beauty. I find such a statement questionable. Why? Let's look at Ezekiel 28 in reference to Satan (Lucifer):

> "Thus said the Lord God; Thou sealest up the sum, full of wisdom, and **PERFECT IN BEAUTY.** Thou hast been in Eden the garden of God....Thou art the anointed cherub that covereth; and I have set thee so: thou wast upon the holy mountain of God....Thou wast perfect in thy ways from the day that thou wast created, till iniquity was found in thee....Thine heart was lifted up **BECAUSE OF THY BEAUTY..."** (Ezekiel 28:12-17, in part).

Since Lucifer was **perfect** in beauty, why would he be jealous of man's beauty?

Another idea presented (which comes from the *Book of Enoch*) is that the so-called mixed offspring were "both spiritual and flesh." Enoch 15:8-9 states:

> "And now, the giants, who are produced from the spirits and flesh, shall be called evil spirits upon the earth, and on the earth shall be their dwelling. Evil spirits have proceeded from their bodies; because they are born from men, [and] from the holy Watchers is their beginning and primal origin; [they shall be evil spirits on earth, and] evil spirits shall they be called."[3] [Brackets in the original translation.]

How can the wicked, fallen angels possibly be called "sons of God" or be termed "holy"? If they are really the sons of God and could reproduce children, why would their children be doomed to supposedly release a **demon** upon the death of the flesh? Even if fallen angels could reproduce, why would their offspring automatically be eternally doomed? This is predestination at its worst!

Since angels do not die, why would it be assumed that their offspring would live an average human lifespan? Wouldn't you assume that the offspring would live a much longer than normal lifespan—or even live forever?

As mentioned before, this idea of the "hybrid" race is not Biblical and neither is the concept that these beings release demons when they die. There are only two destinies for all of mankind and that is either heaven or hell. There is not a third sphere where the flesh dies but the spirit walks the earth for all eternity. John 5:28-29 clearly states that "the hour is coming, in the which **ALL** that are in the graves shall hear His voice, And shall come forth; they that have done good, unto the resurrection of life; and they that have done evil, unto the resurrection of damnation." There is no other alternative. Matthew 25 also only lists two destinations:

> "And He shall set the sheep on His right hand, but the goats on the left. Then shall the King say unto them on His right hand, Come, ye blessed of My Father, inherit the kingdom prepared for you from the foundation of the world:...Then shall He say also unto them on the left hand, Depart from Me, ye cursed, into everlasting fire, prepared for the devil and his angels: And these shall go away into everlasting punishment: but the righteous into life eternal" (Matthew 25:33-34, 41, 46).

DO THE NEPHILIM HAVE SOULS?

In spite of these Scriptures, some evangelicals (and others) are echoing the *Book of Enoch* and teaching that the Nephilim did not have souls or the neshama (also spelled nashamah).[4] Pugh writes:

> "According to the book of *Genesis,* man has a living soul. The *Talmud,* a collection of texts and commentaries on Jewish religious law, calls the living soul the 'neshama.' Without the 'neshama' a man was considered to be not quite human. In the *Talmud* there are ancient references to creatures called 'Beasts' that lacked a 'neshama' to make them human. These beasts, called rulers of the field, were described as being in the image of a man."[5]

To understand this more fully we need to look at the word "neshama." This is a Hebrew word and while it is sometimes translated as soul it actually means "breath." Let's look at a few Bible verses where the word "neshama" is used. We'll start with Genesis 2:7: "And the Lord God formed man of the dust of the ground, and breathed into his nostrils the **breath** [Hebrew: nashamah] of life; and man became a living soul [Hebrew: nephesh]." You can clearly see that the neshama **IS NOT** the soul as there is another Hebrew word for soul. Now look at Genesis 7:21-23 in reference to the flood.

"And **ALL FLESH DIED THAT MOVED** upon the earth, both of fowl, and of cattle, and of beast, and of every creeping thing that creepeth upon the earth, AND EVERY MAN: **ALL** in whose nostrils was the **breath** [Hebrew: nashamah] of life, of ALL that was in the dry land, DIED. And every living substance was destroyed which was upon the face of the ground, both man, and cattle, and the creeping things, and the fowl of the heaven; and they were destroyed from the earth: and Noah only remained alive, and they that were with him in the ark" (Genesis 7:21-23).

NEPHILIM CANNOT RELEASE DEMONS

If these beings had no soul or neshama, the flood would not have had any effect on them because what died in the flood were the beings that had the neshama or breath of life. Pugh, Heron, etc., claim that the flood was sent to destroy the Nephilim so if they died in the flood, they had a neshama which makes Pugh, etc., incorrect. If they had a neshama, these Nephilim could not have released a demon at death since only beings without a neshama supposedly can release a demon. So, either way, Pugh, Heron, and their ilk are incorrect. When we try to go to other sources for "truth" and ignore God's Word, we will always come up with false ideas or contradictory thoughts.

There are other instances in Scriptures where the breath (not the soul) is called the neshama. For instance, in the days of Joshua the Israelites were told to kill all that breathed or had neshama, so we cannot equate the soul (or nephesh) with breath (or neshama). So this theory cannot be correct unless the Bible is wrong (which it is not).

In one interview Joye Pugh stated that

"...we know that in Genesis when God created man in His image, He blew into his nostrils the breath of life and it's like a neshama. It was like a living soul, and I believe that in itself is what is the spiritual part of us that leaves our body when we die."[6]

Pugh frequently says "I believe" but just because a person believes something does not automatically make it true. In this case, Pugh's belief about the Nephilim not having a "neshama" yet releasing a demon once again contradicts the clear teaching of the Bible. Since the Nephilim breathed and moved, and all that breathed and moved were destroyed in the flood, all that died in the flood had to have a neshama. If people would just believe what the Bible says, there would not be such confusion.

The Greek translation of the Hebrew Bible is called the Septuagint. Checking Genesis 2:7 and 7:22 in reference to "the **breath** [nashamah] of life," we find that the Greek word used is "pnoe." "Pnoe" is also used in Acts: "Neither is worshipped with men's hands, as though He needed any thing, seeing He giveth to all life, and **breath** [pnoe] and all things" (Acts 17:25).

"Pnoe" comes from the Greek word "pneo."[7]

"In the New Testament the Greek word 'pneo' (Strong's #4154) is equivalent to the Old Testament 'neshawmaw' [neshama].... and is also the root word for 'pneuma' which means 'spirit' (Strong's #4151)."[8]

HABITATION OF DEVILS

We also find that according to a translation program, the Hebrew word "neshama" is comparable to "pneuma" in the Greek which would be "spirit" or "breath" in English.[9] With this in mind, if the Nephilim had no neshama (spirit), then they could not have released a demon when they died since the demons are spirits. Revelation 16:14 says: "For they are the spirits [pneuma] of devils, working miracles, which go forth unto the kings of the earth and of the whole world, to gather them to the battle of that great day of God Almighty." Revelation 18:2 adds: "Babylon the great is fallen, is fallen, and is become the habitation of devils, and the hold of every foul spirit [pneuma], and a cage of every unclean and hateful bird."

Here are a few more verses showing that demons are spirits (neshama or pneuma):

◆ "When the even was come, they brought unto Him many that were possessed with devils: and He cast out the spirits [pneuma] with His word, and healed all that were sick" (Matthew 8:16).

◆ "And in the synagogue there was a man, which had a spirit [pneuma] of an unclean devil, and cried out with a loud voice" (Luke 4:33).

◆ "And certain women, which had been healed of evil spirits [pneuma] and infirmities, Mary called Magdalene, out of whom went seven devils" (Luke 8:2).

◆ "And as he was yet a coming, the devil threw him down, and tare him. And Jesus rebuked the unclean spirit [pneuma], and healed the child, and delivered him again to his father" (Luke 9:42). (Other verses are: Matthew 10:1; 12:43, 45; Mark 1:23, 26, 27; 3:11, 30; 5:2, 8, 13; 6:7; 7:25; 9:17, 20, 25; Luke 4:33, 36; 6:18; 7:21; 8:2, 29; 9:39, 42; 10:20; 11:24, 26; Acts 5:16; 8:7; 16:16, 18; 19:12, 13, 15, 16; Revelation 13:15; and 16:13.)

◆ "Now the Spirit [pneuma] speaketh expressly, that in the latter times some shall depart from the faith, giving heed to seducing spirits [pneuma], and doctrines of devils" (I Timothy 4:1).

As I Timothy 4:1 shows, spirits can be good or evil. That is why the Bible often gives an identifying word such as "holy" or "unclean" before the word "spirit" so we can know if the spirit being referred to is of God or Satan. I John 4 gives us this warning:

"Beloved, believe not every **spirit** [pneuma], but try the **spirits** whether they are of God: because many false prophets are gone out into the world. Hereby know ye the **Spirit** of God: Every **spirit** that confesseth that Jesus Christ is come in the flesh is of God: And every **spirit** that confesseth not that Jesus Christ is come in the flesh is not of God: and this is that spirit of antichrist, whereof ye have heard that it should come; and even now already is it in the world....We are of God: he that knoweth God heareth us; he that is not of God heareth not us. Hereby know we the **spirit** of truth, and the **spirit** of error" (I John 4:1-3, 6).

However, those who are pushing the idea that the Nephilim do not have souls (or the neshama/pneuma) now proceed to introduce the concept of the golem.

Pugh writes:

"The Jewish Talmud says that a human like being or Golem—a mass of flesh could be created without a soul and that was considered a beast. It would be the same as cloning a person. Each human has only one soul but a person's flesh can be cloned without a soul—making it a beast."[10]

We'll look at the golem in the next chapter.

9. THE GOLEM

What is a golem? To discover the answer to this, we'll look at several definitions first. The dictionary meaning of "golem" is "an artificial human being in Hebrew **folklore** endowed with life."[1]

"In Jewish **folklore,** an image that comes to life. From the Middle Ages stories were told of wise men who could bring clay effigies to life by means of **magic charms** or sacred words. Golems began as perfect servants, whose only fault lay in fulfilling their master's commands too literally or mechanically. Later golems were imagined as protectors of the Jews in times of persecution, but also had a frightening aspect."[2]

"A **golem,** in medieval FOLKLORE, is an animated being made from clay or stone. It is DERIVED FROM HEBREW MYTHOLOGY and is said to contain a scroll with magic or religious words that keep it animated. This included writing the name of God on his forehead, (or on a clay tablet under its tongue) or writing the word Emet (truth in the Hebrew language) on its forehead, and then by erasing the first letter to make it Met (death in Hebrew) it was destroyed. Its existence was a mixed blessing. Although NOT OVERLY INTELLIGENT, a golem could be made to perform simple tasks over and over forever. The problem was getting him to stop. This has been suggested as the inspiration for the Sorcerer's Apprentice segment in Disney's <u>Fantasia</u>."[3] [Caps added.]

The *Grimoire for the Apprentice Wizard* basically gives the same type definition.[4]

Notice that the idea of the golem comes from Jewish **FOLK-LORE.** Remember the warning that the Apostle Paul gave: "Wherefore rebuke them sharply, that they may be sound in the faith; Not giving heed to **JEWISH FABLES,** and commandments of men, that **TURN FROM THE TRUTH"** (Titus 1:13b-14).

The most famous golem story is that of Rabbi Judah Loew ben Bezalel in the late 16th century in Prague.[5]

"Rabbi Judah Loew used information from the Kabalah—the central book of Jewish mysticism—to learn the formula by which God first made man out of clay, and with the help of two other pious men built a man out of clay and brought him to life. The final step of this process was to place God's secret name on a parchment and place it in the forehead of the Golem.

"Loew's **Golem was between seven-and-a-half and nine feet tall** and had tremendous strength, but had a very placid and passive disposition when not under orders to act otherwise. He also lacked the one faculty that only God can give, the power of speech. Because this **giant** was passive and mute, people in the ghetto assumed he was half-witted and the word 'golem' has also come to mean 'idiot.'"[6]

Golems are often portrayed in role-playing games.

"In Dungeons and Dragons **golems are giants (over 7-12 feet tall)** made of various inanimate substances forming the shape of a person and are granted life by a series of spells cast by a magician or priest. The most common of these golems are made of flesh, clay, stone, or iron."[7]

In other words, the golem is a very tall creature (like the Nephilim) who supposedly could follow simple commands. "Sometimes, someone who is large but intellectually slow is called a golem."[8]

"Was the golem human? According to the rabbis, this creature had the same life force of any animal or living being, but it did not possess the same level of intelligence as humans. Stories about the golem's life describe the **creature being dumb,** unable to speak, but capable of understanding basic instructions. There are many discussions among the rabbis over the centuries about the attributes of this manmade creature."[9]

GOLEM IN THE BIBLE

The word "golem" is used one time in the Hebrew Bible in Psalm 139:16: "Thine eyes did see my substance, yet being **unperfect** [Hebrew: golem]; and in Thy book all my members were written, which in continuance were fashioned, when as yet there was none of them." While it is true that the "golem" is unperfect, please note that the Bible says that **ALL** the members were written before they were fashioned. The embryo was also a **LIVING,** breathing baby that was developing. Isaiah 44:24 says that God "formed thee from the womb." Psalm 100:3 adds: "Know ye that the Lord He is God: it is He that hath made us, and not we ourselves...." The forming child had a soul and intelligence. The Biblical golem certainly wasn't a lifeless corpse without a soul or spirit. It also wasn't some 9 foot giant inside its mother's womb. We cannot equate the golem of the Bible to the fictional stories of evil monsters.

It is also claimed that when God created Adam he was a golem for the first twelve hours and then God breathed into him the breath of life.[10] In *Tree of Souls* we find that when Adam was created as a golem,

"...he was as tall as the distance from the earth to heaven, big enough to fill the world from east to west or from north to south. His two eyeballs were like globes of the sun....

"When the angels saw him, they trembled and fled....Then God placed His hand upon Adam and reduced his size until he was no more than a hundred cubits tall, and all the springs of wisdom were closed to him."[11]

Gnosticism also teaches that Adam was a golem and a giant.[12]

Those who push the Nephilim theory tell us that the giants resulted from the fallen angels mating with mankind. However, if God created Adam as a giant and his **REDUCED** stature was still 150 feet tall, why is there such a fuss about the giants in Genesis 6? If Adam had actually been that tall, don't you think his offspring would naturally have also been tall? No fallen angels would have been necessary to produce giant descendants. If giantism was a curse,[13] why would God have made Adam a giant?

While we do not know how tall Adam was, there's no proof that he was a giant. We also know that he wasn't a shapeless mass.

The Bible tells us that "the Lord God **FORMED** man..." (Genesis 2:5). In fact, the Hebrew word for "formed" in Genesis 2:5 is the same Hebrew word for "fashioned" found in Psalm 139:16 (quoted above).

Mankind has been trying to imitate God in creating life but since man is limited in his abilities, his creations supposedly remain mute, dumb, and soulless.

It is claimed that only the most righteous and holy person could make a golem.[14]

"Creation of a golem is a special case. **Only the most righteous of believers are allowed to create them.** Some say that only those who are near to God and his wisdom will be able to follow the ritual to completion."[15]

"Bringing a golem to life was understood to be a process that only those closest to God, the holiest people who had gained some of God's wisdom and power, could accomplish. However, the life that could be created by any man would always be less than that created by God. Thus, a golem was generally unable to speak, and had no free will, always having to obey its maker. However, in many tales the golem outgrows his master physically, becoming dangerous both to people and property, and has to be deactivated."[16]

Another source states that the golems

"...were **a creation of those who were very holy and close to God.** A very holy person was one who strove to approach God, and in that pursuit would gain some of God's wisdom and power. One of these powers was the creation of life. No matter how holy a person became, however, the being they created would be but a shadow of one created by God."[17]

If only the most holy person can create a golem, isn't it strange that golems are such monsters and evil creatures? Also, the method by which these "righteous" people supposedly create these beings is through magic and incantations.[18] The Bible specifically forbids such occultic practices (Deuteronomy 18:10-12; Leviticus 19:26, 31; 20:27;

II Kings 17:17; Galatians 5:19-21), so a truly righteous person would not even try to create such an object as that would make him or her disobey God's Word.

Since the golem was not human we are told that it did not have a soul.[19] This is the same thing that is said of the Nephilim and chimeras—that they did not have a soul.[20] The chimera is described as

> "...any beast constructed of two or more species from any of the numerous planets conquered by the Nephilim. These are the generic minions of almost every Nephilim, and are considered nothing more than **soulless,** thoughtless tools, **brought to life through necromancy.** In almost all cases, they are completely mindless, without a will of their own and are under the complete control of their creator."[21]

Dr. Joye Pugh writes: "A perfect example of a Chimera would be the sexual union between The Fallen Angels and the 'daughters of men,' which produced Giants mentioned in the Book of *Genesis.*"[22] She claims that Goliath was a Chimera because he was supposedly "part human and part Fallen Angel."[23]

We've already looked at the issue of the fallen angels in an earlier chapter and have shown that the "giants" were not produced by the fallen angels. We've also previously covered the topic about Goliath being a man and not a hybrid or a chimera.

Concerning the idea of chimeras, Pugh adds:

> "Some cults teach that Jesus never died on the cross, but was nursed back to health and died a natural death later. Others contend that He was an offspring of man who was created no different than that of the union occurring between the Fallen Angels and the daughters of men, which gave birth to the Giants. In other words, to them, Jesus was a Chimera like the Giants; a mixed human and spiritual being."[24]

The really shocking part is not that the cults believe that Jesus is a chimera but what Pugh interjects at this point. She continues:

"**There is great uniqueness in Jesus being a Chimera,** because **He was truly a 'one-of-a-kind' hybrid.** The major difference between Him versus a Giant is the fact that Jesus' Father was not just a Fallen Angel, but God Almighty incarnate—the Creator of all. Therefore, when Jesus died, He resurrected His body and did not become a spiritual Demon like the Giants, who, upon death of their flesh, walked the Earth without a body because their spirits had already been condemned to eternal damnation. As Fallen Angels, their spirits could not ever re-enter Heaven, but the Spirit and the resurrected body of Jesus could."[25]

In other words, instead of pointing out that the cults are incorrect in their belief, she accepts their belief that Jesus is a hybrid or a chimera! Oh, sure, she does add an evangelical-sounding message, but to me her statement seems like blasphemy—especially when you read her definition of a chimera earlier in her book which she describes as "a **mythical** Greek creature that was said to possess a lion's head, a goat's body, and a Serpent's tail."[26]

CHIMERA AS A SYMBOL OF SATANIC FORCES

A more detailed explanation about a chimera comes from Monstropedia.org where we find:

"Descriptions vary—some say it had the body of a goat, the tail of a snake or European dragon and the head of a lion, though others say it had heads of both the goat and lion, with a snake for a tail. **It is generally considered to have been female,** despite the mane adorning its lion's head. All descriptions, however, agree that it breathed fire from one or more of its heads.

"Sighting the chimera was a sign of storms, shipwrecks, and natural disasters (particularly volcanos). In Medieval Christian art, **the chimera appears as a symbol of Satanic forces.**"[27]

Another reference relates:

"The Chimera is most famous for being a specific female fire-breathing monster in Greek mythology with a lion's head, a goat's body, and a dragon or serpent's tail. The Chimera's tail is often the front part of a serpent including the head.

"Occasionally the front of the Chimera is said to have three heads: the head of a lion, goat, and serpent, but the original myth described it with only the head of a lion....

"Dungeons and Dragons describes chimeras as having dragon wings, a lion body with the hind legs of a goat, and three heads in front of a lion, goat, and dragon. Some of the dragon heads of these chimeras breathe fire, but not all.

"In Dragon Quest, chimeras are giant fire-breathing vultures. It was translated as a wyvern for the US release.

"The word, chimera is now often used to mean a grotesque product of the imagination."[28]

Does any of this describe Jesus in any way?!

Remember, too, we have been told that the golems, chimeras, Nephilim, etc., do not have a soul (or a neshama). The idea of beings without souls is not a Scriptural idea but it can be found in the world of the occult as well as the *Talmud*. Sadly, this idea has now infiltrated the evangelical church.

JESUS IS NOT A CHIMERA

Now, if Jesus is a chimera, He couldn't possess a soul by this theory. However, we have numerous Scripture references telling us that Christ did have a soul (Greek: psuche). For example:

✝ "Then saith He unto them, My **soul** is exceeding sorrowful, even unto death: tarry ye here, and watch with Me" (Matthew 26:38).

✝ "Now is My **soul** troubled; and what shall I say? Father, save Me from this hour: but for this cause came I unto this hour" (John 12:27; see also Mark 14:34).

✝ "Because thou wilt not leave My **soul** in hell, neither wilt thou suffer thine Holy One to see corruption" (Acts 2:27).

✝ "He seeing this before spake of the resurrection of Christ, that His **soul** was not left in hell, neither His flesh did see corruption" (Acts 2:31).

Jesus also possessed a spirit (breath or neshama). The Hebrew word "neshama" is comparable to "pneuma" in the Greek which would be "spirit" or "breath" in English.[29] With this in mind, here are a few verses showing that Jesus also had a spirit. (The Greek word for "pneuma" is boldfaced in the following references.)

✝ "And when Jesus had cried with a loud voice, He said, Father, into Thy hands I commend My **spirit:** and having said thus, He gave up the ghost" (Luke 23:46; see also Matthew 27:50 and John 19:30).

✝ "For I know that this shall turn to my salvation through your prayer, and the supply of the **Spirit** of Jesus Christ" (Philippians 1:19).

✝ "And immediately when Jesus perceived in His **spirit** that they so reasoned within themselves, He said unto them, Why reason ye these things in your hearts?" (Mark 2:8).

✝ "The first man Adam was made a living soul; the last Adam [Jesus] was made a quickening **spirit....**The first man is of the earth, earthy: the second man is the Lord from heaven" (I Corinthians 15:45, 47).

Jesus was not some type of hybrid. He was fully God and fully man. II Timothy 3:16 points out that "God was manifest in the flesh" through Jesus. Matthew 2:23 reveals: "Behold, a virgin shall be with child, and shall bring forth a son, and they shall call His name Emmanuel, which being interpreted is, **God with us.**"

Returning to the idea of the golem, we find: "Similar to the Chimeras, a Golem is a creature made of soil, and brought to life by ancient alchemy....**Not having souls,** their 'alchemy' was limited to manipulating their bodies into disguises or weapons."[30]

The legend of the golem has appeared in various forms in more recent years. Some of these modifications include:

📖 Dr. Frankenstein's monster[31]

❧ "The Incredible Hulk. The Hulk was created by accident but as a result of humans messing around with radioactive materials. The Hulk did not have the power of articulate speech."[32]

❧ The Sorcerer's Apprentice (popularized by Walt Disney's *Fantasia)*[33]

❧ "The Hunchback of Notre Dame. Note that the hunchback Quasimoto fell in love with Esmeralda."[34]

❧ Hal in the movie *2001: A Space Odyssey*[35]

It is interesting to note that some people believe that the Nephilim are "much like the Golem."[36] There is one notable difference as the golems were considered to be dumb, mindless creatures[37] but the Nephilim are usually considered to be very intelligent creatures.

"According to tradition, in addition to being very large and strong, the **Nephilim had enormous psychic abilities.** They performed out of body experiences, levitation, mind control, time travel, mind reading and remote viewing. They had the power of pronouncing and removing curses and diseases, and had ways of knowing and predicting the future....

"**They were also extremely intelligent.** They knew all about science, architecture, and engineering....They drank our blood and slaughtered our babies, and were almost certainly tampering with both human and animal gene pools to pervert the creation and make our redemption impossible. They were the heroes of old, the mighty men of renown, memorialized in every mythology, and the primary reason God had to destroy the world and all its inhabitants in the Great Flood."[38]

"These half-angel half-human babies grew up to be **giants with super human abilities and intelligence.**"[39]

HITLER AND THE MASTER RACE

Adolph Hitler and the Nazis worked on experiments to create a super human master race.

"It may shock people to be told this, but one of the beliefs of the Nazis was that they were descended from the Nepilim (sic), the giants of old. The goal of the Nazi breeding program was to rebuild these old 'Nephilim' genes, thereby producing a race of new 'supermen' equipped with great stature and supernatural and occult powers. The Nazis believed killing the Jews was the required blood-sacrifice needed to animate a new generation of super-men with Luciferian powers."[40]

Hitler said:

"I will tell you a secret...I am founding an Order. It is from there that the second stage will emerge—the stage of the Man-God, when Man will be the measure and center of the world. The Man-God, that splendid Being, will be an object of worship."[41]

"Creation is not yet completed. Man has reached a definite stage of metamorphosis. The ancient human species is already in a state of decline, just managing to survive. Humanity accomplishes a step up once every seven hundred years, and the ultimate aim is the coming of the Sons of God. All creative forces will be concentrated in a new species. The two varieties will evolve rapidly in different directions. One will disappear, and the other will flourish. It will be infinitely superior to modern man. Do you understand the profound meaning of our National-Socialist movement?"[42]

"Anyone who interprets National Socialism merely as a political movement knows almost nothing about it. It is more than religion; it is the determination to create a new man."[43]

We also find:

"The strong parallels between the Nazi creation of a race of demonic super-men and the legends of the Golem should be viewed as no accident. The Nazi SS leaders devoted a lot of effort to studying precisely this kind of material....

"But there is another, more sinister, level to the myth of the Golem. It was to serve as a physical body for the indwelling of Satan. The Golem had no soul of its own to be 'possessed' by Satan, which allowed it to be used in a more complete and powerful manner than in a 'possession.'"[44]

Sherry Shriner claims: "The antichrist will be Satan's seed—a Nephilim....This will probably include cloning and a hybrid or of the serpent seed illuminati-bloodline."[45]

HYBRID RACE THROUGH CLONING

Some evangelicals also believe we will once again have a hybrid race through cloning. For instance, John Torell writes:

"This is another step in the direction of cloning of a human being. By bypassing the use of a sperm from a man, and instead 'gutting' the egg from a woman and then inserting 'the guts' from another human's cell, they are hoping to be able to produce a copy of the person who gave the cell. If this is successful, it will **produce a humanoid; it will be a human body with no soul. This will be a specie not seen on earth since the days of Noah before the flood, when fallen angels came into women and impregnated them and the offspring were called 'giants'**....

"Satan had by now created a half human/half demonic race and **for such a being there was no salvation.**"[46]

Since the Nephilim are supposedly soulless beings, can they reproduce? If they can't reproduce they will die out quickly. If they can, will their offspring also be soulless? If a Nephilim would mate with a human being, would that "child" have a soul since he's half human or would he be soulless since he's half Nephilim? At what point would a soul enter into the offspring or are all the offspring eternally doomed?

Harry Walther claims:

"In reality, every infant born to these Alien/human hybrids will not have a human soul, but the SOUL of an Ancient Demon! Remember back in the Days of Noah, The Alien/Human hybrid race was destroyed in The Great Flood. But their souls, being neither human or martian were doomed to roam the earth and they became the DEMONS that JESUS exorcized (sic) from possessed people.

"Satan will use the human womb to bring these ancient demons back to walk the earth in human-hybrid form."[47] [Emphasis in the original.]

"The second stage is for the extraterrestrials (AKA fallen angels) to create a race of beings that though they appear to be human in every aspect are really just shells of humans with no soul. This is the reason why the eggs and sperm are collected from the abductees. These materials allow them to create beings that can be inhabited by the demonic hordes that long for bodies."[48]

Pugh alleges:

"Presently, our generation is perfecting that capability. The acknowledgement of the first human Clone will pave the way for others to jump on the bandwagon. It is a tightly guarded secret that one of the oldest, successfully living Clones is a Chimera who is now over 21 years of age. His debut to the world will soon be an eye opener as to how perfect the process of Cloning really is."[49]

Olaf Hage asks:

"If you were seeking a body, a vessel to occupy for the grand finale of human history, would you settle for some moldy sixteenth century Golem, or might you prefer a more princely portion: handsome, rich and powerful?

"Former mighty ones cast from the high battlements of Heaven must surely select a succulent slice of Scottish laddie over even the best-preserved Medieval Golem.

"And what if that Highlander were an 'immortal' as the old clan legends tell? Perhaps there's more to all these ancient claims of 'Mighty Men of old, the men of renown' than we have dared suspect. Can a child be brought into the world without a soul? Are the Nephilim genes still with us? Does the blood of angels flow in our veins? Do giants walk among us? Are our dreams haunted by the auld din of warring seraphim?

"Can a handsome young man truly be a Golem?

"Does evil prefer beauty and glamour over ugliness? Is our naive habit of equating wickedness with warts leading us into deception? Perhaps the truth is too obvious:

"The Golem hides."[50]

We will look a little closer at cloning later in this book but first we need to study Daniel 2 so we will be better able to understand how these verses are being used to explain cloning—and what is supposed to transpire from such a technique.

10. WHAT ABOUT DANIEL 2?

King Nebuchadnezzar had requested that certain Israelites "in whom was no blemish, but well favoured, and skilful in all wisdom, and cunning in knowledge, and understanding science, and such as had ability in them to stand in the king's palace, and whom they might teach the learning and the tongue of the Chaldeans" (Daniel 1:4) be brought to Babylon. The young man, Daniel, was one such person who was taken to stand before the king.

In the second year of Nebuchadnezzar's reign he had a dream which troubled him greatly. Of course, being a pagan king, he called his magicians, astrologers, and sorcerers and asked for the interpretation of his dream. The problem was that Nebuchadnezzar had forgotten the dream yet he still wanted an interpretation. He told the men:

> "The thing is gone from me: if ye will not make known unto me the dream, with the interpretation thereof, ye shall be cut in pieces, and your houses shall be made a dunghill. But if ye shew the dream, and the interpretation thereof, ye shall receive of me gifts and rewards and great honour: therefore shew me the dream, and the interpretation thereof. They answered again and said, Let the king tell his servants the dream, and we will shew the interpretation of it. The king answered and said, I know of certainty that ye would gain the time, because ye see the thing is gone from me. But if ye will not make known unto me the dream, there is but one decree for you: for ye have prepared lying and corrupt words to speak before me, till the time be changed: therefore tell me the dream, and I shall know that ye can shew me the interpretation thereof. The Chaldeans answered before the king, and said, There is not a man upon the earth that can shew the king's matter: therefore there is no king, lord, nor ruler, that asked such things at any magician, or astrologer, or Chaldean. And it is a rare thing that the king requireth, and there is none other that can shew it before the king, except the gods, whose dwelling is not with flesh. For this cause the king was angry and very furious, and commanded to destroy all the wise men of

Babylon. And the decree went forth that the wise men should be slain; and they sought Daniel and his fellows to be slain" (Daniel 2:5-13).

Daniel asked Arioch, the captain of the king's guard, why the decree was so hasty so Arioch told him what the king had demanded. When Daniel heard the story, he asked the king for some time and promised to give him the interpretation. Daniel then told his three Hebrew friends about the decree and all of them prayed that God would reveal the dream and He answered their prayers. Arioch took Daniel to the king and Daniel said:

"The secret which the king hath demanded cannot the wise men, the astrologers, the magicians, the soothsayers, shew unto the king; But there is a God in heaven that revealeth secrets, and maketh known to the king Nebuchadnezzar what shall be in the latter days" (Daniel 2:27-28).

Here is what Daniel revealed to Nebuchadnezzar:

"Thou, O king, sawest, and behold a great image. This great image, whose brightness was excellent, stood before thee; and the form thereof was terrible. This image's head was of fine gold, his breast and his arms of silver, his belly and his thighs of brass, His legs of iron, his feet part of iron and part of clay. Thou sawest till that a stone was cut out without hands, which smote the image upon his feet that were of iron and clay, and brake them to pieces. Then was the iron, the clay, the brass, the silver, and the gold, broken to pieces together, and became like the chaff of the summer threshingfloors; and the wind carried them away, that no place was found for them: and the stone that smote the image became a great mountain, and filled the whole earth....And whereas thou sawest iron mixed with miry clay, they shall mingle themselves with the seed of men: but they shall not cleave one to another, even as iron is not mixed with clay" (Daniel 2:31-35, 43).

"MINGLE THEMSELVES WITH THE SEED OF MEN"

Before looking at the interpretation of the dream, we're going to focus in on part of verse 43 for a while: "they shall mingle themselves with the seed of men...."

Many evangelicals today are using this phrase to try to prove that the Nephilim will return and once again mingle with mankind. For instance, Pastor Michael Hoggard and Thomas Horn teach this viewpoint as well as Chuck Missler who declares:

"As he [Daniel] switches to a personal pronoun, they, 'shall mingle themselves with the seed of men....' This is extremely suggestive when viewed in light of the warning of our Lord in Luke 17:26, ostensibly directing us to look more closely at Genesis 6.

"Just what (or who) are 'mingling with the seed of men?' These would seem to refer to some beings who are not the seed of men themselves!

"Could this be a hint of a return to the mischief of Genesis 6? It staggers the mind to consider the potential significance of Daniel's passage and its implications for the future global governance.

"Are these 'aliens' so prolific that they constitute a political constituency?

"Will there be UFO incidents as part of a carefully orchestrated program to lead us toward a political agenda? Or has it started already? Are the UFOs, and the increasingly widespread abductions, part of the preparations for this scenario?"[1]

Jack Kelley remarks:

"The Aramaic word for seed means offspring so seed of men is a way of saying mankind, and the fact that 'they' are differentiated from mankind hints that 'they' may not be human. Also, the mixing will not be successful, just as trying to mix iron with pottery is not successful, underscoring their difference. So it's possible to infer from this that there could be a non-human element trying to mix itself into the general population....

"If that's the case then the phrase 'as it was in the days of Noah' that Jesus used in Matt. 24:37 takes on an even more literal meaning. And in those days the Nephilim were considered 'Heroes, men of renown' (Gen. 6:4) so it's likely that this would be the case in the future as well. As to when they're revealed and what their specific role will be, we're not told."[2]

"Some commentators use this verse to support a view that in the last days non-humans will once again practice cross breeding with humans as in the days of Noah. They point to documented cases of alien abduction that show an unusual interest in our reproductive systems. Some even speculate that there are large numbers of these hybrids among us now, just waiting for the signal to go into action."[3]

DEMON-ALIEN INVASION

Another person declares:

"Frightening, and yet it is very true. But Genesis is not the only area that speaks of the demon-alien invasion. The feet and 10 toes formed by a blend of ceramic clay and iron in the colossal and splendid statue in Nebuchadnezzar's fantastic dream symbolizes the FINAL UNIFIED EARTHLY GOVERNMENT, formed by a 'planetary takeover' by an ALIEN RACE, headed by Lucifer (Satan). Have you ever read Daniel 2:43 with 'new eyes'?

"'As you saw iron mixed with ceramic clay, THEY will MINGLE WITH THE SEED OF MEN; but they will not adhere to one another, just as iron does not mix with clay.'

"The 'IRON' is in reference to an 'EXTERNAL RACE' outside of the 'CERAMIC CLAY,' being the 'RACE OF MAN.' This external demon-alien race can be called the 'Iron People.' The word 'they' is referencing this demon-alien race. Daniel is telling us that the demon-alien race will genetically intermingle its DNA with the DNA (seed) of our race, precipitating the creation of a 'NEW HYBRID RACE' of 'IRON-CLAY PEOPLE'; this is the blending of ceramic clay (man) with iron (demon-aliens) that Daniel describes, but says will not adhere for long.

"The New Hybrid Race will be 'Neo Preterhumans' (New Super Humans) that will become the new 'men of renowned,' a replication of events mirroring the events in the Days of Noah. 'For as in the days of Noah, so shall be when cometh the Son of Man.'"[4] [Emphasis in the original.]

Sherry Shriner writes:

"The Prophet Daniel prophesied that the last days ruling kingdom would be iron mixed with miry clay and in Daniel 2:43 he warns, 'they shall mingle with the seed of men.' This is literal DNA tampering and hybridization to living and cohabitation with humans."[5]

Dr. Joye Pugh comments:

"The kingdoms made of Iron and Clay will fall, just like all the kingdoms before them—by the hand of God. The Gold kingdom of the Fallen Angels, the Silver kingdom of the Fallen Angels mating with humans to produce the Giants before the Flood, the Bronze race of the Demigods with the remnant of the Giants, the Iron race of Demigods mixing with pagans like the Canaanites, and the Clay and Iron race consisting of the mixing between the good seed of Abraham and Satan's evil lineages all will be destroyed. Scripture plainly states that mixing Fallen Angel genetics and mankind will not hold together; yet Satan, through the ages, has tried and tried to remake mankind to his pleasing."[6]

Notice that Pugh insists that "Scripture PLAINLY STATES that mixing fallen angel genetics and mankind will not hold together." Where does the Bible PLAINLY state such nonsense? Couldn't she at least give the verse—if there were such a verse? The Bible DOES PLAINLY state the meaning of these kingdoms—but IT IS NOT at all what Pugh claims it is. Look carefully at Daniel 2:36-45:

"This is the dream; and **we will tell the interpretation thereof** before the king. Thou, O king, art a king of kings: for the God of heaven hath given thee a <u>kingdom,</u> power, and strength, and glory....**Thou art this head of gold.** [*Joye claims that this is the kingdom of the fallen angels but the Bible says that the Gold kingdom was Nebuchadnezzar himself. She next claims that the Silver kingdom is the mating of the fallen angels with humans to produce the Giants but let's look at the Bible:*] And **after thee** shall arise another <u>kingdom</u> inferior to thee [*The Silver kingdom ONLY comes AFTER King Nebuchadnezzar's reign—not before the flood*], and another third <u>kingdom</u> of brass, which shall bear rule over all the earth. And the fourth <u>kingdom</u> shall be strong as iron: forasmuch as iron breaketh in pieces and subdueth all things:

and as iron that breaketh all these, shall it break in pieces and bruise. And whereas thou sawest the feet and toes, part of potters' clay, and part of iron, the kingdom shall be divided; but there shall be in it of the strength of the iron, forasmuch as thou sawest the iron mixed with miry clay. And as the toes of the feet were part of iron, and part of clay, so the kingdom shall be partly strong, and partly broken. And whereas thou sawest iron mixed with miry clay, they shall mingle themselves with the seed of men: but they shall not cleave one to another, even as iron is not mixed with clay. And **in the days of these kings** *[kings, plural, hence the "they" of v. 43]* shall the God of heaven set up a kingdom, which shall never be destroyed: and the kingdom shall not be left to other people, but it shall break in pieces and consume all these kingdoms, and it shall stand for ever. Forasmuch as thou sawest that the stone was cut out of the mountain without hands, and that it brake in pieces the iron, the brass, the clay, the silver, and the gold; the great **God hath made known to the king what shall come to pass** <u>hereafter</u> *[not thousands of years before]*: and the **dream is certain, and** *the interpretation thereof sure."*

SILVER KINGDOM WAS NOT PRIOR TO THE FLOOD

According to the Bible, the Gold Kingdom was during Nebuchadnezzar's reign which was around 580 BC. The Silver Kingdom came AFTER that, yet Pugh claims that the Silver Kingdom was BEFORE the Flood which was almost 1000 years PRIOR to Nebuchadnezzar's reign. Not only does her interpretation defy Scripture, her time line doesn't agree with the Scripture.

Every person is free to believe or disbelieve the Bible (although there are consequences if we do not believe it). However, I am greatly saddened by those (such as Pugh) who claim they believe the Bible but who continually ignore the explicit Scriptural references. There is no indication in these verses to alien beings intermingling with mankind. The text is clear that **KINGDOMS** are being referenced here. Agreements and alliances between nations can be made but many times the nations are not really united in heart. "They speak vanity every one with his neighbor: with flattering lips and with a double heart do they speak" (Psalm 12:2). Daniel refers to two kings whose "hearts shall be to do mischief, and they shall speak lies at one table; but it shall not prosper..." (Daniel 11:27).

Furthermore, in this very chapter (Daniel 2) that is supposed to "prove" that angels will once again mate with humans, we find just the opposite! When Nebuchadnezzar dreamed the dream about the kingdoms, he could not remember the dream and called the Chaldeans, astrologers, magicians, and sorcerers to show him the dream. They answered:

> "O king, live for ever: tell thy servants the dream, and we will shew the interpretation. The king answered and said to the Chaldeans, The thing is gone from me: if ye will not make known unto me the dream, with the interpretation thereof, ye shall be cut in pieces, and your houses shall be made a dunghill. But if ye shew the dream, and the interpretation thereof, ye shall receive of me gifts and rewards and great honour: therefore shew me the dream, and the interpretation thereof. The king answered and said, I know of certainty that ye would gain the time, because ye see the thing is gone from me. But if ye will not make known unto me the dream, there is but one decree for you: for ye have prepared lying and corrupt words to speak before me, till the time be changed: therefore tell me the dream, and I shall know that ye can shew me the interpretation thereof" (Daniel 2:4b-9).

Now, look at the rest of the answer that the Chaldeans gave Nebuchadnezzar:

> "The Chaldeans answered before the king, and said, There is not a man upon the earth that can shew the king's matter: therefore there is no king, lord, nor ruler, that asked such things at any magician, or astrologer, or Chaldean. And it is a rare thing that the king requireth, and there is none other that can shew it before the king, **EXCEPT THE GODS, *WHOSE DWELLING IS <u>NOT</u> WITH FLESH*"** (Daniel 2:10-11).

Here are the magicians and sorcerers who are in contact with evil forces of the spirit world and yet they stated that the gods do not dwell with flesh. Why, then, would the dream's interpretation be used to "prove" that the gods (or angels) will dwell or intermingle with flesh? If only this **entire** chapter had been read and studied, the conclusion that some evangelicals have reached, would have been easily disproved—not just once but twice (Daniel 2:10-11 **and** 36-45).

To try to make Daniel 2:43 fit in with an alien agenda and to postulate that this verse suggests humans intermating with angels shows how desperate some people are to try to prove a theory that they cannot prove by the Bible.

Before discussing cloning, we need to look at another text in Daniel which concerns the "Watchers."

11. WHO ARE THE "WATCHERS"?

King Nebuchadnezzar had another dream which is recorded in Daniel 4. In his dream he saw "a watcher and an holy one" (Daniel 4:13).

Who are the watchers? Luciferian Michael Ford asserts:

> "In certain rabbinical literature, the Daughters of Cain were those who joined in sexual union with the **Fallen Angels, the Watchers,** and gave birth to the Nephilim, the Giants who were war like and brutal."[1]

The Temple of the Black Light "is an international temple dedicated to the...Tradition of Luciferianism/Satanism."[2] They report that "the leaders of the order of angels called The **Watchers**...chose to break free...and **acted in accordance with the will of Lucifer.**"[3]

Occult writer, Richard Cavendish, "lists the Watchers as the Fallen Angels that magicians call forth in ceremonial magick."[4]

Raven Grimassi notes that "every act of magick that a Wiccan performs is observed and noted by the Watchers."[5] He adds: "There is a definite link between the 'powers' of a Wiccan and their rapport with the Watchers."[6]

Seeming to agree with Satanists and occultists, Dr. Joye Pugh purports:

> "Another historical work, *The Book of Enoch,* calls Fallen Angels the 'Watchers.' These 'Watchers' are described as Satan and his Fallen Angels who engaged in sexual relationships with earthly women against Jehovah's wishes. The term 'Watcher' appears in the Bible's Book of *Daniel.*"[7]

Before continuing with this thought, let me state that the *Book of Enoch* **IS NOT** a historical work. (We will look at this book in detail in a later chapter.)

She also claims:

"The 'Watcher's' (sic) offspring were (sic) the Nephilim, who are also referred to as the Giants. The Fallen Angels' involvement in the affairs of mankind has been an ongoing battle between the forces of good and evil ever since the Garden of Eden."[8]

"As you will recall, in ancient times, the 'Watchers' (Fallen Angels) and human women produced hybrids that the Bible recorded as Giants. Alien hybrids, Fairy changelings, and the Giants have always been alluded to as existing. They are mentioned in the Bible, as well as in literary words of mythology and folklore as being offspring from the sexual relations between Demons, gods, and humans."[9]

Pugh forthrightly states that the Bible mentions these hybrids but she fails to provide the Bible reference for her statement. Where does the Bible speak about "Alien hybrids, Fairy changelings," etc.? What Bible is Joye reading?

Another source asks: "Who were these Watchers or Heavenly Beings? According to the Book of Daniel they were fallen angels (Daniel 4:13,17, 23)."[10]

ENOCH AND THE WATCHERS

Did the idea of watchers being fallen angels come from Daniel—or is there another source for this notion? Actually, this concept is taken from the *Book of Enoch*. We are told: "The First Book of Enoch was the first piece of Jewish literature to describe a class of angels, the Watchers, who are positively evil and who lead the dead to a place of eternal torment."[11]

"It is in Enoch where we first learn about the rebellion of the Watchers, the angels assigned to watch over and guard over the earth."[12]

"According to the Book of Enoch, these Watchers instructed the people of Earth in many studies, including the use of charms and enchantments, the arts of magic, and the secrets of the cosmetic trade."[13] [Emphasis in the original.]

"Another study in which the Watchers instructed earthlings was astrology, with all its concomitant evils."[14]

The idea of evil watchers was mentioned in the *Book of Enoch*. It was then picked up by the occult world, and now this conjecture is being propagated by the church world. Some evangelicals (such as Thomas Horn, Patrick Heron, Dr. Joye Pugh, etc.) insist that these watchers were the "sons of God" mentioned in Genesis 6.

For instance, Pugh claims:

"At the beginning of Creation, Satan and his followers took oaths and bound themselves by curses to rebel against God Almighty and descend upon His creation of man. These wicked Angels, called 'Watchers,' actively tempted women. They blatantly taught mankind many evils and twisted versions of the secrets of Heaven to their benefit. Women, who accepted the invitation of the 'Watchers,' bore their children, which produced many evil Giants, called Nephilim, before the Flood."[15]

Thomas Horn writes:

"The familiar Genesis story of Watchers cohabiting with women parallels the modern 'abduction' reports in that the '...sons of God...took them wives of all which they chose.' The implication here is that, as in alien abduction, this was not by mutual agreement or harmony of wills, but that **these women were taken ('took') forcibly at the sole discretion of the powerful beings.** As a result of the abduction-marriages, hybrids were born of the genetic interruption called 'Nephilim.'"[16]

What does the Bible **actually** tell us about the watchers? Were the watchers mentioned in Daniel good or evil beings? Let's take a look.

WATCHER--AN HOLY ONE

Nebuchadnezzar had a dream that troubled him greatly. Once again he called for the magicians, astrologers, Chaldeans, and soothsayers to give him an interpretation but they could not. Finally, he called for Daniel and told him what he dreamed. In his vision he saw a goodly and tall tree. He also saw a **"watcher and an holy one"** who commanded that the tree be cut down but that the stump of it should remain. He added:

> "This matter is by the decree of the watchers, and the demand by the word of the holy ones: to the intent that the living may know that the most High ruleth in the kingdom of men, and giveth it to whomsoever He will, and setteth up over it the basest of men" (Daniel 4:17).

We can clearly see that the watcher is referred to as **AN HOLY ONE.** To get around this clear meaning, Pugh states: "Daniel separated the two and said a watcher AND an holy one. The Watcher is a fallen angel."[17] Notice, however, the wording in Daniel: "I saw in the visions of my head upon my bed, and, behold, <u>A</u> watcher and an holy one came down from heaven; <u>HE</u> cried, and said thus..." (Daniel 4:13-14a). If there were two entities here the pronoun would have been **THEY** instead of **HE.** *Albert Barnes' Notes on the Bible* mentions that only **ONE** angel is being referred to in this passage. He remarks:

> "And, behold, a watcher and an holy one—Or rather, perhaps, 'even a holy one'; or, 'who was a holy one.' He evidently does not intend to refer to two beings, a 'watcher,' and 'one who was holy;' but he means to designate the character of the watcher, that he was holy, or that he was one of the class of 'watchers' who were ranked as holy—as if there were others to whom the name 'watcher' might be applied who were not holy. So Bertholdt, 'not two, but only one, who was both a watcher, and was holy; one of those known as watchers and as holy ones.'"[18]

Likewise, the *Jamieson-Fausset-Brown Bible Commentary* states: "watcher and an holy one—rather, 'even an holy one.' Only one angel is intended, and he not one of the bad, but of the holy angels. Called a 'watcher,' because ever on the watch to execute God's will."[19]

Notice, too, that the watcher came **FROM HEAVEN.** Heaven is a holy place for a holy people. Revelation 21:27 tells us that "there shall in no wise enter into it any thing that defileth, neither worketh abomination, or maketh a lie...." So, if the watcher came from heaven, it had to be a holy being. Psalm 103:20 says: "Bless the Lord, ye His angels, that excel in strength, that do His commandments, hearkening unto the voice of His word." Furthermore, in Daniel's interpretation we see that the watcher's declaration was **"the decree of the most High..."** (Daniel 4:24). The watcher was **NOT** a fallen angel but one of God's **holy** messengers. In Daniel 4:17 we have the plural "watchers" along with the plural "holy ones."

When Daniel heard the dream, he, too, was troubled. He told Nebuchadnezzar that the tree represented the king and that he was going to be abased until he knew "that the most High ruleth in the kingdom of men, and giveth it to whomsoever He will" (Daniel 4:25). Daniel pleaded with him: "Wherefore, O king, let my counsel be acceptable unto thee, and break off thy sins by righteousness, and thine iniquities by shewing mercy to the poor; if it may be a lengthening of thy tranquillity" (Daniel 4:27).

In spite of Daniel's warning, Nebuchadnezzar continued in his sinful ways. A year after this vision he was walking in the palace at Babylon and he bragged:

> "Is not this great Babylon, that I have built for the house of the kingdom by the might of my power, and for the honour of my majesty? While the word was in the king's mouth, there fell a voice from heaven, saying, O king Nebuchadnezzar, to thee it is spoken; The kingdom is departed from thee" (Daniel 4:30-31).

For the next seven years, Nebuchadnezzar lived with the beasts of the field.

> "And at the end of the days I Nebuchadnezzar lifted up mine eyes unto heaven, and mine understanding returned unto me, and I blessed the most High, and I praised and honoured Him that liveth for ever, whose dominion is an everlasting dominion, and His kingdom is from generation to generation:...At the same time my reason returned unto me; and for the glory of my kingdom, mine honour and brightness returned unto me; and my counsellors and my lords sought unto me; and I was established in my kingdom, and excellent majesty was added unto me. Now I

Nebuchadnezzar praise and extol and honour the King of heaven, all whose works are truth, and His ways judgment: and those that walk in pride He is able to abase" (Daniel 4:34, 36-37).

The purpose of the dream was to show Nebuchadnezzar that God ruled in men's affairs. After Nebuchadnezzar was abased, he realized that God was in control and he acknowledged God's power. Would fallen angels give a decree that would result in God's name and majesty being magnified? Of course not!

The Watchers mentioned in Daniel were holy angels which came from heaven with a message from God. They were not fallen angels as some individuals claim.

12. THE NEPHILIM, CLONING, AND THE ANTICHRIST

The idea of golems, chimeras, aliens, and Nephilim is appearing more and more frequently in movies, TV programs, novels, role-playing games, and video games. Obviously, the world is being prepared for a great deception. Remember, deception will play a large role in the end times scenario. Jesus' disciples asked Him: "What shall be the sign of Thy coming, and of the end of the world?" His answer was:

> "Take heed that no man **deceive** you. For many shall come in My name, saying, I am Christ; and shall **deceive** many....And many false prophets shall rise, and shall **deceive** many....For there shall arise false Christs, and false prophets, and shall shew great signs and wonders; insomuch that, if it were possible, they shall **deceive** the very elect" (Matthew 24:4, 5, 11, 24; see also Mark 13:5, 6; Luke 21:8).

☞ "But evil men and seducers shall wax worse and worse, **deceiving, and being deceived**" (II Timothy 3:13).

☞ "Let no man **deceive** you by any means: for that day shall not come, except there come a falling away first, and that man of sin be revealed, the son of perdition" (II Thessalonians 2:3).

☞ "Let no man **deceive** you with vain words: for because of these things cometh the wrath of God upon the children of disobedience" (Ephesians 5:6).

☞ "For they that are such serve not our Lord Jesus Christ, but their own belly; and by good words and fair speeches **deceive** the hearts of the simple" (Romans 16:18).

Notice that the deception includes false teachers and false Christs. Part of this deception is coming from the so-called evangelical world. Using the verse in Daniel 2:43, but ignoring the Biblical interpretation, we now encounter the idea of cloning. Chuck Missler writes:

> "To 'mingle themselves with seed of men,' they have to be something other than the seed of men. What can they be? Are they hybrids produced by cloning? Are they Nephilim produced by fallen angels? Whatever they are, they apparently are prolific enough to be included within the idioms of a vision dealing with global political power in the last days!"[1]

In reference to Daniel 2:43, Larry Taylor says:

> "Daniel is an end-time book revealing here that in the end-time, SEED or DNA mixture will be attempted between Mankind (clay) and Fallen Beings (iron) or as some call them: extraterrestrials or alien beings. This will produce a hybrid or cloned being that will be as the Nephilim or Giants in Genesis 6."[2]

Ralph Davenport speculates:

> "The fallen sons of God will once again attempt to corrupt the human race with their offspring, the Nephilim. I believe the sons of God may be using cloning/DNA technology as well—this may account for the so called alien abductions, but its (sic) still mating with humans, even if indirectly. God consigned the fallen angels to Tartarus who were involved in this sin during the days of Noah, but there is nothing in scripture that would prevent subsequent fallen angels from repeating the behavior of the first...."[3]

Another source claims:

> "In the past, scholars speculated that one day it would be hybridization which would create the antichrist and that these fallen angel-Aliens would develop and produce a creature that is fully fallen angel and fully man....
>
> "The antichrist will be Satan's seed—a Nephilim/Gibborim....This will probably include cloning and a hybrid. Or, of the serpent seed illuminati-bloodline."[4]

Missler states:

"The convolutions that current biotechnologies may hold for the future cannot help but impact our conjectures regarding the bizarre prophecies which the Bible spells out for the coming climax of human history: directable pestilences, the mixing of non-seeds with the seed of men, injectable microchips, images that speak (and enforce). Several prominent Bible commentators have openly conjectured that this Coming World Leader (commonly called 'the Antichrist') may be an 'alien' or have some kind of alien connection. Could this also involve some perversion of biotechnological manipulations?"[5]

"The possibility that the Coming World Leader might boast of an 'alien' connection has been a popular conjecture among prophecy buffs. The fact that he might be a clone of some kind is also hinted at:

"And the beast that was, and is not, even he is the eighth, and is of the seven, and goeth into perdition.—Revelation 17:11

"The beast's definition as being 'an eighth, but of the seven,' is suggestive. Could he be a clone of one of the leaders of the past?"[6]

CLONED BEAST POSSESSES BLOOD OF JESUS

Taking this idea to an extreme, Joye Pugh believes that Satan (whom she identifies as the Antichrist) will actually inhabit the cloned body of Jesus Christ! She was contemplating "how Satan could live in the flesh." She had consulted the *Talmud* and read stories there about the beasts of the field that didn't have a "neshama," that is a beast that supposedly didn't have a soul. She writes:

"According to the book of *Genesis,* man has a living soul. The *Talmud,* a collection of texts and commentaries on Jewish religious law, calls the living soul the 'neshama.' Without the 'neshama' a man was considered to be not quite human. In the *Talmud* there are ancient references to creatures called 'Beasts' that lacked a 'neshama' to make them human. These beasts, called rulers of the field, were described as being in the image of a man. **IF SATAN WERE TO INHABIT THE CLONED BODY OF**

JESUS, HE WOULD BE LIVING IN A HUMAN BODY WITH NO 'NESHAMA.' He would truly fulfill prophecy by being a beast in the image of a man. **THAT BEAST WOULD POSSESS THE BLOOD OF JESUS,** whose blood is considered by many to be a spark of the divine, and immediately be heralded as the Messiah. He would fulfill the Dragon King's Blood Lineage of being half-man and half-god—the beast the New Age is waiting for."[7]

She also states:

"A Clone would be an example of an artificial life. Born without a soul, through fission, a Clone would not be eternal or immortal, but continually living in an undead state. A Cloned body would be a perfect vehicle for Satan to take a ride in. He could totally inhabit a Cloned body, as there is no soul to compete with. In a normal body, Satan can only attempt to possess the body if the soul allows it to happen. With competition of the person's soul, Satan must contend with the fact at any given moment he can be exorcised out by a Priest, as well as through the individual's choice for him to leave, therefore losing control of the body.

"Being the Antichrist requires Satan to find a vehicle that no human can remove him from. The only possibility for this scenario to happen is through a Cloned body that has no soul. The soul or spirit of the body, genetically, cannot be replicated. It leaves the body at death and exists only within the original host; it can not be duplicated."[8]

Could the Antichrist actually be the **CLONED IMAGE OF JESUS?** Before we consider that possibility, we need to look more closely at Pugh's presumptions.

IS SATAN THE ANTICHRIST?

One of Pugh's misconceptions is that Satan is the Antichrist or the Beast.[9] The Bible clearly shows that this is not the case. Turn to Revelation 20:10: "And the DEVIL that deceived them was cast into the lake of fire and brimstone, where the BEAST and the FALSE

PROPHET are, and shall be tormented day and night for ever and ever." We clearly see 3 separate entities here: the devil or Satan, the beast (also known as the Antichrist), and the false prophet so Satan cannot be the Antichrist in the flesh. Revelation 13 tells us that the dragon gives the beast his great power, his seat, and great authority. Verse 4 states: "And they worshipped the dragon which gave power unto the beast: AND they worshipped the beast, saying, Who is like unto the beast?" It is obvious that the beast or the Antichrist is not Satan although the Antichrist does receive his power from Satan. In spite of these clear references, Pugh claims otherwise: "Even the Book of *Revelation* informs believers that **the coming Antichrist will be Lucifer in the flesh of a man,** therefore the spiritual uniting/mixing with earthly flesh."[10]

If the Bible really did say this, as Pugh claims, couldn't she at least give the Bible verse to back up her statement?

Pugh then adds: "Prepare yourself to meet Satan in the flesh. He is alive and walking in a physical body among mankind."[11]

We find that II Thessalonians 2 refers to the Antichrist and it clearly tells us that his "coming is AFTER THE WORKING OF SATAN" but he IS NOT Satan! (See II Thessalonians 2:8-10.)

Proceeding with her false and unscriptural theory, she writes:

"Therefore, the High Priest that the Sanhedrin is eagerly seeking will turn out to be a Clone of Jesus—an evil re-creation of his Image, the Antichrist; but not Jesus. The world will be deceptively told that this re-created Jesus is returning for his so-called second time just as he promised—with the assistance of Cloning technology. They will add that historical records unearthed prove his return is no different than that of the Fallen Angels where, in ancient times, in order to walk on Earth they united/mixed their spiritual side with the flesh and were born from a woman—'As Above, So Below.' Therefore, taking a chimeric cell identified as a mixture of human and the divine from the Holy Shroud to re-birth Jesus will be touted as one and the same. When this Cloned Antichrist eventually does sit in the final Temple proclaiming that he is God, then he and the Temple will be annihilated by the real Jesus at His Second Coming for standing on God's Holy Mount and deceitfully parading in the flesh as 'I AM.'"[12]

She adds: "This diabolical entity is none other than Satan, who has been regenerated in the Cloned image of Jesus Christ."[13]

The reason why Pugh believes Satan will use a cloned body is because

"...there is no soul to compete with....With competition of the person's soul, Satan must contend with the fact at any given moment he can be exorcised out by a Priest, as well as through the individual's choice for him to leave, therefore losing control of the body....The **only possibility** for this scenario to happen is through a Cloned body that has no soul."[14]

CLONE IS IN AN UNDEAD STATE

Pugh claims the clone is in an "undead" state. On page 358 of her book she said: "A Clone would be an example of an artificial life. **Born without a soul,** through fission, a Clone would not be eternal or immortal, **but continually living in an undead state."**[15]

The assumption that this Satanic "undead" clone **CANNOT** have a soul is vital to Pugh's theory. Remember she said: "The **only possibility** for this scenario to happen is through **a Cloned body that has no soul."**[16]

Strangely, on page 357, just one page before the above quote, Pugh explains the "undead" state like this: "It is a condition of being **undead;** a body of this world with the **soul** of one not from this world."[17]

Does the "undead" have a soul or doesn't it? Pugh doesn't even seem to know—yet she continues to push her theory all across America and, sadly, even some evangelicals have been promoting her book.

Continuing with her false theory she asserts that Satan would not only use the "cloned body of Jesus" but that he would actually "possess the blood of Jesus" by cloning the blood on the Shroud of Turin. She believes this is the only way the Antichrist will be able to prove his Merovingian lineage.[18]

DOES SATAN POSSESS THE BLOOD OF JESUS?

Now, if Satan possesses the actual blood of Jesus, and it is only through Christ's blood that we can be saved, will Satan become our Savior? Will Christ's blood—which is supposed to be flowing through Satan's veins—bring redemption? Such a thought is detestable.

While such an idea should be repugnant to true Christians, we do find a somewhat related concept in occult teachings. For instance, there is a poem by Charles Peguy which basically states that the same blood flows through Satan's and Christ's veins:

> "The arms of Jesus are the Cross of Lorraine,
> Both the blood in the artery and the blood in the vein,
> Both the source of grace and the clear fountaine;
> The arms of Satan are the Cross of Lorraine,
> And the same artery and the same vein,
> And the same blood and the troubled fountaine."[19]

In an article by Tracy R. Twyman we find:

> **"The reference to Satan and Jesus sharing the same blood is very important.** A tradition exists, one which **finds support among the Book of Enoch** and many others, that **Jesus and Satan are brothers,** both sons of the Most High God, and they both sat next to his throne in Heaven, on the right and left sides, respectively, prior to Satan's rebellion and the War in Heaven....It makes sense that Satan should both be a direct son of God, since he is described as God's 'Most Beloved Angel' and 'The Brightest Star in Heaven.'"[20]

Twyman, by the way, is the Grand Master of the Dragon Court and Exalted Grand Master of the Ordo Lapsit Exillis.[21]

"The Ordo Lapsit Exillis is named after the Stone that fell from Heaven, the fabled jewel that is said to have fallen from Lucifer's crown during the war in Heaven, and which in the occult is used as a symbol of enlightenment—of the descent of divine light form (sic) the mind of God into the mind of Man. As such it symbolizes Venus, the Morning Star, as well as the Luciferian doctrine of the initiates, the secret knowledge which men are not allowed, and which Lucifer's angels were cast from Heaven for sharing with man....

"For us, the Lapsit Exillis is also a cornerstone, for it is the solid rock upon which our ideals stand, and upon which we have built our work. For us, the Stone that fell from Heaven provides the foundation of our fraternity, and is certainly a jewel most valued."[22]

In other words, Tracy is a follower of Lucifer. Why does the viewpoint of a Luciferian seem to mesh so closely with the viewpoint of a so-called evangelical Southern Baptist by the name of Joye Pugh? Isn't there a problem here?

SHROUD OF TURIN

Now let's consider if there is a possibility that the Antichrist could be the **CLONED IMAGE OF JESUS** with DNA taken from the Shroud of Turin. Pugh claims: "The greatest evidence of Jesus' resurrection is the Holy Shroud of Turin, which today is housed in Turin, Italy. This 2,000 year old faded, linen burial cloth has the imprint of the full body of Jesus on it."[23]

"The reason it is so important is that as the Holy Grail it may very well unlock the secrets of immortality. The presence of God's blood and Jesus' DNA is all over it."[24]

First of all, there is much controversy over the shroud and the exact dating of it has never been proven conclusively. Multiple carbon dating tests have been performed on the shroud and many believe that it dates to about 1260-1390 A.D.[25] However, the carbon dating method has many problems of its own. For instance, **"LIVING** snails were carbon dated at 27,000 years old" and **"LIVING** mollusk shells were dated to be 2,300 years old as well...."[26]

Even if carbon dating did suggest a date of 2000 years for the shroud, that wouldn't prove that it was Christ's shroud. Furthermore, the Shroud of Turin is one piece but the Bible indicates that there were several pieces (more than just a shroud and a napkin) to Christ's grave clothes. John 20:6-7 reveals: "Then cometh Simon Peter following him, and went into the sepulchre, and seeth the **LINEN CLOTHES** lie, **AND** the napkin, that was about His head, not lying with the linen clothes, but wrapped together in a place by itself." The napkin around Christ's head was separate from the other pieces of linen clothes. Luke 24:12 explains: "Then arose Peter and ran unto the sepulchre; and stooping down, he beheld the linen **CLOTHES** laid by **THEMSELVES....**" This certainly doesn't sound like the Shroud of Turin to me since the shroud is one large piece!

Moreover, John 19:40 says: "Then took they the body of Jesus, and wound it in **linen clothes** *with the spices,* as the manner of the Jews is to bury." Let's notice several things about this verse. The linen clothes (plural) were wound or tied about the body. This is the same Greek word as when Jesus told the disciples to go and find the donkey that was **tied.** Notice also that there were spices used. Verse 39 says that it was about an 100 pound weight. Finally, notice that this burial was done according to the Jewish custom of burying. The custom of the first century was to usually wash and straighten the body then to bandage it tightly from the armpits to the ankles in strips of linen about a foot wide. The spices were placed between the wrappings or folds of the linen. These spices served as a preservative as well as a cement to glue the cloth into a solid form. The head was not wrapped like the rest of the body and the Bible does specifically refer to a napkin being around the face and separate from the burial linen. When Lazarus was raised from the dead, he "came forth, bound hand and foot with graveclothes: and his face was bound about with a napkin" (John 11:44).

The Shroud of Turin seems to show wounds that were not washed but the Jewish custom was to wash the body. For instance, in Acts 9:37 we find that Tabitha (who was also called Dorcas) was sick and died and they washed her and "laid her in an upper chamber." Also, with all the spices applied, the burial cloth of Jesus would have been quite stiff but the Shroud of Turin is fairly flexible. So, the Shroud of Turin doesn't fit the Biblical description or the Jewish custom in any way.

FACE NAPKIN

Pugh does mention a "face napkin" (also called a Sudarium) which is kept in Oviedo, Spain. There are claims that the face napkin belongs with the shroud, but wouldn't the face napkin have taken away from the imprint of the face on the shroud? Even stranger, the face napkin doesn't even have an image on it.[27]

The person who was buried in the shroud was approximately 6'2". Although the Bible does not give us Jesus' height we do know that Jews, for the most part, are SHORTER than the average male. According to JewishEncyclopedia.com we find:

> "Measurements of Jews have been taken sporadically in most European countries with the following results: The average height of Jews is 162.1 cm. [approximately 5'3"]; span of arms, 169.1 cm.; and girth around the chest, about 81 cm.: so that they are the **SHORTEST** and narrowest of Europeans."[28]

Could Jesus have been taller than the average Jewish male? While it is possible, it certainly is not likely because Judas had to identify Jesus when he betrayed Him. "Now he that betrayed Him gave them a sign, saying, Whomsoever I shall kiss, that same is He" (Matthew 26:48; see also Mark 14:44 and Luke 22:47-48). (Had Christ been about a foot taller than the average person, He would not have needed to be identified. Judas could have just said to look for the tallest person in the garden.)

Remember, too, the shroud shows a person who had long hair. I Corinthians 11:14 (which was given by inspiration of the Holy Spirit) says: "Doth not even nature itself teach you, that, if a man have long hair, it is a shame unto him?" Do you think that this long-haired man could be Jesus when the Bible condemns long hair on a man?

WAS JESUS A NAZARITE?

Some people have argued that Jesus was a Nazarite[29] and therefore He would have had long hair because the Nazarites were under a vow not to cut their hair. It is true that a Nazarite took a vow not to cut his hair: "All the days of the vow of his separation there shall no razor come upon his head" (Numbers 6:5). We do see, however, that this vow was only for a certain amount of time. It was not a life-long vow (except in a few instances such as Samuel and Samson) and at the end of the vow, the hair was cut and a burnt offering, sin offering, and a peace offering were also presented. Numbers 6 reveals:

> "[T]his is the law of the Nazarite, when the days of his separation are fulfilled: he shall be brought unto the door of the tabernacle of the congregation....And the **Nazarite shall shave the head of his separation at the door of the tabernacle of the congregation, and shall take the hair of the head of his separation, and put it in the fire** which is under the sacrifice of the peace offerings" (Numbers 6:13, 18).

Jesus, however, was not a Nazarite. He was a **Nazarene** because He was from the town of Nazareth. Matthew 2:23 states: "And He came and dwelt in a city called Nazareth: that it might be fulfilled which was spoken by the prophets, He shall be called a Nazarene." (See also Matthew 4:13; 21:11; 26:71; Mark 1:9, 24; 10:27; 14:67; 16:6; Luke 1:26; 2:4, 39, 51; 4:16, 34; 18:37; 24:19; John 1:45; 18:5, 7; 19:19; Acts 2:22; 3:6; 4:10; 6:14; 10:38; 22:8; 26:9.)

Could Jesus the Nazarene have taken the vow of a Nazarite sometime during His life and been under this vow when He was crucified? Searching the Scriptures gives us some answers. We do know that Jesus was not under a Nazarite vow at either the beginning nor the ending of His ministry. How do we know? We find that the Nazarite vow included some stringent requirements: "He shall separate himself from wine and strong drink, and shall drink no vinegar of wine, or vinegar of strong drink, neither shall he drink any liquor of grapes, nor eat moist grapes, or dried. All the days of his separation shall he eat nothing that is made of the vine tree, from the kernels even to the husk" (Numbers 6:3-4). What was the first miracle Jesus performed? He turned the water into wine (John 2:11). Right before His death we see that Jesus gave communion to His disciples (Mark 14:23-25). Both grape juice and wine were forbidden items to a Nazarite while he was under this vow so we know that Jesus could not have been under a Nazarite vow at the beginning nor the end of His ministry. He offered the communion right before His death so His hair would not have been long when He died. (Had Christ had long hair in the Garden, Judas would not have had to identify Him to the soldiers because the custom was short hair and Jesus would have easily been identified as being different.)

Furthermore, part of the Nazarite vow included this command: "All the days that he separateth himself unto the Lord he shall come at no dead body" (Numbers 6:6). Throughout Christ's ministry He touched the dead. He laid His hand upon Jairus' dead daughter and raised her from the dead (Matthew 9:18-25; Mark 5:22-42; Luke 8:41-56). He touched the bier of the widow's son and he was raised (Luke 7:12-15). He also raised Lazarus from the dead (John 11:11-44). These resurrections took place at various times during Jesus' ministry so He could not have been under a Nazarite vow at any of these times.

In Ezekiel 44:20 we see that the **priests were forbidden to have long hair:** "Neither shall they shave their heads, nor suffer their locks to grow long...." In Hebrews we are repeatedly told that **Christ is our high priest.** "Wherefore, holy brethren, partakers of the heavenly calling, consider the Apostle and High Priest of our profession, Christ Jesus" (Hebrews 3:1). "Seeing then that we have a great high priest, that is passed into the heavens, Jesus the Son of

God..." (Hebrews 4:14; see also Hebrews 2:17; 4:15; 5:1, 5-6; 7:17, 21, 26; 8:1; 9:11). Do you really think that Christ would have long hair?

SHROUD SHOWS BEARDED MAN

The shroud also shows a bearded man but, according to a Messianic prophecy found in Isaiah 50:6, we find: "I gave My back to the smiters, and My cheeks to them that PLUCKED OFF THE HAIR: I hid not My face from shame and spitting."

In Isaiah we find a Messianic prophecy which states that Christ's "visage was so marred more than any man, and His form more than the sons of men" (Isaiah 52:14). This means that His appearance was greatly disfigured. This probably occurred during His trial and beatings. Matthew tells us: "Then did they spit in His face, and buffeted Him; and others smote Him with the palms of their hands" (Matthew 26:67; see also Luke 22:64). The following day they scourged Him, put a crown of thorns on His head, spit on Him, and took a reed "and smote Him on the head" (Matthew 27:27-30). The shroud does not seem to show evidence of such excessive abuse.

Pugh believes that the Knights Templar were trying to gain possession of the shroud. She writes:

> "The Templar Order did not actually protect pilgrims on their way to worship at Jerusalem, as has been promoted in history books. Instead, they were on the destroyed Temple site to try and find the 'Secret Pillar,' ancient scrolls, Ark of the Covenant, and the Holy Shroud, which were believed to be hidden beneath the rubble of the Temple. It was their search for this Enochian vault of secrets, temple treasures, and the Holy Shroud for which they formed the Crusades."[30]

Actually, such a supposition seems ludicrous. The Jewish leaders did not believe that Jesus was the Messiah and that was part of the reason why they had wanted Him crucified. John 5:18 states:

"Therefore the Jews sought the more to kill Him, because He not only had broken the sabbath, but said also that God was His Father, making Himself equal with God." At Jesus' trial, the Jews told Pilate: "We have a law, and by our law He ought to die, because He made Himself the Son of God" (John 19:7).

After He was crucified, the chief priests and Pharisees came to Pilate and said:

> "Sir, we remember that **THAT DECEIVER** [referring to Jesus] said, while He was yet alive, After three days I will rise again. Command therefore that the sepulchre be made sure until the third day, lest His disciples come by night, and steal Him away, and say unto the people, He is risen from the dead: so the last error shall be worse than the first. Pilate said unto them, Ye have a watch: go your way, make it as sure as ye can. So they went, and made the sepulchre sure, sealing the stone, and setting a watch" (Matthew 27:63-66).

When Jesus did rise from the dead

> "...behold, some of the watch came into the city, and shewed unto the chief priests all the things that were done. And when they were assembled with the elders, and had taken counsel, they gave large money unto the soldiers, Saying, Say ye, His disciples came by night, and stole Him away while we slept. And if this come to the governor's ears, we will persuade him, and secure you. So they took the money, and did as they were taught: and this saying is commonly reported among the Jews until this day" (Matthew 28:11-15).

SOLDIERS BRIBED

The chief priests thought that Jesus was a deceiver and they had actually bribed the soldiers to lie about Jesus' resurrection. So, why would they want to have Christ's shroud buried in the Temple? The enemies of Christ would not have wanted to keep the cloth because that would have only proved Christ's resurrection which they had denied. The Jews who had Jesus crucified wanted His memory blotted out, so why would they want to keep His shroud as a memorial? Burying His shroud in the temple would not serve their purpose in covering up Christ's resurrection. In fact, it would only **PROVE** His resurrection—which they **DID NOT** want to happen. The disciples wouldn't keep the shroud since the Jews were forbidden to handle bloodstained clothes and they would have broken the Jewish custom by keeping or hiding the cloth. The Levitical law stated that "whosoever touched one that is slain with a sword in the open fields, or a dead body, or a bone of a man, or a grave, shall be unclean seven days" (Number 19:16). After this seven day period, the person needed to be purified and he that "purifieth not himself, defileth the tabernacle of the Lord; and that soul shall be cut off from Israel" (Number 19:13). Every time the shroud would have been touched would have rendered the person who touched it unclean for seven more days.

Additionally, the disciples would not have had access to the Temple area to bury it. Remember that the disciples were behind **closed doors** for fear of the Jews (John 20:19). Can you imagine them asking for permission to access the Temple area by the same Jews that they feared? Also, if the shroud was in their possession, this would only serve the Jewish leaders' purpose and could supply the implied "proof" that the disciples had actually stolen Christ's body.

Furthermore, as already mentioned, the Jews were not allowed to handle bloody clothes so why would they save a bloody (and prohibited) item and allow such an object to be put in their sacred, holy, and purified Temple? This just is not a very likely scenario.

Continuing with her theory, Pugh writes that the Templars

"...became secretly known as the guardians of the Holy Grail, the owners of the Blood of Jesus. His blood was obtained from that which was spilt on the Holy Burial Shroud following His crucifixion. The Crusaders did not want the world to know that they had stolen the Holy Shroud for the purpose of one day regenerating Jesus' Divine Blood through a Noble and Royal Bloodline.

"The Shroud is first believed to have been in the possession of Joseph of Arimathea (sic). According to Scripture, it was he who had wrapped Jesus in a linen burial cloth and placed Jesus in his tomb. Some believe Magdalene is really worshipped by the Templar (sic) because she was the first to have possession of the Shroud when she came to the tomb and found it empty. Scripture verifies that the burial cloth and Face Napkin were all that remained in the tomb after the resurrection. Mary would have had first access to the Shroud and may have possibly taken it when she returned with two of the Disciples to prove to the others that Jesus had indeed resurrected."[31]

DID MARY MAGDALENE POSSESS THE SHROUD?

Could it be possible that Mary Magdalene took the shroud as suggested by Pugh? First of all, Mary was not the only woman at the tomb after the resurrection. According to Luke 24:10 we find: "It was Mary Magdalene, and Joanna, and Mary the mother of James, and other women that were with them" that told the apostles that the Lord was risen. If Mary Magdalene took the shroud she did so with a group of witnesses. Additionally, the grave clothes were still in the tomb when Peter and John later came on the scene. John 20:4-8 reveals:

"So they ran both together: and the other disciple did outrun Peter, and came first to the sepulchre. And he stooping down, and looking in, saw the linen clothes lying; yet went he not in. Then cometh Simon Peter following him, and went into the sepulchre, and seeth the linen clothes lie, And the napkin, that was about his head, not lying with the linen clothes, but wrapped together in a place by itself. Then went in also that other disciple, which came first to the sepulchre, and he saw, and believed."

It is highly doubtful that Mary Magdalene would have kept the shroud to show to the disciples. Just touching it would have made her unclean for seven days. Also, if she did have the shroud as proof of Christ's resurrection, why did Thomas still doubt it (John 20:24-29)? When he finally saw the risen Lord, Jesus said to him: "Thomas, because thou hast seen Me, thou hast believed: BLESSED are they that HAVE NOT SEEN, and yet have believed" (John 20:29). Why would Jesus gently admonish Thomas but not the other disciples if they had only believed He resurrected because they had seen the burial shroud? If Jesus reprimanded Thomas, what would He say to those who were depending on seeing a relic before believing? Hebrews 11:1 tells us that "faith is the substance of things hoped for, the EVIDENCE OF THINGS NOT SEEN" and "without faith it is impossible to please" God (Hebrews 11:6).

Pugh writes:

"Whoever possessed the Shroud following the resurrection allowed it to later resurface and become widely known as the 'Cloth of Edessa.' The Cloth was said to bring healing to anyone who beheld it or touched it. As we have already discussed, the Shroud bears the imprint of the crucified Christ. It was hidden in the walls at Edessa, during the Crusades, in an effort to keep it secure. Unfortunately, the Cloth was discovered by the warring Knights Templar and taken into their possession. The Templar (sic) made sure at the right time that the Holy Shroud would become the sole possession of the Vatican."[32]

SHROUD AS A RELIC

Again, we see a problem with Pugh's idea that this shroud is the shroud of Christ. This cloth supposedly brought healing to anyone who touched it but, by Jewish law, touching such an object was forbidden and caused uncleanness which required a purification ceremony. How could such a prohibited object bring healing? Furthermore, veneration of objects is strictly forbidden since this is idolatry.

Continuing with her unfounded fabrication, Pugh claims:

"The quest of the Templar (sic) during the Crusades was to secure the Holy Blood of Jesus and one day produce from it their Canaanite Messiah, i.e. Evil Twin.

"The Templar (sic) and their Jewish founders knew full well that Jesus was divine. They thought if they could push Jesus to the limit through threatening him with crucifixion that he would choose to bring in his troupes of Angels instead of just dying. He fooled them and chose death in order to offer the entire world salvation because his own race denounced him. When news of His body's resurrection spread far and wide, those who knew the true Mosaic teachings had no doubt that Jesus had indeed been the Son of God. The Templar (sic) wanted access to His divine blood and sought out every relic that had blood on it, such as the Shroud, Face Napkin, Spear, Robe, and Cross. All the while they refused to proclaim their mistake openly because Jesus had refused to give them the materialistic world that they desired most. They began their alchemical experiments so that one day in the future the divine blood could be made to live again."[33]

Let's once again pause and look more closely at several of Pugh's assumptions. How could the Templars threaten Jesus with crucifixion since they were not even in existence in Jesus' day? Furthermore, let's see what the Bible says. Pugh says that they knew that Jesus was the Son of God but I Corinthians 2:8 says: "Which **NONE OF THE PRINCES** of this world **KNEW: for** *HAD THEY KNOWN IT, THEY* ***WOULD NOT HAVE CRUCIFIED THE LORD OF GLORY.*** *"* John 7:47-48: Then answered them the Pharisees, Are ye also deceived? Have ANY of the rulers or of the Pharisees believed on Him?" "For they that dwell at Jerusalem, and their rulers, because THEY KNEW HIM NOT, nor yet the voices of the prophets which are read every sabbath day..." (Acts 13:27). Once again, the Bible proves Pugh is wrong.

As already mentioned, Pugh believes that Satan will live in the cloned body of Jesus and actually possess His blood yet she claims that the Templars wanted Christ's blood to produce "their CANAAN-ITE Messiah."[34] Since when was Jesus—or for that matter, Satan—a CANAANITE? Once again we see that Pugh's theory is all mixed up—and INCORRECT.

Not only is Pugh's theory irrational but she even contradicts herself on numerous occasions. For instance, she tells us that the cloned being will be a "twin in the image of Jesus"[35] and will "be deceptively posing as His Twin,"[36] yet she also claims that the cells that housed the DNA on the shroud

"...have the potential to be used to Clone another human being identical to the man on the Shroud. Each individual human cell is a holographic image of the complete body. Once the cell is coaxed into dividing through an electrical shock, it will grow into the exact image of the body from which it was originally taken—**not a twin.**"[37]

It can't be both ways—yet she claims both ways.

She continues:

"That is the reason why the blood of Jesus on the Holy Shroud became the 'Holy Grail' of the Knights Templar. They taught that through a mystical form of Alchemy, which induced rejuvenation, that this Holy Blood would one day live again. The Templar (sic) believed that through scientific advancement, their ability to identify the spark of the divine in Jesus' blood would forever change mankind's destiny from mortal to immortal. **The blood taken from the Shroud would allow future alchemists to birth a child from its cellular samples.** In doing this, their goal to manipulate and control the genetic blueprint of mankind would be achieved. Possession of the blood belonging to the Son of God would offer the potential of locating the key to the hidden doorway between what is of man and what is of God. The DNA of Jesus would be a unique Tree of Life, with properties not found in that of sinful man, because part of His genetic makeup came directly from the divine."[38]

"Prepare yourself to meet Satan in the flesh. **He is alive** and walking in a physical body among mankind."[39]

WHO IS THE ANTICHRIST?

So, **WHO** does Pugh believe is the Antichrist parading around in the body of Jesus? To her, the child birthed from the DNA on the Shroud of Turin is none other than Prince William! She records:

"As far back as the early 1960's, Professor Lorenzo Ferri, with permission from the Vatican, studied the height of the man on the Shroud. He estimated the height of Jesus to be around 6'2"—the same height as that of Prince William. Ferri also estimated the weight of Jesus to be about 175 pounds and William is already over 160 pounds. Facial features appearing on the Shroud are remarkably similar to early paintings of Jesus and to those of Prince William....The facial dimensions of the Prince and Jesus are remarkably similar."[40]

Once again we find that there is a theological problem with Pugh's aberration. As mentioned earlier, Pugh mistakenly believes that Satan and the Antichrist are the same entity which is not true according to the Bible. Also, we know that Satan is not omnipresent so he is limited to one place at any one time. If Satan is the Antichrist and he is living in Prince William's body he would not have been able to be anywhere other than where William has been for the past 26 years. The Bible, however, tells us that Satan is walking about as a roaring lion seeking whom he may devour (I Peter 5:8). Ephesians 2:2 tells us that Satan is "the prince of the power of the **AIR....**" He is not confined to a body.

If Prince William is Satan in the flesh, what do we do with Revelation 20? We find:

"And I saw an angel come down from heaven, having the key of the bottomless pit and a great chain in his hand. And he laid hold on the dragon, that old serpent, which is the Devil, and Satan, and bound him a thousand years, And cast him into the bottomless pit, and shut him up, and set a seal upon him, that he should deceive the nations no more, till the thousand years should be fulfilled: and after that he must be loosed a little season....And when the thousand years are expired, Satan shall be loosed out of his prison, And shall go out to deceive the nations which are in the four quarters of the earth, Gog and Magog, to gather them to battle: the number of whom is as the sand of the sea" (Revelation 20:1-3, 7-8).

Does this mean that Prince William will be bound in the bottomless pit for a thousand years and then released for a little season? Will Satan/Prince William return in the cloned body of Christ? Such ideas are ludicrous!

Revelation 17:8 reveals that the beast "shall ascend out of the bottomless pit, and go into perdition...." Where does cloning the DNA from the Shroud of Turin fit into this picture?

We've already gone through several factors to show that the Shroud of Turin is not Christ's shroud. We also have scriptural proof that Christ's DNA will not be cloned. In John 14:9 Jesus told His disciples: "Yet a little while, and the world seeth Me **NO MORE.**" If Satan is walking around in Christ's body, wouldn't the world be seeing "Jesus"? John 16:10 also reminds us: "...I go to My Father, and ye [shall] see Me **NO MORE.**"

Completely ignoring the Scripture, Pugh announces:

> "Because the body of the Prince has been fissioned from the blood of Jesus, **he will look identical to the image imprinted on the Holy Shroud of Turin.** Everyone will be pleased that the Messiah has returned to the Temple in Jerusalem to regain his rightful home and to rule as king. Satan will have completed his task to be worshipped as the Savior of mankind. He will be sitting in the rebuilt Temple in Jerusalem, as well as residing in the rebuilt (Cloned) temple of Jesus."[41]

Pugh also believes that the blood of Mary, the mother of Jesus, is flowing through Prince William's veins.[42] She writes:

> "Of course, if Charles is not his real father, and William is a Clone from the Shroud of Turin, then it is understandable that he would take a symbol from the lineage of his mother's Crest. William, in a strange twist of theory, would be like Jesus, who took His lineage from His Virgin Mother, Mary, because Joseph was not truly His real father, even though both Mary and Joseph were descendents (sic) of the lineage of David from Adam's son Seth."[43]

Again, we see a problem with Pugh's thinking both Scripturally and scientifically. If William has Mary's blood flowing through his veins, how can he also be of the lineage of Cain as Pugh claims? She writes: "This modification in Prince William's pedigree is an attempt to prove that **he has the blood of the lineage of Cain** flowing through his veins....Cain's lineage was tainted by Satan and his Fallen Angels."[44] Mary came from Seth's lineage so Cain's blood was not in her veins in any way, shape, or form.

As already mentioned, Pugh claims Prince William has the blood of Christ in his veins[45] yet here she claims he also has Mary's blood. Both of these cannot be correct. Why? When a firstborn child is conceived, **the blood source comes from the father.** M. R. DeHaan, a medical doctor, states:

> "The mother provides the foetus (the unborn developing infant) with the nutritive elements for the building of that little body in the secret of her bosom, **but all the blood which forms in that little body is formed in the embryo itself and only as a result of the contribution of the male parent. From the time of conception to the time of birth of the infant not ONE SINGLE DROP OF BLOOD ever passes from mother to child....All the blood which is in that child is produced within the child itself as a result of the introduction of the male sperm. The mother contributes no blood at all.**"[46] [Emphasis added.]

The *Nurse's Handbook of Obstetrics* also says: "When the circulation of the blood begins in the embryo, it remains separate and distinct from that of the mother."[47]

IS PRINCE WILLIAM A CLONE?

Since Pugh claims that Prince William was cloned from the Shroud of Turin, his blood source could not be from Mary. Of course, since the Shroud of Turin is not Christ's shroud, William's blood could not be from Christ, either. In fact, there is no proof that William was even cloned from the shroud.

The blood source of Jesus is of vital importance to the Christian. This is the significance of the virgin birth. Since the blood of a firstborn comes **ONLY** through the Father, Jesus' blood source was provided by God alone. Jesus took on human flesh or a body (Hebrews 10:5) but He did not partake of the sinful human nature.

Remember Judas said that he betrayed innocent blood (Matthew 27:4). This is why Christ's blood could atone for our sins. I Peter 1:18-19 says: "Forasmuch as ye know that ye were not redeemed with corruptible things, as silver and gold,...But with the **precious blood of Christ,** as of a lamb **without blemish** and without spot...." (See also Ephesians 1:7; 2:13; Colossians 1:14, 20, etc.)

This firstborn issue is of vital importance in the area of the fallen angels as well. The Bible tells us that "flesh and blood CANNOT inherit the kingdom of God" (I Corinthians 15:50). Since angels dwell in heaven (Matthew 22:30; 24:36; Mark 12:25; 13:32; Luke 2:15; John 1:51; II Thessalonians 1:7), we know that they can't have blood so how could the angels intermingle with human women and pass their blood to their offspring since the firstborn's blood comes from the FATHER?

SHROUD OF TURIN HAS TYPE AB BLOOD

We are told that the blood on the Shroud of Turin is type AB.[48] The National Blood Society reveals: "The newest and rarest group, AB, only **appeared between 1000 and 500 years ago,** and is believed to have occurred as a response to the mixing of existing blood groups on a major scale."[49] Do you see a problem with this? If this blood type only appeared about 500-1000 years ago, the shroud **CANNOT** be Christ's shroud as He was crucified almost 2000 years ago.

Let's now return to Prince William. Since Pugh claims that the Antichrist/Satan/Prince William "will be deceptively posing as [Christ's] twin,"[50] let's take a look at some of the features of Prince William. As already mentioned, Pugh claims that he has Christ's blood flowing through his veins because he was supposedly cloned from the shroud. Now, since the blood on the shroud is AB and that is only a more recent discovery, Prince William cannot be the cloned image of Jesus. Furthermore, we know that Prince Charles' blood type is O negative.[51] A DNA test was done on Prince William (as well as on

Prince Harry) and the results came back that both children were fathered by Prince Charles.[52] Since the blood of the firstborn comes from the father, then Prince William must have type O blood. Type O blood is **NOT** the blood type that appears on the shroud.

We also know that Jesus was of the lineage of David (Matthew 1:1, 17; 12:23; Luke 1:32; John 7:42; II Timothy 2:8; Revelation 22:16) and from the tribe of Judah which made him a Jew by earthly and human standards.

According to the JewishEncyclopedia.com we find:

"As regards complexion, JEWS ARE DARKER than the surrounding peoples in Europe, except Galicia. THE HAIR IS ALSO DARKER; and the average 15 per cent having black hair as against 3 to 4 per cent in the general European popula-tions....The nose is generally considered the characteristic feature of the Jews, who have, on the average, the longest (77 mm.) and narrowest (34 mm.)....The lips of Jews are also characteristic, as large a proportion as 48 per cent being thick."[53]

Do any of these features fit Prince William. His hair color is listed as blonde or sandy blonde and he has hazel/blue eyes.

Pugh also writes that William "is a very handsome young man...."[54]

Since William is supposedly the clone of Christ and has His features, we need to notice that Jesus had no physical beauty or any outstanding characteristics in His fleshy body. Isaiah 53:2 says that Christ "hath no form nor comeliness; and when we shall see Him, there is no beauty that we should desire Him." The meaning in the Hebrew is that Christ had no splendour or handsomeness to His appearance. We also know that when Judas was ready to betray Jesus that he had to identify Him to the soldiers. It was only Jesus and His disciples in the Garden but the soldiers didn't know Jesus from the others. Judas told the soldiers that the person he would kiss would be the man to take.

On the other hand, the world whole will wonder after the beast and worship him. They will admire the Antichrist. Revelation 13:8 says: "And all that dwell upon the earth shall worship him whose names are not written in the book of life of the Lamb slain from the foundation of the world."

The worship of the Antichrist (the beast) will be short-lived as he will be destroyed with the brightness of Christ's coming (II Thessalonians 2:8-10). His fate is described in Revelation 19:20:

> "And the beast was taken, and with him the false prophet that wrought miracles before him, with which he deceived them that had received the mark of the beast, and them that worshipped his image. These both were cast alive into a lake of fire burning with brimstone."

If Pugh's theory is correct, we have just encountered some more Scriptural problems. For one thing, this so-called cloned Antichrist supposedly has no soul. How then can he be sent to hell? Matthew 10:28 says: "[F]ear Him which is able to destroy BOTH **SOUL** AND **BODY** in hell." Furthermore, if the Antichrist has the cloned body of Jesus, are we to assume that Jesus' body will spend eternity in hell? If not, will His cloned body return to dust? When these questions were posed to Dr. Pugh, she responded: "If William is a clone—the beast has no soul. At death, the body returns to the dust. A clone is just an empty vehicle."[55] She added (about his physical body): "It will return to dust. There is nothing to resurrect—no soul."[56]

JESUS' BODY WILL NOT SEE CORRUPTION

There are several verses in the Bible that tell us that Jesus' body did not see corruption so if Prince William is Satan in the flesh living in the cloned body of Jesus, then Jesus body will return to dust—at least according to Pugh. The Bible, however, tells us differently.

✟ "He seeing this before spake of the resurrection of Christ, that His soul was not left in hell, neither His flesh did see corruption" (Acts 2:31).

✜ "For Thou wilt not leave My soul in hell; neither wilt Thou suffer Thine Holy One to see corruption" (Psalm 16:10).

✜ "That He should still live for ever, and not see corruption" (Psalm 49:9).

✜ "Because Thou wilt not leave My soul in hell, neither wilt Thou suffer Thine Holy One to see corruption" (Acts 2:27).

✜ "Wherefore He saith also in another psalm, Thou shalt not suffer Thine Holy One to see corruption" (Acts 13:35).

If, as Pugh claims, Satan is living in Christ's body in the form of Prince William (or anyone else for that matter), this body will see corruption. Therefore, on the basis of Scripture, we know that Prince William/Satan/Antichrist CANNOT be inhabiting the cloned body of Jesus.

PRINCE WILLIAM AS MESSIAH?

Now, will the Jews accept Prince William as their Messiah? Remember, Pugh wrote:

> "Because the body of the Prince has been fissioned from the blood of Jesus, **he will look identical to the image imprinted on the Holy Shroud of Turin.** Everyone will be pleased that the Messiah has returned to the Temple in Jerusalem to regain his rightful home and to rule as king. Satan will have completed his task to be worshipped as the Savior of mankind. He will be sitting in the rebuilt Temple in Jerusalem, as well as residing in the rebuilt (Cloned) temple of Jesus."[57]

Once again, we have a problem. Jesus Himself told the Jews in John 5:43: "I am come in My Father's name, and ye receive Me not: **if another shall come *in his own name*, him ye will receive.**" So we know that the Antichrist who is posing as the Messiah will not come in the name of Jesus Christ. We also know that the Jews on a whole have nothing whatsoever to do with Christ. In the Scriptures they referred to Him as a deceiver (Matthew 27:63), blasphemer (Mark

3:28-30), Beelzebub (the prince of the devils, Mark 3:22), etc., and today it is still the same thing.

Rabbi Simmons explains:

"It is important to understand why Jews don't believe in Jesus....

"Jews do not accept Jesus as the messiah because:

"1) Jesus did not fulfill the messianic prophecies.

"2) Jesus did not embody the personal qualifications of the Messiah.

"3) Biblical verses 'referring' to Jesus are mistranslations.

"4) Jewish belief is based on national revelation."[58]

If they don't believe Jesus fulfilled the prophecies or had the qualifications to be the Messiah, they won't accept a person who comes claiming to be Christ. In fact, we are told that one reason Jesus doesn't qualify is because His followers claim that He had a virgin birth and the Jews are expecting a person whose **father** came from the tribe of Judah which leaves Jesus out because He didn't have an earthly father.

Rabbi Simmons also states:

"According to Torah sources, the Messiah will be born of human parents and possess normal physical attributes like other people. He will not be a demi-god, nor will he possess supernatural qualities."[59]

We are also told:

"According to Christianity, Jesus had no human father. Therefore, **the discussion of Jesus as the Messiah stops here. Nowhere in Hebrew Scriptures does the Royal Blood Line continue by adoption.** The Jewish Scriptures clearly state that a person's genealogy and tribal membership is transmitted exclusively through one's PHYSICAL father....Judaism understands the Messiah to be a human being with no connotation of deity or divinity."[60] [Caps and underline in the original.]

So, we have both the Scripture and writings from a Rabbi to show that the "Messiah" (the Antichrist) will not come in the name of Jesus.

ANOTHER "JESUS"

The Jews are not the only ones who are looking for a Messiah but who are <u>not</u> looking for Jesus Christ. Mary Bailey of Lucis Trust said: "If we look for the Christ as He was two thousand years ago, we will fail to recognise Him."[61] Ruth Montgomery, one of the "heralds of the New Age,"[62] tells us that Jesus is not the Christ and that it will be a DIFFERENT Christ than in the Bible who will come to bring world peace. While in a trance, she asked her Spirit Guide (a demon) about the Second Coming of Christ. She said: "I asked if Jesus of Nazareth would again reincarnate, in order to 'prepare the body for the Christ Spirit,' and the Guides said that he would NOT."[63] The Guides continue:

> "'In the twenty-first century, the soul of ANOTHER PER-FECTED BEING will return to human incarnation...and...Christ will arrive at the beginning of a NEW ERA after the shift and the chaos. But it WILL NOT be the man who was ONCE incarnate and known as...JESUS. It will be another Wise One.'"[64]

While New Ager Benjamin Creme claims that Maitreya is the Messiah that the Jews are awaiting, the Christ of the Christians, the Imam Mahdi of the Muslims, etc., he also claims that "Jesus of Nazareth and the Christ are not *one* and the same person."[65] [Emphasis in the original.] According to Maitreya, Jesus was nothing more than a man that allowed Maitreya to use His body. Benjamin Creme claims that Maitreya will come under a different name.[66] He says that if Maitreya comes as Maitreya there will be a division among the Buddhists. If he comes as Christ, there will be a division among Christians, etc. I'm not saying that Maitreya is the Antichrist figure that is going to come, but I am trying to point out that many people in the world today will not accept a person by the name of Christ so for the Antichrist to be a cloned image of Christ would really not be to his advantage in his role as deceiver.

Muslims believe that their Mahdi or prophesied redeemer of Islam will work alongside Jesus to restore righteousness so a cloned image of Jesus will not be sufficient to many Muslim minds, either. In fact, an Islamic website specifically states that the Mahdi will "NOT be the same individual as the Promised Messiah (Jesus)."[67] [Emphasis in the original.]

So, we can see that even if a person could actually clone an exact image of Christ, this idea won't help in getting mankind to accept the Antichrist as the Messiah.

To briefly recap, many people are claiming that the Antichrist will be one of the Nephilim and that he will probably be a clone. Dr. Pugh, in particular, goes so far as to claim that this clone will be taken from the Shroud of Turin which she claims is Christ's shroud. These ideas, as have been proven in this chapter, are based on faulty and unscriptural conjectures, opinions, speculations, assumptions, and suppositions.

I'm pleading with my readers to go back to the Bible and when beliefs like this are presented you'll be able to spot the counterfeit.

13. IS THE *BOOK OF ENOCH* SCRIPTURE?

The *Book of Enoch* has been mentioned several times throughout this book. Thomas Horn, Patrick Heron, Dr. Joye Pugh, and others within the Christian church today are embracing many ideas from the *Book of Enoch*. Lynn Marzulli says that he appreciates this book "for its historicity," although he doesn't "view it as canon."[1] Tom Brown writes:

> "Several years back, I came across the book of Enoch. The book claims to have been written by Enoch himself. I'm always suspicious of any non-canonical book. This book was no exception. I read it with deep cynicism. However, I did not read anything that would not be in accord with sound doctrine. It confirmed all the basic doctrines that Christians and Jews believe today."[2]

Patrick Heron proclaims: "...I have found **nothing** in the Book of Enoch that contradicts anything in scripture, rather it enhances and copper fastens the revealed Word of truth."[3]

They use this book to "prove" that the fallen angels mated with humans and then produced the race of the Nephilim. In this chapter, we will look a little more closely at the *Book of Enoch* and see how it compares to the Bible.

The *Book of Enoch* is believed to have been written about 100 to 200 years before Christ and is considered to be an apocryphal book.[4] The word "apocryphal," according to the Merriam-Webster Dictionary, means "of doubtful authenticity" or "spurious." It is also called a "pseudepigraphic work"[5] which means that it was a writing that is falsely attributed to a biblical character—in this case, Enoch, the great-grandfather of Noah.

We do know that the early church fathers were aware of this book. Some Christians today tell us that these church fathers accepted the *Book of Enoch* as inspired. It is true that Tertullian was one who believed that Enoch was inspired,[6] but what the "Christian" leaders fail to also tell us is that Tertullian admitted that most church fathers of his day **REJECTED** this book and that it **WAS NOT** included in the canon of Scriptures.[7] Remember, too, Tertullian was also a proponent of the **heresy** known as Montanism[8] so this endorsement for the *Book of Enoch* comes from someone who had already embraced heretical doctrines. Can we trust his endorsement?

We also know that other church fathers such as Origen and Jerome did not believe that the *Book of Enoch* was canonical. "In fact it appears that only Tertullian and Augustine thought the work was inspired and Augustine waffled on the point."[9] The early church was certainly aware of this book and some leaders did quote from it but quoting from a book does not necessarily mean an endorsement of the book. Many occult books are well-known and have been quoted from but that doesn't mean that they are inspired.

The book was well-known during the first few centuries after Christ, but the *Book of Enoch* and "many other books became discredited after the Council of Laodicea. And being under ban of the authorities, afterwards it gradually passed out of circulation."[10] In fact, this book was considered lost for over 1000 years until 1773 when the explorer James Bruce brought three Ethiopian copies back with him. The first English translation was published in 1821 by Richard Laurence.[11]

Today, the *Book of Enoch* is the main source being used to try to prove that the fallen angels mated with mankind and produced the Nephilim.

DOES JUDE QUOTE FROM THE *BOOK OF ENOCH*?

Those who refer to this book try to authenticate it by saying that the Bible mentions the *Book of Enoch* and claim that Jude quoted from it. Enoch 1:9 says:

> "And behold! He cometh with ten thousands of His holy ones to execute judgment upon all, and to destroy all the ungodly:

and to convict all flesh of all the works of their ungodliness which they have ungodly committed, and of all the hard things which ungodly sinners have spoken against Him."

Pointing to Jude 1:14, these advocates claim that this is proof that Jude quoted Enoch 1:9. For instance, Patrick Heron remarks:

"It is important to reiterate that Jude, one of the sons of Mary and Joseph, quoted directly from this most ancient of books. For this gives the writings of Enoch gravitas and informs us that it is indeed a **divinely inspired book** from which we can learn."[12]

The truth, however, is that Jude **did not** mention the *Book of Enoch.* Jude 1:14 simply states that "Enoch also, the seventh from Adam, prophesied of these, saying, Behold, the Lord cometh with ten thousands of His saints...." Jude does not reference any particular book nor does he say that he was quoting from a book. He merely remarks that Enoch PROPHESIED about the Lord coming again. Prophesies are not always contained in books. In fact, the Greek word used in Jude for "prophesied" means to "SPEAK under inspiration." So, the mention of Enoch's prophecy in Jude is no proof whatsoever for the veracity of the *Book of Enoch.*

What is of interest is that none of the Aramiac or Greek fragments contain Enoch 1:9. The only copy to have it is the Ethiopian copies so there "is insufficient evidence whether the phrase is in the original Book of Enoch or whether a person knowledgeable of Christianity 'enhanced' an older version."[13]

Now, if the *Book of Enoch* were written by the godly Enoch, it would have to agree with the Bible, wouldn't it? Let's see how it lines up with Scripture.

➤ In Enoch 60 we read: "In the year 500, in the seventh month, on the fourteenth day of the month in the life of Enoch." Do you see a problem here? Genesis 5:23 says: "And all the days of Enoch were three hundred sixty and five years." If this were an inspired book, don't you think Enoch would at least know his own age?

➤ Enoch 107:2-3 records an incident where Enoch speaks to Methuselah:

> "'And now, my son, go and announce to thy son Lamech, that this son who is born is really his, and that this is not a falsehood.' And when Methuselah had heard the words of his father Enoch—for he had shown him everything that was secret—he returned, after his having seen him, and called the name of that son Noah, for he will make glad the earth for all destruction."

Is it possible that Enoch spoke to Methuselah about Noah's birth? Let's go to Genesis 5 and check it out. We see that Adam was 130 when Seth was born. Seth was 105 when Enos was born, Enos was 90 when Cainan was born, Cainan was 70 when Mahalaleel was born, Mahalaleel was 65 when Jared was born, Jared was 162 when Enoch was born, Enoch was 65 when Methuselah was born, Methuselah was 187 when Lamech was born, and Lamech was 182 when Noah was born.

FATHER	AGE AT SON'S BIRTH	SON'S NAME
Adam	130	Seth
Seth	105	Enos
Enos	90	Cainan
Cainan	70	Mahalaleel
Mahalaleel	65	Jared
Jared	162	Enoch
Enoch	65	Methuselah
Methuselah	187	Lamech
Lamech	182	Noah

By adding the years from Adam to Enoch (130 + 105 + 90 + 70 + 65 + 162) we see that 622 years had lapsed since creation. Enoch lived for 365 years so that would make 987 years. So, by the Genesis account, God took Enoch 987 years after creation. The problem with the above scenario is that Noah was not born until 1056—69 years

AFTER Enoch was translated. In other words, the event described in Enoch 107 could not have happened according to the Bible since Enoch was not here to deliver such a message.[14]

➤ In Enoch 106 we find the birth of Noah:

"And after some days my son Methuselah took a wife for his son Lamech, and she became pregnant by him and bore a son. And his body was white as snow and red as the blooming of a rose, and the hair of his head and his long locks were white as wool, and his eyes beautiful. And when he opened his eyes, he lighted up the whole house like the sun, and the whole house was very bright. And thereupon he arose in the hands of the midwife, opened his mouth, and conversed with the Lord of righteousness. And his father Lamech was afraid of him and fled, and came to his father Methuselah. And he said unto him: 'I have begotten a strange son, diverse from and unlike man, and resembling the sons of the God of heaven; and his nature is different and he is not like us, and his eyes are as the rays of the sun, and his countenance is glorious. And it seems to me that he is not sprung from me but from the angels, and I fear that in his days a wonder may be wrought on the earth....And he [Noah] arose in the hands of the midwife, and opened his mouth and blessed the Lord of heaven" (Enoch 106:1-7, 11-12).

NOAH STARTS TALKING AT BIRTH

This passage has Noah talking from his birth and when he opened his eyes, the whole house lit up like the sun. Stories of a fantastical, fanciful, far-fetched nature abound in pagan mythology but we find nothing of this sort in the Scriptures.

Noah was so extraordinary that his father thought that he was born from an angel. This scenario raises more questions. Can righteous angels produce children? If they can, how would the righteous angels' offspring differ from the fallen angels' offspring? If only the evil angels supposedly mated with mankind, and Lamech thought that Noah was from an angel, wouldn't this make Noah one of the Nephilim? If Noah were a Nephilim then he wasn't perfect in his generations. Also, why would God send a flood to destroy the Nephilim yet spare Noah if he were a Nephilim? This passage in Enoch presents a number of problems.

➤ In Enoch 9 we read: "And then **Michael, Uriel, Raphael, and Gabriel** looked down from heaven and saw much blood being shed upon the earth..." but the Bible says in Genesis 6:12 that **"God looked upon the earth."** Enoch 10 says God sent **Uriel** to Noah to tell him to hide himself and that a flood would destroy the earth but Genesis 6:13-14 says that **God** told Noah to build the ark. Chapter 67 of the *Book of Enoch* says: "And in those days the word of God came unto me, and He said unto me:...now **the angels are making a wooden (building),** and when they have completed the task I will place My hand upon it and preserve it, and there shall come forth from it the seed of life, and a change shall set in so that the earth will not remain without inhabitant." On the other hand, Genesis 6:14 says that **God told Noah to make the ark** and verse 22 says: "Thus did Noah, according to all that God commanded him, so did he." Hebrews 11:7 also says that Noah prepared an ark.

➤ The *Book of Enoch* has Noah communicating with the dead on numerous occasions. Since this is a forbidden practice (Leviticus 19:31; 20:6, 27; Deuteronomy 18:10-12; II Kings 21:6; I Chronicles 10:13; II Chronicles 33:6), and since Noah was a righteous person, do you think that Noah would commit such a sin?

➤ Enoch 8 tells about several angels and how they corrupted mankind:

> "And Azazel taught men to make swords, and knives, and shields, and breastplates, and made known to them the metals of the earth and the art of working them, and bracelets, and ornaments, and the use of antimony, and the beautifying of the eyelids, and all kinds of costly stones, and all colouring tinctures. And there arose much godlessness, and they committed fornica-tion, and they were led astray, and became corrupt in all their ways. Semjaza taught enchantments, and root-cuttings, Armaros the resolving of enchantments, Baraqijal (taught) astrology,

Kokabel the constellations, Ezeqeel the knowledge of the clouds, Araqiel the signs of the earth, Shamsiel the signs of the sun, and Sariel the course of the moon" (Enoch 8:1-3).

Michael, Uriel, Raphael, and Gabriel then went to God and gave a report of the wickedness. "And again the Lord said to Raphael: 'Bind Azazel hand and foot, and cast him into the darkness....And on the day of the great judgement he shall be cast into the fire....And the whole earth has been corrupted through the works that were taught by Azazel: **to him ascribe all sin**'" (Enoch 10:4, 8-9).

DID THE ANGELS BRING SIN?

Does the Bible teach that sin entered the world because of the fallen angels? No, it does not! Romans 5:12 clearly reveals: "Wherefore, as by **one man** sin entered into the world, and **death by sin;** and so death passed upon all men, for that all have sinned." According to the Biblical account, there was no death prior to Adam's and Eve's sin. After their sin, we see that Abel was killed by Cain in Genesis 4. Lamech (Cain's great-great-great-grandson, not Noah's father who was also named Lamech) had killed a man (Genesis 4:23). Genesis 5 gives a list of deaths—and this is all BEFORE Genesis 6. Since death came because of sin, then the so-called "fallen angels" did not bring sin and corruption to the earth. Sin was already quite evident in the lives of mankind. In fact, I John 3:4 says that "sin is the transgression of the law" and we know that a transgression occurred in the Garden of Eden when Adam and Eve partook of the tree of the knowledge of good and evil in direct disobedience to God's command (Genesis 2:17). Romans 5:19 tells us that "by one man's disobedience many were made sinners" and James 1:15 states that "sin, when it is finished, bringeth forth death," "[f]or the wages of sin is death..." (Romans 6:23).

We know from Genesis 6 that it was the wickedness of man (not the angels) that angered God: "And God saw that the wickedness of MAN was great in the earth, and that every imagination of the thoughts of his heart was only evil continually. And it repented the Lord that He had made MAN on the earth..." (Genesis 6:5-6).

➤ Enoch 2:3 states that "the whole earth is filled with water, and clouds, and dew and rain lie upon it." According to the Bible, there was no rain until the flood: "[T]he Lord God had not caused it to rain upon the earth....But there went up a mist from the earth, and watered the whole face of the ground" (Genesis 2:5-6).

It wasn't until the flood that rain came upon the earth and "all the fountains of the great deep [were] broken up, and the windows of heaven were opened" (Genesis 7:11). Since Enoch died before the flood came, he would not have even seen rain much less the whole earth full of water.

➤ The *Book of Enoch* said that man "hope[d] to live an eternal life, and that each one of them will live five hundred years" (Enoch 10:10-11). First of all, 500 years isn't eternal life and people at this time were living 800 and 900 years so living only 500 years would seem to be more of a punishment than it would be living an eternal life!

➤ Enoch 77:1 says that the Most High will descend from the south but Matthew 24:27 says: "For as the lightning cometh out of the east, and shineth even unto the west; so shall also the coming of the Son of man be."

➤ Enoch 100:10 teaches that God inquires of the angels about mankind's deeds but Romans 14:23 says that "every one of us shall give account **of himself** to God." (See also I Peter 4:3-5.) Furthermore, we know that God already knows our hearts and does not need an angel to tell Him about it. I Chronicles 28:9 says that "the Lord searcheth all hearts, and understandeth all the imaginations of the thoughts." (See also Isaiah 66:18; Psalm 94:11; Matthew 12:25; Luke 5:22; 6:8; 11:17; and I Corinthians 14:25.) During the days before the flood we see that "God saw that the wickedness of man was great in the earth, and that every imagination of the thoughts of his heart was only evil continually..." (Genesis 6:5). Psalm 44:21 asks: "Shall not God search this out? for He knoweth the secrets of the heart." David declared: "O Lord, Thou hast searched me, and known me....Thou understandest my thought afar off...and art acquainted with all my ways. For there is not a word in my tongue, but, lo, O Lord, Thou knowest it altogether" (Psalm 139:1-4). Romans 2:16 adds that "God shall judge the secrets of men by Jesus Christ." The angels don't enter into this at all. Furthermore, according to I Corinthians 6:3, we find that in heaven the Christians will be judging the angels, not the angels judging men.

➤ Enoch 40 tells about the angel Phanuel "who is set over the repentance unto hope of those who inherit eternal life..." (Enoch 40:9). Jesus Christ is the only Mediator between God and man (I Timothy 2:5). Wouldn't this angel be usurping Christ's place?

TALL TALE

➤ In reference to the giants, the *Book of Enoch* tells us that they were 3000 ells tall (Enoch 7:2-3). An ell varies from 27-45 inches so that would make these giants anywhere from 6,750 to 11,250 feet tall or approximately 1 to 2 miles in height. To reach this height, the giant would have to grow **OVER 1 FOOT EVERY SINGLE MONTH FOR MORE THAN 900 YEARS** (1 foot x 12 months x 900 years = 10,800 feet)! Is such a "tall tale" even plausible? Remember, these were normal women who supposedly gave birth to the Nephilim. Would a normal woman be able to carry an excessively heavy or extremely long baby? Unless the Guinness World Record has recently been broken, the heaviest baby on record at birth was 22 1/2 pounds.[15]

The tallest living man who is 7 foot, 9 inches recently married and on November 20, 2008 an article appeared in the paper with the title "World's Tallest Man Now the World's Tallest Dad." The boy, born on November 19, 2008, "was a very average 22-inches in height."[16] It's obvious that almost all growth would have to occur outside of the womb.

➤ The book also teaches that these giants, which were supposedly produced from the mating of angels and humans, do not have a soul and when they die a demon is released. Their fate is to walk the earth forever after the body dies but this is an extra Biblical teaching and does not parallel with Scriptures.

➤ Additionally, the *Book of Enoch* also has contradictions throughout its text. For instance Enoch 72:37 tell us that the sun and moon differ in the intensity of the light they produce "but as regards **size they are both equal."** The very next verse, however, mentions "the **smaller luminary,** which is named the Moon..." (Enoch 73:1). Are the sun and moon the same or different sizes?

WHICH ANGEL IS WHICH?

➤Another contradiction within the *Book of Enoch* is in Enoch 6:78 where we find a list of 19 angels that took an oath to come to earth and defile the women and each of them was a chief of ten. Chapter 69 gives a list of almost 30 angels who were supposed to have defiled the women and taught various other evils to them. Some of these angels were chiefs over 100s, 50s, and 10s. Not only do the numbers differ but so do most of the names. In Enoch 6:1-7 we are told that **Semjaza** was the leader who lusted after the earthly women. Since he didn't want to be the only angel reprimanded for his sin, he took an oath of the other angels to sin with him and a total of 200 angels came to earth. If there are 19 chief angels (as listed in Chapter 6) and each one had 10 angels under him, that would make 209 angels (190 + 19 leaders)—not the 200 which is recorded.

➤ According to Enoch 69 we see that **Jeqon** is "the one who led astray [all] the sons of God, and brought them down to the earth, and led them astray through the daughters of men. And the second was named **Asbeel:** he imparted to the holy sons of God evil counsel, and led them astray so that they defiled their bodies with the daughters of men" (Enoch 69:4-6). Which angel (Semjaza, Jeqon, or Asbeel) led the other angels astray?

Going the Bible, we find that there is no indication that the angels were ever sent to earth to watch over mankind. We also know from the Scriptures that 1/3 of the angels fell (Revelation 12:4) so if 200 fell that would make a total of 600 angels but the Bible tells us that Jesus could have called "more than twelve legions of angels" (Matthew 26:53). During the time of Christ, a legion consisted of 6,000 or more men so Jesus could have called more than 72,000 angels just to deliver Him. Also, John says in Revelation 5:11: "I heard the voice of many angels round about the throne...and the number of them was ten thousand times ten thousand, and thousands of thousands." The number of angels given in the *Book of Enoch* just doesn't fit with the Biblical record.

➤ Enoch 69:11 states: "For men were created exactly like the angels...."

Are men created exactly like the angels? Not according to the Bible. Psalm 104:4 and Hebrews 1:7 tells us that the angels are spirits. II Peter 2:11 says that angels are greater in power and might. Psalm 8 and Hebrews 2 mention that God made man "a little lower than the angels" (Psalm 8:5; Hebrews 2:7). Hebrews also reveals that Jesus "was made a little lower than the angels for the suffering of death..." (Hebrews 2:9), so angels do not die but man does. Continuing on in Hebrews we see men "are partakers of flesh and blood" and that Jesus "likewise took part of the same....For verily He took not on Him the nature of angels; but He took on Him the seed of Abraham" (Hebrews 2:14, 16). Luke 24:39 reminds us that "a spirit hath not flesh and bones." Obviously, then, man was not "created exactly like the angels."

Luke 20:36 does have the phrase "they are equal unto the angels" but this is not the same as "created exactly like the angels." First of all, we need to look at the context of Luke 20. It is in reference to the resurrection and the Sadducees, who did not believe in the resurrection, were trying to ensnare Jesus. They said unto Jesus:

"Master, Moses wrote unto us, If any man's brother die, having a wife, and he die without children, that his brother should take his wife, and raise up seed unto his brother. There were therefore seven brethren: and the first took a wife, and died without children. And the second took her; and in like manner the seven also: and they left no children, and died. Last of all the woman died also. Therefore in the resurrection whose wife of them is she? for seven had her to wife" (Luke 20:28-32).

Jesus explained:

"The children of this world marry, and are given in marriage: But they which shall be accounted worthy to obtain that world, and the resurrection from the dead, neither marry, nor are given in marriage: Neither can they die any more: for they are equal unto the angels; and are the children of God, being the children of the resurrection" (Luke 20:34-36).

The message is quite clear. We were NOT created like the angels but in the resurrection we will be like the angels in that we no longer marry and will not die. (See also Matthew 22:23-30 and Mark 12:18-25.)

BOOK OF ENOCH AND THE CABALA

Additionally, it is the *Book of Enoch* that "influenced the kabbalistic tradition and is considered part of the Merkabah mystical literature."[17]

Since this book influenced the kabbalistic tradition, let's briefly look at what the Cabala (also spelled Cabbala, Cabbalah, Kabala, Kabbala, Kabbalah, Kabalah, Kaballa, Quabalah, Qabala, etc.) is. According to *Webster's Dictionary,* the Cabala is "a medieval and modern system of Jewish **THEOSOPHY,** mysticism, and thaumaturgy marked by belief in creation through emanation and a cipher method of interpreting Scripture" and "a traditional, **ESOTERIC, OCCULT, OR SECRET** matter."[18] **REINCARNATION, MAGICAL POWER OF WORDS AND SIGNS, THE POWER OF AMULETS, DIVINATION, CONJURATIONS OF SPIRITS, AS WELL AS OTHER OCCULTIC PRACTICES, PLAY AN**

IMPORTANT ROLE IN THE CABALA AND CABALISTIC TEACHINGS.[19]

One occult magazine discloses that the Cabala "is a very powerful system, and Pagans should take advantage of it. Witches do, after all, steal (er, borrow) anything that works, regardless of the tradition....It may well bring Pagans closer their (sic) Gods."[20]

A description for the book, *A Kabbalah for the Modern World,* by Migene Gonzalez-Wippler, urges: "This book needs to be in the library of every **OCCULTIST, PAGAN, KABBALIST, MYSTIC** and person involved in the **NEW AGE.** The Kabbalah is the basic form of Western mysticism."[21]

Another occult catalog indicates:

"The Qabalah, whose disciplines includes the **OCCULT** sciences of **ASTROLOGY AND TAROT,** forms the basis of the Western Mystery Tradition. It is a system of mystical knowledge and spiritual development in the same way that **YOGA** is the mystical system of the East. The **TREE OF LIFE**—a diagram consisting of ten circles connected by twenty-two 'paths' is the heart of Qabalistic teaching."[22]

In an article entitled "Jung and the Qabalah," we are told:

"The Qabalah is one of the most ancient Western philosophical systems. **IT FORMS MUCH OF THE INNER FOUNDATIONS UPON WHICH ASTROLOGY, TAROT, ALCHEMY, NUMEROLOGY, MYTHOLOGY AND CEREMONIAL MAGIC ARE BASED.**"[23]

From the *Dictionary of Mysticism,* we discover that the **CABALA "IS AN ESSENTIAL ELEMENT IN MOST SCHOOLS OF OCCULTISM."**[24]

There are many other problems with the *Book of Enoch.* My question is: "How can any true Christian go to this unscriptural book to glean truth"? We know that Satan is a liar and the father of lies so why would we trust a book to give us truth when it is in direct conflict with God's Word? When we realize that people like Anton LaVey (the founder of the Church of Satan), Aleister Crowley (known as the "wickedest man in the world" and the "Great Beast 666"[25]), Albert Pike (well-known Mason and occultist[26]), Helena Petrovna Blavatsky (occultist, New Ager, and founder of the Theosophical Society[27]), Elizabeth Clare Prophet (New Ager, astrologer, and communicator with the ascended masters[28]), and others of like mind, advocate and use the *Book of Enoch,* we have to wonder why a Christian would use the same book to find truth and then promote the **same ideas** as the Satanists.

One Satanic bookstore sells books like *The Satanic Screen, Secret Life of a Satanist, The Devil's Notebook, The Satanic Witch, Satan Speaks, The Satanic Bible, The Satanic Rituals, Encyclopedia of Hell,* and—believe it or not—*The Book of Enoch* which it claims "is a rare and **important resource** that was suppressed by the early church and thought destroyed."[29]

Psychic Edgar Cayce thought the book was "a **valid source** for higher spiritual knowledge."[30]

In an ad for Helena Petrovna Blavatsky's one book we find that the partial contents include:

> "The ABC of Magic; Chaldean Oracles; The Book of Hermes;...**The Book of Enoch;** Hermetic and Kabalistic Doctrines; Numbers and Magic; Occult Weapons; The Duty of the True Occultist;...Magical Statutes; Masonry and Jesuits; Mysteries and Masonry; Egyptian Initiation;...Christian Star Worship; Defense of Astrology;...Swedenborg; Occult Secrecy; and much more."[31]

WAS ENOCH CONFUSED?

Now, if "Enoch" did not know his own age, recorded an event that could not have happened, mentions communication with the dead as an acceptable practice, doesn't know which angel was in charge of defiling the women, and so forth, how could we trust what he has to say about the angels mating with women? Remember, it is from the *Book of Enoch* that the idea of the fallen angels mating with women, as well as the idea of the Nephilim, the hybrids, etc., has gained popularity with the occult world. Sadly, many in the church who profess to be Christians, have joined the ranks of the Satanists and occultists in promoting this unscriptural viewpoint.

The *Book of Enoch* deals extensively with spirit entities such as angelic visitations, communication with angels, functions of angels, etc. Since this book influenced the kabbalistic tradition, it is interesting to note that in the book entitled *Magical Arts* we find that the **"CABALA INCLUDED SPELLS** *designed to induce an unseen population of spirits to carry out the magician's wishes."*[32]

Galatians 1:8 forewarns us: "But though we, **or an angel from heaven,** *preach any other gospel unto you* than that which we have preached unto you, let him be accursed." Remember, too, that there "are false apostles, deceitful workers, transforming themselves into the apostles of Christ. And no marvel; Satan himself is transformed into an angel of light. Therefore it is no great thing if his ministers also be transformed as the ministers of righteousness; whose end shall be according to their works" (II Corinthians 11:13-15).

Seeing that the *Book of Enoch* teaches another gospel, why are so many evangelical authors resorting to such a work and accepting it as "truth"? Remember, Patrick Heron declared: "...I have found **nothing** in the Book of Enoch that contradicts **anything** in scripture, rather it enhances and copper fastens the revealed Word of truth."[33] If he couldn't find anything that contradicted the Bible, we have to wonder how closely he has read the Bible or the *Book of Enoch*. We also should be cautious and question his viewpoint on the fallen angels mating with mankind which is taken from the *Book of Enoch*.

As one person remarked:

"The reason why the early church fathers and the King James Bible translators rejected the Book of Enoch as inspired of God, WASN'T to hide the truth; BUT, because it isn't the truth. The Book of Enoch is a fraud, an imposter (sic), and straight from Hell."[34] [Emphasis in the original.]

14. IS THE *BOOK OF JASHER* SCRIPTURE?

The *Book of Jasher* is another book that is often referenced to "prove" that the fallen angels mixed with mankind and tampered with the DNA.[1] Mormons, as well as some others, believe that this book is Scripture.[2] Others, such as Thomas Horn, Wayne Simpson, Ted Weiland, Steven Collins, Chris Ward, and Timothy Couche do not claim the *Book of Jasher* is Scripture but they do promote or reference it. They are quick to add that the Bible mentions the *Book of Jasher* in Joshua 10:13 and II Samuel 1:18.[3] What they fail to mention is that the Hebrew word "Jasher" (yasher) means upright, right, or righteous and is used in 119 verses. A few such verses are:

➜ "And thou shalt do that which is **right** and good in the sight of the Lord: that it may be well with thee, and that thou mayest go in and possess the good land which the Lord sware unto thy fathers..." (Deuteronomy 6:18).

➜ "He is the Rock, His work is perfect: for all His ways are judgment: a God of truth and without iniquity, just and **right** is He" (Deuteronomy 32:4).

➜ "There was a man in the land of Uz, whose name was Job; and that man was perfect and **upright,** and one that feared God, and eschewed evil" (Job 1:1).

➜ "The statutes of the Lord are **right,** rejoicing the heart: the commandment of the Lord is pure, enlightening the eyes" (Psalm 19:8).

➜ "Good and **upright** is the Lord: therefore will He teach sinners in the way" (Psalm 25:8).

➜ "For the word of the Lord is **right;** and all His works are done in truth" (Psalm 33:4).

→ "Righteous art thou, O Lord, and **upright** are Thy judgments" (Psalm 119:137).

What most of those who promote the *Book of Jasher* also will not tell you is that there is disagreement over what this "book" actually is. The JewishEncyclopedia.com reveals that the Rabbis and Jerome "translated 'Sefer ha-Yashar' by 'Book of the Righteous'" but

> "...they did not agree as to which book was meant. R. Johanan referred it to Genesis, finding there allusions both to the title ('Book of the Righteous') and to the incidents in connection with which it is quoted; R. Eleazar referred it to Deuteronomy; and Samuel b. Nahmani to the Book of Judges ('Ab. Zarah 25a). Sixtus Senensis ('Bibl. Sanct.' book ii.) states that some Hebrew writers (whose names he does not give) understand by the 'Book of Jasher' the twelve Minor Prophets.
>
> "Levi b. Gershon was the only commentator who thought that the 'Sefer ha-Yashar' was a special book, lost during the Captivity. His opinion has been adopted by Junius, Hottinger...and many others."[4]

In other words, only one commentator thought that the *Book of Jasher* was a lost book yet this is the opinion that has been adopted by many.

WHICH *BOOK OF JASHER?*

Another issue is that there are several books which carry this name.[5] The copy that is often used today was printed in 1887 in Salt Lake City by J. H. Parry and Company (which has printed many Mormon books). The title page states:

> "This is one of the **apochrypal** (sic) *Books of Jasher.* There are several (as many as five) separate works by this title, **all composed much later than Biblical times.** This particular one is a translation of a Hebrew book printed in 1613. Sepir Ha Yasher, the Hebrew title of this book, means the 'Book of the Upright,' or 'the Upright or Correct Record.' This title was misread as

'Jasher,' and at some point Jasher was treated as a proper name; however the pronoun 'the' (hebrew 'ha') never preceeds (sic) proper names."[6]

Notice that all these books were composed **MUCH LATER than Biblical times** so how could have the Bible quoted from any of these books? For instance, this

"...book in its entirety cannot be so old as shown by chapter 10, covering the descendants of Noah, which contains medieval names for territories and countries, perhaps mostly (sic) obviously *Franza* for France and *Lumbardi* in *Italia* for Lombardy. The text of this chapter closely follows the beginning of Josippon, a tenth century rabbinic text that lists the various peoples living in Europe in ca. 950.

"Most of its extra-Biblical accounts are found in nearly the same form in either other medieval compilations, or in the Talmud, or in other midrash or in Arabic sources. For example it contains the common tale that Lamech and his son Jabal accidentally killed Cain, thus requiting his wickedness for slaying Abel."[7]

Regardless of these facts, John Pratt (a Mormon) claims:

"Most reviewers grant that there are no significant disagreements between Book of Jasher and the Bible....The few disagreements between Jasher and the Bible are insufficient to disqualify it from being the authentic lost book mentioned in the scriptures."[8]

Really? Is this true? Are there only insignificant disagreements between the Bible and the *Book of Jasher?* Can this book be trusted? We'll see how this book compares to the Bible very shortly but, contrary to what is claimed (by Thomas Horn and others), the *Book of Jasher* **DOES NOT** "prove" that fallen angels mated with humans and produced the Nephilim. Thomas Horn quotes Jasher 4:18 as follows: "After the **fallen angels** went into the daughters of men, the sons of men taught the mixture of animals of one species with the other, in order to provoke the Lord."[9] Sounds fairly convincing, doesn't it? The problem is that Jasher 4:18 **DOES NOT** say what Horn claims it does.

If you go to the *Book of Jasher* you will find that Jasher 4:18-19 really says:

> "And **their judges and rulers** went to the **daughters of men** and took their wives by force from their husbands according to their choice, and the **sons of men** in those days took from the cattle of the earth, the beasts of the field and the fowls of the air, and taught the mixture of animals of one species with the other, in order therewith to prove the Lord; and God saw the whole earth and it was corrupt, for all flesh had corrupted its ways upon earth, all men and all animals. And the Lord said, **I will blot out man that *I* created from the face of the earth, yea from man to the birds of the air, together with cattle and beasts that are in the field for I repent that I made them.**"

It should be quite obvious that humans are being referred to in the above instance. There is no mention of "angels" or "sons of God." There is no mention of the "Nephilim" or "giants" or strange creatures. In fact, verse 19 says that the Lord will blot out man that **HE** created—not a hybrid race that supposedly came from a mixture of angels and humans.

So, even though the *Book of Jasher* is far from a Biblical book, it cannot honestly be used to promote the Nephilim theory as many are doing today.

Now, let's look at a number of specific examples and see how this book compares to the Bible. Some of the following discrepancies may be somewhat boring but a few of them are being listed in order to show how far-fetched the *Book of Jasher* really is.

INCORRECT AGES GIVEN

Book of Jasher	*Bible*
"... Methuselah lived eighty-seven years and he begat Lamech" (Jasher 3:13)	He was 187 years (Genesis 5:25)

Lamech was 160 when Seth died (Jasher 4:9)	He was 168 years
Lamech was 770 when he died (Jasher 5:20)	He was 777 (Genesis 5:31)
Methuselah was 960 (Jasher 5:36)	He was 969 (Genesis 5:27)
Terah was 38 when he begat Haran and Nahor (Jasher 7:22)	Terah was 70 (Genesis 11:26)
Abram leaves Haran at the age of 50 (Jasher 13:5)	Abram leaves Haran at 75 (Genesis 12:4)

OTHER DISCREPANCIES

➡ Jasher 2:3 says: "And it was in the days of Enosh [Enos] that **the sons of men continued to rebel and transgress against God,** to increase the anger of the Lord against the sons of men." Genesis 4:26 reveals: "And to Seth, to him also there was born a son; and he called his name Enos: **then began men to call upon the name of the Lord.**"

➡ Jasher 9 refers to the Tower of Babel and its destruction: "And they ceased building the city and the tower; therefore he called that place Babel, for there the Lord confounded the Language of the whole earth..." (Jasher 9:37). What happened to the tower? Jasher 9:38 declares: "And as to the tower which the sons of men built, **the earth opened its mouth and swallowed up one third part thereof,** and a fire also descended from heaven and burned another third, and the other third is left to this day...."

Could this really have happened? Not if you believe the Bible for there we find that the **FIRST** earthquake did not occur until Numbers 16:30 which was several hundred years after this incident.

➡ In Jasher 15 we find the narration of Lot and Abraham. Both men possessed much cattle and strife arose between their herdmen. Jasher 15:40 claims: **"And Abraham quarrelled daily with Lot** on account of this...." On the other hand, the Bible account mentions that there was strife between the herdmen but **Abraham said: "Let there be no strife..."** (Genesis 13:8). Abraham suggested that they separate and he kindly told Lot that if he wanted to go to the left, then he'd move to the right or if Lot wanted the right side, then Abraham would take the land to the left.

SHEM WAS MELCHIZEDEK

➔ Jasher 16 tells us that Abram met Adonizedek: "And Adonizedek king of Jerusalem, the same was Shem, went out with his men to meet Abram and his people, with bread and wine, and they remained together in the valley of Melech. And Adonizedek blessed Abram, and Abram gave him a tenth from all that he had brought from the spoil of his enemies, for Adonizedek was a priest before God" (Jasher 16:11-12). Several people such as Helena Lehman, Stephen E. Jones, and Marshall W. Best use this passage to "prove" that Melchizedek, Adonizedek, and Shem are all the **SAME** person. For instance, Marshall Best writes: "The important point...is that Melchizedek, also called Adonizedek, is Shem of all people!"[10] Helena Lehman states: "As explained in the Book of Jasher, Melchizedek, the king of Salem, was none other than Shem."[11] Stephen Jones says: "To show that Shem was the Melchizedek of Gen. 14:18, we will quote from Jasher 16:11, 12, which tells us the story of Abram's meeting with Melchizedek after freeing Lot...."[12]

Once again, we see that the Bible and the *Book of Jasher* are at odds. First of all, Adonizedek **WAS NOT** Melchizedek as the individuals mentioned above claim. Abram met Melchizedek in Genesis 14 which is several hundred years before Adonizedek is even mentioned in Joshua 10. Furthermore, Melchizedek was a righteous man but Adonizedek made war with a city that had made peace with the Israelites and he was killed and hung on a tree by the Israelites in this war (Joshua 10:23-26). We also know that Shem was dead long before Adonizedek was born so Adonizedek was not the same person as Shem. Additionally, Hebrews gives us more information about Melchizedek. There we find that this person was "Without father, without mother, without descent, having neither beginning of days, nor end of life; but made like unto the Son of God; abideth a priest continually" (Hebrews 7:3). It is also related to us that Levi "was yet in the loins of his father, when Melchisedec met him" (Hebrews 7:10). In other words, Levi was not yet born at this point but the Levites are mentioned in Joshua 8 which is 2 chapters before Adonizedek is mentioned which again shows that Adonizedek and Melchizedek **ARE NOT THE SAME PERSON.** Remember, too, Shem was dead long before Adonizedek was born so Shem could not have been Adonizedek. Notice also that Melchizedek did not have a father or mother, he was without descent, and he did not have a beginning of days nor end of life. Shem's father was Noah (Genesis 5:32), he was born, he had several children (Genesis 10:22), and he died (Genesis 11:11). Shem could not possibly be Melchizedek.

If individuals would simply read the Bible more thoroughly, they would never fall for the falsehoods presented in the *Book of Jasher* and other apocryphal literature.

➔ Jasher 29 relates the account of Jacob and Esau when Jacob received the blessing from his father that was meant for Esau. "And Jacob was very much afraid of his brother Esau, and he rose up and fled to the house of Eber the son of Shem, and he concealed himself there on account of his brother, and Jacob was sixty-three years old when he went forth from the land of Canaan from Hebron, and Jacob was concealed in Eber's house fourteen years on account of his brother Esau..." (Jasher 29:11). After fourteen years Jacob returned and Esau sought to slay him so Rebecca then sent Jacob to her brother's home. (Jasher 29:20-30). According to Genesis 27 and 28 we find that Rebecca told Jacob to go to her brother's home when Esau said that he planned to kill Jacob. Jacob did not spend fourteen years with Eber. He went directly to Laban's place as advised by his mother.

➜ Jasher 41:22 says an **ANGEL** saw Joseph wandering in the field. Genesis 37:17 says it was a **MAN.**

➜ When Joseph was in prison and the butler and baker each dreamed a dream, Joseph gave the correct interpretation to them and said that in three days the butler would be restored to his former position but that the baker would be hanged. According to Jasher 46:15-16 the third day was the day that the Queen gave birth to Pharaoh's first-born son and he made a feast. Genesis 40:20 tells us that this day was Pharaoh's birthday and that was why he made the feast.

➜ The chronology in Jasher records Isaac's death in chapter 47. This is after Joseph interpreted the dreams for the butler and the baker. However, according to the Bible, Isaac died in Genesis 35 which is before Joseph was even sold into Egypt. Jasher 43:35 also claims that Isaac wept when he had heard that Joseph was killed by a beast. As just mentioned, Isaac's death was recorded in Genesis 35 and this incident is found in Genesis 37.

PHARAOH'S DREAM

➜ When Pharaoh had his dream, the account in Jasher 48 says that the magicians, wise men, and sorcerers came and gave various interpretations for it. "And the king heard all the words of the wise men of Egypt and their interpretation of his dreams, and none of them pleased the king" (Jasher 48:24), so he ordered all of them to be killed. It was then that the butler remembered that Joseph had correctly interpreted his dreams so Pharaoh sent his servants "and the king's servants shaved him" (Jasher 48:41) and he came before Pharaoh. Going to the Bible we see a completely different description. Genesis 41:7-8 states: "And Pharaoh awoke, and, behold, it was a dream. And it came to pass in the morning that his spirit was troubled; and he sent and called for all the magicians of Egypt, and all the wise men thereof: and Pharaoh told them his dream; **BUT THERE WAS NONE THAT COULD INTERPRET THEM** unto Pharaoh." The butler told Pharaoh about Joseph and when he was brought out of the dungeon, Joseph "shaved **HIMSELF**" and came before Pharaoh.

→ Jasher 51:26-32 tells us that when Jacob's ten children went to Egypt to buy food they told Joseph (whom they didn't recognize) that they were looking for their brother. Genesis 42:6-14 gives a completely different picture. The ten brothers told Joseph that they were "twelve brethren, the sons of one man in the land of Canaan; and, behold, the youngest is this day with our father, and **ONE IS NOT.**" They were certainly not trying to find Joseph in Egypt. This same chapter also tells us that Simeon **could not be bound.** Jasher gives a very fanciful account of this. It tells us that Joseph called 70 valiant men to seize Simeon but when Simeon shrieked, they became afraid of their lives and fled and left Joseph and his five-year-old son Manassah alone with his brothers. At this point "Manassah smote Simeon a heavy blow with his fist against the back of his neck....And Manassah laid hold of Simeon and he seized him violently and he bound him..." (Jasher 51:42-43). Genesis 42:24 tells us that Joseph "turned himself about from them, and wept; and returned to them again, and communed with them, and **took from them Simeon, and bound him**" before their eyes." There was no heavy-handed struggle involved in any way.

→ According to Jasher 55:20 Joseph took Reuben, Issachar, Zebulun, and Benjamin unto Pharaoh. Genesis 47:2 says that he took **FIVE** (not four) of his brothers to Pharaoh.

→ In Jasher 56 we have the account of Jacob's imminent death. He commanded his sons to carry his body back to his burying place at Machpelah. He also commanded Levi and his sons to carry the ark of the covenant. This could not have occurred since the ark was not even made until over 400 years later. The ark was only constructed **AFTER** the children of Israel left Egypt and they remained in Egypt for over 400 years after Jacob's death. Exodus 25 is where we find the Lord's command for the ark to be built: "And let them make Me a sanctuary; that I may dwell among them....And they shall make an ark of shittim wood" (Exodus 25:8, 10).

TUSSLE AT JACOB'S BURIAL

➜ Jasher 56 also contains a fanciful tale about how Esau refused to let Jacob be buried at Machpelah claiming that he owned it and Jacob did not. A bitter fight broke out and Jacob's sons killed 40 of Esau's men. Jacob's grandson, Chushim, then killed Esau with a sword and cut off his head. "And when Chushim did this thing the sons of Jacob prevailed over the sons of Esau, and the sons of Jacob buried their father Jacob by force in the cave, and the sons of Esau beheld it" (Jasher 56:65). Another battle ensued and Jacob's sons killed 80 more of Esau's men and took 50 other men captive to Egypt. In the meantime the children of the east went to Egypt to help Esau's men and Joseph and his brethren "slew of them six hundred thousand men" (Jasher 57:9) and pursued them and slew 30 more men. More war and more bloodshed follows this account. The Bible gives no indication that any such thing happened. It simply states: "For his sons carried him [Jacob] into the land of Canaan, and buried him in the cave of the field of Machpelah, which Abraham bought with the field for a possession of a buryingplace of Ephron the Hittite, before Mamre. And Joseph returned to Egypt, he and his brethren, and all that went up with him to bury his father, after he had buried his father" (Genesis 50:13-14).

➜ Jasher 71 claims that **Moses was 18 years old when he killed the Egyptian.** At this point Pharaoh ordered him slain and "the angel of the Lord took hold of the right hand of Moses, and brought him forth from Egypt, and placed him from without the borders of Egypt, a distance of forty days' journey" (Jasher 71:11). After fleeing Egypt, he went to Cush and soon became the king of Cush at the age of 27 and "forty years did he reign" (Jasher 73:2). After 40 years "the people of Cush gave many presents to Moses, and sent him from them with great honor. So Moses went forth from the land of Cush, and went home and ceased to reign over Cush, and Moses was sixty-six years old when he went out of the land of Cush..." (Jasher 76:11-12).

After this Moses went to Midian and Reuel put him in prison for ten years but Reuel's daughter, Zipporah, fed him with bread and water during this time. Her father did not know that she was sustaining Moses. After ten years Zipporah suggested that they check on Moses to see if he was dead or alive and Reuel was surprised to find him alive since he was unaware that Zipporah had fed him during this time. (Jasher 76:1-23; 77:27-37). Reuel then gave Moses Zipporah for a wife.

The Bible tells us that when Moses "was full **forty years old, it came into his heart to visit his brethren the children of Israel. And** seeing one of them suffer wrong, he defended him, and avenged him that was oppressed, and smote the Egyptian....Then fled Moses at this saying, and was a stranger in the land of Madian [Midian], where he begat two sons. And when forty years were expired, there appeared to him in the wilderness of mount Sina an angel of the Lord in a flame of fire in a bush" (Acts 7:23-24, 29-30). We also know from Exodus 2:15 that when Moses fled from Pharaoh he went and dwelt in the land of Midian (Exodus 2:15). The *Book of Jasher* and the Bible certainly do not coincide.

MOSES AS KING OF CUSH

Furthermore, Jasher 81:3-4 claims that the Israelites stayed in Egypt for 210 years but the Bible tells us several times that they were there for 430 years. Exodus 12:40-41: "Now the sojourning of the children of Israel, who dwelt in Egypt, was four hundred and thirty years. And it came to pass at the end of the four hundred and thirty years, even the selfsame day it came to pass, that all the hosts of the Lord went out from the land of Egypt" (see also Galatians 3:17). According to Jasher, Moses reigned in Cush in the 157th year after the Israelites went down to Egypt (Jasher 73:1). Since the Israelites were in Egypt 430 years and Moses was 80 years old when he led them out of Egypt (see Exodus 7:7 and Acts 7:23-24, 29-30), Moses would not even have been born in the 157th year, much less be a reigning king! Moses' birth was yet almost 200 years in the future.

➡ Jasher 78:12-13 asserts that Pharaoh ordered that no more straw be given to the Israelites **before** Moses went to him (Jasher 79:4). Exodus 5 tells us that this command from Pharaoh only happened **after** Moses and Aaron confronted Pharaoh.

➡ After Moses' rod became a serpent, Jasher 80:1 says that it was **two years** before the Lord sent Moses back to Pharaoh. However, Exodus 7:14-15 says: "The Lord said unto Moses get thee unto Pharaoh **in the morning.**"

PHARAOH SPARED

➡ When God sent the plagues upon the Egyptians, Jasher 80 alleges that Pharaoh's daughter (who is called Bathia in Jasher) who had raised Moses, asked him why he brought evil upon the Egyptians after she did good for him. Moses asked if any of the ten plagues (which differ greatly from the Bible account) affected her and she said "No." Moses then promised her that even though she was the firstborn, she would not die. Moses also "said to Pharaoh, Behold though thou art thy mother's first born, yet fear not, for thou wilt not die, for the Lord has commanded that thou shalt live, in order to show thee his great might and strong stretched out arm" (Jasher 80:57). Jasher 81:40-41 claims: "And when the children of Israel had entered the sea, the Egyptians came after them, and the waters of the sea resumed upon them, and they all sank in the water, and not one man was left **excepting Pharaoh,** who gave thanks unto the Lord and believed in him....And the Lord ordered an angel to take him from amongst the Egyptians, who cast him upon the land of Ninevah and he reigned over it for a long time."

Is this what the Bible teaches us? Let's look at Exodus 11:5: "And **ALL** the firstborn in the land of Egypt shall die, **FROM THE FIRSTBORN OF PHARAOH** that sitteth upon his throne, even unto the firstborn of the maidservant that is behind the mill; and all the firstborn of beasts." Exodus 12:29 also reveals: "And it came to pass, that at midnight **the Lord smote all the firstborn in the land of Egypt, from THE FIRSTBORN OF PHARAOH** that sat on his throne unto the firstborn of the captive that was in the dungeon; and all the firstborn of cattle."

Concerning Pharaoh himself we find in Psalm 136:15: "But overthrew Pharaoh and his host in the Red sea..." and Exodus 14:28 states "all the host of Pharaoh that came into the sea after them; **there remained not so much as one of them.**"

RACHEL TALKS FROM THE GRAVE

Not only do we discover contradiction after contradiction, we also find many problematic areas. For instance in Jasher 42 there is the story of Joseph being sold. There are so many discrepancies in this story (which I won't mention) but on his way to Egypt, the company passed near where Rachel, Joseph's mother, was buried. Joseph ran to her grave and talked to her. Jasher 42:30-41 has Rachel responding to Joseph from the grave and giving him advice. This is necromancy and is strictly forbidden by God in Deuteronomy 18:11-12.

Jasher 44 contains a peculiar passage about Potiphar's wife trying to entice Joseph. After she accused Joseph of trying to seduce her, Potiphar ordered that Joseph be beaten. While he was crying out that he was innocent, an eleven month old baby began to talk and said that Joseph was innocent and "the child told them accurately all that happened, and all the words of Zelicah [Potiphar's wife] to Joseph day after day did he declare unto them" (Jasher 44:66). Strangely, even though Joseph was found to be innocent, he was still placed in prison.

In Jasher 53 Benjamin uses a "map of the stars" to find out where Joseph is. This is a form of astrology and a practice which is also forbidden in Deuteronomy 18:10. Jasher also claims that Joseph told Benjamin that he was going to send him away and then bring him back. This chapter continues with the narrative of how Benjamin was found to have the silver cup in his sack. When the brothers came before Joseph, he "rose up and caught hold of Benjamin and took him from his brethren with violence..." (Jasher 53:32). Judah then threatens Joseph and said that he could slay all Egypt and Joseph then tries to intimidate his brothers but threatening to kill them. After more verbal exchanges, Judah

> "...was exceedingly wroth and his anger burned within him, and there was before him in that place a stone, the weight of which was about four hundred shekels, and Judah's anger was kindled and he took the stone in one hand and cast it to the heavens and caught it with his left hand. And he placed it afterward under his legs, and he sat upon it with all his strength and the stone was turned into dust from the force of Judah. And Joseph saw the act of Judah and he was very much afraid, but he commanded Manassah his son [who was only five years old!] and he also did with another stone like unto the act of Judah..." (Jasher 54:28-30).

FIVE YEAR OLD ASSEMBLES AN ARMY

Judah now commands his brothers to destroy Egypt so Joseph sent his five year old son to gather all the valiant men together.

> "And their number was five hundred cavalry and ten thousand infantry, and four hundred men who could fight without sword or spear, only with their hands and strength....Then Judah hastened and drew his sword, and uttered a loud and bitter scream, and he smote with his sword....And they all fled at the sound of the shouting, and they were terrified and fell one upon the other, and many of them died as they fell, and they all fled from before Judah and his brethren and from before Joseph. And whilst they were fleeing, Judah and his brethren pursued them unto the house of Pharaoh, and they all escaped, and Judah again sat before Joseph and roared at him like a lion, and gave a great and tremendous shriek at him.And the shriek was heard at a distance, and all the inhabitants of Succoth heard it, and all Egypt quaked at the sound of the shriek, and also the walls of Egypt and of the

land of Goshen fell in from the shaking of the earth, and Pharaoh
also fell from his throne upon the ground, and also all the pregnant
women of Egypt and Goshen miscarried when they heard the
noise of the shaking, for they were terribly afraid" (Jasher 54:39,
43, 45-47).

Since Pharaoh was so terrified, he told Joseph to release
Benjamin and send him back with his brothers. Pharaoh then gives
Joseph an ultimatum:

"And if thou desirest not to do this thing, cast off from thee
all my valuable things, and go with them to their land, if thou
delightest in it, for they will this day destroy my whole country
and slay all my people; even all the women of Egypt have
miscarried through their scream; see what they have done merely
by their shouting and speaking, moreover if they fight with the
sword, they will destroy the land; now therefore choose that which
thou desirest, whether me or the Hebrews, whether Egypt or the
land of the Hebrews....And Joseph was greatly afraid of his
brethren and on account of Pharaoh, and Joseph sought a pretext
to make himself known unto his brethren, lest they should destroy
all Egypt" (Jasher 54:50, 52).

A completely different picture is portrayed in Genesis 44. After
the cup was found in Benjamin's sack, all the brothers returned to
Joseph. "And Judah said...we are my lord's servants, both we, and he
also with whom the cup is found." There was no harsh exchange, no
contest showing who was mightier and more powerful, no threats of
killing. There was just a simple submission. After Joseph said that he
would only retain Benjamin, Judah made a plea to release Benjamin
and he said that he became the surety for him. Judah said: "Now
therefore, I pray thee, let thy servant abide instead of the lad a bondman
to my lord; and let the lad go up with his brethren" (Genesis 44:33).
It was at this point that Joseph revealed himself to his brethren. It is
obvious that both accounts cannot be correct.

These are just a few (and I mean **A FEW!**) of the problems
with the *Book of Jasher*. With such discrepancies, fancies, and
inaccuracies in the *Book of Jasher,* why would any person who claims
to believe the Bible resort to such a book to find "truth"?

Once again, I'm urging all my readers to get back to the Bible. Read it through from cover to cover, Genesis to Revelation, and then start over again. Each time you do so you'll learn more and more. Remember Proverbs 3:5-6: "Trust in the Lord with all thine heart; and lean not unto thine own understanding. In all thy ways acknowledge Him, and He shall direct thy paths."

To conclude this chapter, I think it might be of interest to know that Ye Olde Magick Shoppe, a pagan website, sells the *Book of Jasher*.[13] It just happens to be listed under the section called "Occult Books." Do **YOU** want to stake your eternal destiny on such a book?

15. CONCLUSION

Using the Bible as our source for truth and information, we have detected that the popular teaching of the Nephilim is not a Scriptural idea. We've looked at the concept of the serpent seed and see that there is no basis in the Bible for such a notion. Sin started in the Garden of Eden but the sin was disobedience to God not a sexual relationship between Eve and Satan. The problem wasn't the apple on the tree, it was the "pair" on the ground.

We studied the context surrounding the verse "Ye are of your father the devil" and found that it is not referring to a physical lineage. We've seen the reason why Cain's name is not mentioned in the genealogy of Jesus.

We learned that the fallen angels did not mate with humans to produce the Nephilim and we discovered why God sent the flood. We compared the days of Noah and the days of Lot with the end times.

There was in-depth coverage of the idea of the golem and beasts which supposedly have no souls. We've looked at the concept of cloning and the Shroud of Turin and we took a glimpse into Daniel to see who the watchers were.

Although these are all important issues that are pertinent to today, the most important topic has to do with our eternal destiny. Where will you spend eternity?

Because of Adam's and Eve's sin, sin has been passed on to all of us. Romans 5:12 states: "Wherefore, as by one man sin entered into the world, and death by sin; and so death passed upon all men, for that all have sinned." "For the wages of sin is death; but the gift of God is eternal life through Jesus Christ our Lord" (Romans 6:23).

This is the importance of the virgin birth. Since the blood of a firstborn comes **ONLY** through the Father, Jesus' blood source was provided by God alone. Jesus took on human flesh or a body (Hebrews 10:5) but He did not partake of the sinful human nature. II Corinthians 5:21 states: "For He hath made Him to be sin for us, who knew no sin; that we might be made the righteousness of God in Him." This is why Christ's blood could atone for our sins. I Peter 1:18-19 says: "Forasmuch as ye know that ye were not redeemed with corruptible things, as silver and gold,...But with the **precious blood of Christ,** as of a lamb **without blemish** and without spot...."

"In whom we have redemption through His blood, the forgiveness of sins, according to the riches of His grace" (Ephesians 1:7; Colossians 1:14).

"But now in Christ Jesus ye who sometimes were far off are made nigh by the blood of Christ" (Ephesians 2:13).

Even though **ALL** of us are born in sin, the good news is that "Christ Jesus came into the world to save sinners" (I Timothy 1:15). If you have never accepted Christ as your **PERSONAL** Savior and would like to do so, the first step is to be born again. John 3:3 emphasizes: **"EXCEPT** a man be born **AGAIN,** he **CANNOT** see the kingdom of God." How can one be born **AGAIN?** We all know that we were born once, our physical birth, but can we enter into our mother's womb and be born the second time (see John 3:1-17)? No. The second birth comes by being born into the family of God. John 3:16: "For God so **LOVED** the world that He **GAVE** His only Begotten Son, that **WHOSOEVER BELIEVETH** in Him should not perish, but have everlasting life."

All you need to do is sincerely believe with all your heart that Jesus is the Son of God and be willing to turn from your sins, whatever they are—big or small. Ask Jesus to come into your heart and help you to live for Him, and He **WILL** do it. "He that covereth his sins shall not prosper: but whoso **CONFESSETH AND FORSAKETH** them shall have mercy" (Proverbs 28:13). John 6:37 promises: "Him that cometh to Me I will **IN NO WISE** cast out." Romans 10:9 states: "If thou shalt **CONFESS** with thy mouth the Lord Jesus, and shalt

BELIEVE in thine heart that God hath raised Him from the dead, thou **SHALT** be saved."

If you would like to be born again, pray your own prayer or sincerely pray the following:

> *Dear Jesus, I realize that I am a sinner. I believe that You died for my sins. Please forgive me of my past sins and come into my heart. Save me for Your sake, and help me to live for You. I ask this in Your name. Amen.*

If you sincerely prayed and asked Jesus to forgive you of your sins, you will have the assurance that you are now a child of God. John 1:12 reveals: "But **AS MANY AS RECEIVED HIM,** to them gave He power to become the sons of God, even to them that **BELIEVE** on His name." Read your Bible **EVERY** day (start with the book of John), and find a Bible-believing church where you can worship God with other born again believers.

"Therefore being justified by faith, we have peace with God through our Lord Jesus Christ" (Romans 5:1), "and the peace of God, which passeth all understanding, shall keep your hearts and minds through Christ Jesus" (Philippians 4:7). "If the Son [Jesus Christ] therefore shall make you free, ye shall be free indeed" (John 8:36).

GLOSSARY

✎ *Alien abduction*

Kidnapping of an individual by non-human entities or extraterrestrials. The individual claims to have been taken to unfamiliar surroundings and usually forced to undergo a medical examination that often includes the individual's reproductive system.

✎ *Anunnaki* or *Annunaki*

Mythological beings from Sumeria. The name is roughly translated to mean "those who came from heaven to Earth."

✎ *Apocryphal*

Writings (such as the *Book of Enoch,* the *Book of Jasher,* etc.) that are of doubtful authenticity or questionable accuracy.

✎ *Book of Enoch*

An apocryphal book (often quoted by occultists) but not included in the canon of Scriptures.

✎ *Clone*

"A copy of a sequence of DNA, as from a gene, that is produced by genetic engineering. The clone is then transplanted into the nucleus of a cell from which genetic material has been removed."[1]

✎ *Edinburgh Manuscript*

A Masonic manuscript written in 1696.

✎ *Gibbor, Gibborim,* or *Gibbowr*

Hebrew word for "mighty."

✎ *Golem*

In Jewish folklore, a clay or stone image that is endowed with life through magic charms.

✎ *Greys*

One type of humanoid extraterrestrial that often appears in supposed alien abductions or encounters with UFOs.

✎ *HVHI*

The incommunicable name of Samael or Satan.

✎ *Hybrid*

A mixture of two different things. One example would be the mule which is the offspring of a male donkey and a female horse. Most hybrids are sterile.

✎ *Iysh*

Hebrew word for "a man as an individual or a male person."

✎ *Lilith*

In folklore, Lilith is considered the "Bride of the Devil" and the Jewish version refers to her as "the patroness of witches." In witchcraft teachings, Cain is considered to be the son of Lilith and Satan.

✎ *Merkabah* or *Merkava*

"Throne or chariot of God, as described by Ezekiel. It became an object of visionary contemplation for Jewish mystics in Palestine in the 1st century AD; in the 7th-11th century, Merkabah mysticism was centered in Babylonia. Merkabah mystics courted ecstatic visions that involved a dangerous ascent through celestial hierarchies to the throne of God. Hostile angels guarded the gates to the seven 'heavenly dwellings,' and a successful journey required magical formulas. The Talmud warns that of four men who engaged in Merkabah, only one had a true vision; of the others, one died, one went mad, and one became an apostate."[2]

✎ *Midrash*

Rabbinical exegesis, exposition, or interpretation of the Hebrew Scriptures. It can also refer to a book such as a compilation of Midrashic teachings.

✎ *Montanism*

A heretical teaching from the 2nd century promulgated by Montanus "who believed that the Holy Spirit, or Paraclete, dwelt within him and made him its instrument for guiding men in the Christian way."[3]

✎ *Nephilim* or *Nefilim*

The word comes from the Hebrew and means "bully," "tyrant," or "giant." Some teach that the Nephilim are the fallen angels or the offspring of the fallen angels and human women. This idea comes from the *Book of Enoch,* but such a concept is not found in the Word of God.

✎ *Nephesh*

The Hebrew word for "soul."

✎ *Neshama, Neshamah, Nashamah* or *Neshawmaw*

The Hebrew word for "breath."

✎ *Pneuma*

The Greek word for "spirit" or "breath."

✎ *Pseudepigrapha*

Spurious or false writings often attributed to biblical times. One such pseudepigrapha is the *Book of Enoch.*

✎ *Samael* or *Sammael*

Another name for Satan. Samael means "Poison of God." He is also called the "Angel of death." Some Luciferians believe that Samael fathered Cain with Lilith.

✎ *Sefer haYashar*

"...a Hebrew midrash known in English translation mostly as *The Book of Jasher.*"[4]

✎ *Serpent Seed*

There are various aspects and perspectives to this belief, but basically the "serpent seed" theory teaches that when Eve partook of the tree of the knowledge of good and evil in the Garden of Eden, she had actually engaged in a sexual relationship with the serpent or Satan and from this illicit relationship Cain was born. Such a theory is not Biblical.

✎ *Sumerian Clay Tablets*

Cuneiform (or wedge-shaped) writing developed by the Sumerians and preserved on clay tablets.

✎ *Tablet of Destinies*

"In Mesopotamian mythology, the **Tablet of Destinies** (not, as frequently misquoted in general works, the 'Tablets of Destiny') was envisaged as a clay tablet inscribed with cuneiform writing, also impressed with cylinder seals, which, as a permanent legal document, conferred upon the god Enlil his supreme authority as ruler of the universe."[5]

✎ *Talmud*

A collection of Rabbinic writings which consists of the Mishnah and the Gemara. It is the primary source of Jewish religious authority, law, customs, and history. It is a very important text for Rabbis and is a sacred book to the Jews. The *Talmud* teaches "that Mary, the Mother of Jesus Christ, was a whore and an adulteress who bore Jesus by a Roman soldier named Pandera."[6] According to the "uncensored" text of the Talmud we find that Jesus' mother (called Miriam) had sex with many men.[7] The *Talmud* also teaches that "Jesus is now burning in hot excrement in Hell."[8]

✎ *Targum*

"Targum" means "translation" or "interpretation" and is the Aramaic translation of the Hebrew Bible.

✎ *Tartaroo*

Greek word translated as "hell." It is a special place where the fallen angels are confined until the day of judgment (II Peter 2:4).

✎ *Zera*

Hebrew word meaning "seed."

ENDNOTES

Chapter 1: Let's Start with the Scriptures

[1] http://www.challies.com/archives/articles/counterfeit-det.php

Chapter 2: The Serpent Seed Doctrine

[1] http://www.serpentseedline.com/; http://www.gotquestions.org/serpent-seed.html; http://www.sherryshriner.org/sherry/serpent-seedline.htm; http://www.unification.org/ucbooks/intro.html; http://www.watchman.org/cat95.htm; http://www.watchman.org/cat95.htm; http://www.letusreason.org/moon2.htm; http://thechurchofjesuschrist.wordpress.com/2008/08/12/arnold-murray-secret-identity/; http://en.wikipedia.org/wiki/Serpent_seed; http://en.believethesign.com/index.php?title=Serpent's_Seed; http://www.propheticrevelation.net/branhamism.htm; http://www.deceptioninthechurch.com/williambranham1.html; http://www.letusreason.org/Poptea4.htm; http://www.dishangel.com/study.htm; http://www.thehomeland.org/tempold/kenites1.htm; http://www.forgenerations.net/falsemessiahs/FalseTeachers/arnoldmurray.html; http://www.stargods.org/SellerSerpentSeed.htm; http://petragrail.tripod.com/lilith.html; http://www.wfial.org/index.cfm?fuseaction=archives.index; http://www.experiencefestival.com/unification_church; http://abominationnation.blogspot.com/2008/05/who-is-todd-bentley.html; http://www.apologeticsindex.org/b05.html; http://www.gospelassemblyfree.com/facts/branham.htm; http://www.biblemaster.com/qanda/display_topic_threads.asp?ForumID=2&TopicID=6571&PagePosition=1; http://www.teachinghearts.org/dre00glossary.html#twoseed; http://home.online.no/~raygd/tale2.htm; http://www.endtimez.com/nephilim.html; http://www.congregator.net/topical/bible-believers-newsletter-242.htm; http://www.biblestudysite.com/migrationmap.htm; http://michaelsheiser.com/PaleoBabble/2008/06/was-cain-fathered-by-the-devil-no-wait-extraterrestrials/; http://www.riseofthefallen.com/htm/history.htm; http://www.raidersnewsnetwork.com/full.php?news=9210; http://www.hartsvillenewsjournal.com/main.asp?Search=1&ArticleID=2821&SectionID=4&SubSectionID=4&S=1; http://www.splcenter.org/intel/intelreport/article.jsp?aid=916

[2] http://www.serpentseedline.com/

[3] http://www.biblitecapleyades.net/sociopolitica/the_experiment/experiment13.htm

[4] http://forbiddenfruitjam.wordpress.com/2008/07/26/seedline-theory-another-reply/

[5] http://www.sherryshriner.org/sherry/serpent-seedline.htm

[6] http://www.youtube.com/watch?v=qGvUwiHpM_M&feature=related (approximately 7 minutes into the interview); Joye Jeffries Pugh, *Eden: The Knowledge of Good and Evil: 666* (Mustang, Oklahoma: Tate Publishing, 2006), p. 31.

[7] http://www.wildernesschurch.com/articles/twoseeds.htm

[8] http://www.thewatcherfiles.com/sherry/cain.htm; http://www.sherryshriner.org/sherry/serpent-seedline.htm; http://www.serpentseedline.com/

[9] http://en.wikipedia.org/wiki/Michael_S._Heiser

[10] http://michaelsheiser.com/PaleoBabble/2008/06/was-cain-fathered-by-the-devil-no-wait-extraterrestrials/

[11] *Ibid.*

[12] *Ibid.* See also: http://virtualreligion.net/iho/targum.html; http://www.jewishencyclopedia.com/view.jsp?artid=24&letter=F

[13] http://en.wikipedia.org/wiki/Targum

[14] http://michaelsheiser.com/PaleoBabble/2008/06/was-cain-fathered-by-the-devil-no-wait-extraterrestrials/

[15] Michael W. Ford, *Liber HVHI: Magick of the Adversary* (Houston, Texas: Succubus Publishing, 2005), p. 23. See also: http://petragrail.tripod.com/lilith.html

[16] http://www.paganwiki.org/index.php?title=Lilith; http://www.chaostatic.com/paradigm/writings/black-witchcraft.php; Michael W. Ford, *Black Witchcraft: Foundations of the Luciferian Path,* p. 5.

[17] http://www.chaostatic.com/paradigm/writings/black-witchcraft.php

[18] Ford, *Liber HVHI, op. cit.,* p. 87.

[19] http://www.chaostatic.com/paradigm/writings/black-witchcraft.php. See also: *Ibid.,* p. 30; Michael W. Ford, *Black Witchcraft: Foundations of the Luciferian Path,* p. 6-7.

[20] *Ibid.*

[21] http://www.biblestudygames.com/biblestudies/gardenofeden.htm

[22] http://www.israelect.com/reference/WillieMartin/Genesis41.htm; http://www.thewatcherfiles.com/sherry/cain.htm; http://www.sherryshriner.org/sherry/serpent-seedline.htm; http://www.serpentseedline.com/

[23] http://eword.gospelcom.net/comments/1john/mh/1john3.htm

[24] http://www.israelect.com/reference/WillieMartin/Genesis41.htm; http://www.mission.org/jesuspeople/arnmuray.htm

[25] *Ibid.;* http://www.satansrapture.com/satanseed.htm; Joye Jeffries Pugh, *Eden: The Knowledge of Good and Evil: 666* (Mustang, Oklahoma: Tate Publishing, 2006), p. 32, 35, 36, 41; http://people.delphiforums.com/johnk63/serpent%20seed.html; http://www.sherryshriner.org/sherry/serpent-seedline.htm; http://www.serpentseedline. com/; http://www.biblestudygames.com/biblestudies/parabletares.htm; http:// www.sherryshriner.org/sherry/serpent-seedline.htm; http://www.biblestudysite.com/ realsin.htm; http://en.believethesign.com/index.php?title=Serpent's_Seed; http:// www.visi.com/~steved/cam/Murray.htm; http://mystery-babylon.org/cain.html; http:// www.biblebelievers.org.au/bb981121.htm; http://newsfromthewest.blogspot.com/2008/ 02/jewish-magazine-shows-how-to-cook.html; http://www.officialnewworldorder.com/ html/jewish_bankers.html.

[26] http://www.thewatcherfiles.com/stargates/part-thirteen.htm; http:// www.bibliotecapleyades.net/stargate/stargate06_13.htm; http://www.sherryshriner.org/ sherry/serpent-seedline.htm. See also: http://www.raidersnewsnetwork.com/ full.php?news=9210; http://www.echoesofenoch.com/abductions.htm

Chapter 3: "Ye Are of Your Father the Devil"

[1] http://www.watchman.org/cat95.htm

[2] http://www.biblebelievers.org.au/jew.htm; http://thechurchofjesuschrist. wordpress.com/2008/08/12/arnold-murray-secret-identity/;http:// www.arguewitheveryone.com/judaism-israel/19828-satan-his-children-jews.html; http://newsfromthewest.blogspot.com/2008/02/jewish-magazine-shows-how-to-cook.html; http://www.biblestudygames.com/biblestudies/gardenofeden.htm; http:// www.watchman.org/cat95.htm; http://www.endtimeschristianity.com/cgi-bin/ webbbs_files/webbbs_config.pl?noframes;read=291 [3] http://www.satansrapture.com/ satanseed.htm

[4] http://www.arguewitheveryone.com/judaism-israel/19828-satan-his-children-jews.html

[5] http://www.biblebelievers.org.au/jew.htm

[6] http://www.biblebelievers.org.au/bb981121.htm. See also: http:// www.biblebelievers.org.au/nl039.htm; http://www.thewatcherfiles.com/sleep.htm; http:// www.serpentseedline.com/control_factor.htm

[7] http://www.sherryshriner.org/sherry/serpent-seedline.htm; http:// www.goodnewsaboutgod.com/studies/spiritual/home_study/new_religion1.htm

[8] *Ibid.;* http://petragrail.tripod.com/lilith.html

Chapter 4: Is Cain Missing from Adam's Lineage?

[1] Joye Jeffries Pugh, *Eden: The Knowledge of Good and Evil: 666* (Mustang, Oklahoma: Tate Publishing, 2006), p. 35. See also: http://www.serpentseedline.com/; http://members.tnns.net/wordweb/genesis7.htm

[2] http://www.gotquestions.org/Jesus-genealogy.html; http://bibletools.org/index.cfm/fuseaction/Bible.show/sVerseID/25049/eVerseID/25064; http://www.geocities.com/cobblestoneministries/2006/GenealogiesofJesusInMatthew1andLuke3.html

[3] http://www.biblestudygames.com/biblestudies/gardenofeden.htm; http://www.stargods.org/SellerSerpentSeed.htm; http://www.theseason.org/genesis/genesis4.htm; http://www.loveyah.com/day8.htm; http://www.letusreason.org/Poptea4.htm; http://www.ccel.org/s/schaff/encyc/encyc02/htm/iv.vi.xv.htm; http://trescx.splinder.com/post/17496359/ath+thiest+%3D+athiest+%3D+son+of+; http://www.angelfire.com/ca6/sunnysweb/kenites.html

[4] http://www.mission.org/jesuspeople/arnmuray.htm

[5] http://www.letusreason.org/Poptea4.htm. See also: http://www.1911 encyclopedia.org/Kenites

[6] http://www.stargods.org/SellerSerpentSeed.htm; http://www.angelfire.com/ca6/sunnysweb/garden.html; http://www.biblestudysite.com/migrationmap.htm; http://www.dishangel.com/study.htm; http://www.stormfront.org/forum/showthread.php?t=375707; http://www.thewatcherfiles.com/royal_battle_partthree.htm; http://www.hartsvillenewsjournal.com/main.asp?Search=1&ArticleID=2821&SectionID=4&SubSectionID=4&S=1

Chapter 5: The Nephilim

[1] http://www.answersingenesis.org/articles/aid/v2/n1/who-were-the-nephilim

[2] http://www.jewishencyclopedia.com/view.jsp?artid=24&letter=F

[3] http://www.jewishpath.org/parshanoach.html

[4] http://www.gotquestions.org/Printer/Nephilim-PF.html. See also: http://www.thewatcherfiles.com/sleep.htm

[5] *Ibid.;* http://home.flash.net/~saints/deceive.htm; Mark Hitchcock and Scot Overbey *Extraterrestrials: What on Earth Is Going On?* (Oklahoma City, Oklahoma: Hearthstone Publishing Ltd., 1997), p.176-177; Zecharia Sitchin, *The End of Days: Armageddon and Prophecies of the Return* (William Morrow, 2007), p. 2, 53-55; http://watch.pair.com/dragon-lineage.html; http://www.newsguide.us/art-entertainment/books/Due-to-Increasing-Demand-Arrival-of-the-Prince-a-Progressive-Christian-Book-is-Now-Available-Via-the-AuthorHouse-Book-Return-Program/

[6] Michael W. Ford, *Liber HVHI: Magick of the Adversary* (Houston, Texas: Succubus Publishing, 2005), p. 87. See also: http://www.gotquestions.org/Nephilim.html

[7] http://www.riseofthefallen.com/htm/nephilim.htm

[8] http://en.wikipedia.org/wiki/Fields_of_the_Nephilim; http://www.last.fm/music/Fields+of+the+Nephilim; http://www.spookhouse.net/angelynx/nephilim/neph.html; http://www.musicemissions.com/artists/Fields+Of+The+Nephilim

[9] http://www.musicemissions.com/artists/Fields+Of+The+Nephilim. See also: http://www.spookhouse.net/angelynx/nephilim/neph.html

[10] http://www.book-of-thoth.com/thebook/index.php/Nephilim; http://www.avoo.com/wiki/Basic_Role_Playing

[11] http://www.magicdeckvortex.com/DDB/the_nephilim_deck_v11.htm; http://www.gamingetcstore.com/mg-gp-rm-138.html; http://forums.gleemax.com/wotc_archive/index.php/t-638009; http://ww2.wizards.com/gatherer; http://www.mtgontario.com/index.php?name=News&file=article&sid=589

[12] http://www.book-of-thoth.com/thebook/index.php/Nephilim; http://www.last.fm/music/Behemoth/_/The+Nephilim+Rising

[13] *Ibid.*

[14] *Ibid.*

[15] http://scifipedia.scifi.com/index.php/Nephilim_(movie)

[16] http://www.amazon.com/Last-Red-Hot-Vampires-Katie-MacAlister/dp/0451220854

[17] http://www.book-of-thoth.com/thebook/index.php/Nephilim

[18] http://www.monstropedia.org/index.php?title=Nephilim

[19] Joye Jeffries Pugh, *Eden: The Knowledge of Good and Evil: 666* (Mustang, Oklahoma: Tate Publishing, 2006), p. 44. See also: Personal letter from Dr. Pugh to a friend; http://www.delusionresistance.org/christian/noah01%20-%20nephilim.html; http://www.raidersnewsnetwork.com/editoral.php?feature=11868; http://www.kingdom-gospel.com/ufo.html; http://ldolphin.org/nephilim.html; http://home.att.net/~warplover/06_the_nephilim.html#nine; http://www.shangrala.org/RELIGIONS/1Christianity/GodsCovenants.html; http://www.endtimez.com/nephilim.html; http://www.thewatcherfiles.com/sherry/who-is-what.html; http://www.bcrevolution.ca/secret_societies.htm; http://www.rainbowcircle.net/forum/topic/show?id=1986923%3ATopic%3A19499; http://www.paradoxbrown.com/Chapter_4.htm;

http://www.logoschristian.org/aliens.html; http://www.thewatcherfiles .com/ aliens_are_coming.html; http://www.thegreatseparation.com/newsfront/2005/02/ the_nephilim_bu.html; http://www.riseofthefallen.com/htm/nephilim.htm; http:// thestrongdelusion.com/index.php?option=com_content&task=view&id=440&Itemid=9; http://www.raidersnewsnetwork.com/full.php?news=19591; http://mysterial.org.uk/cgi-bin/index.cgi?action=viewnews&id=1210; http://www.tbm.org/origindemons.htm; http://www.paradoxbrown.com/chapter_guy.htm; http://home.att.net/~warplover/ 06_the_nephilim.html#nine; http://www.seancasteel.com/angels_and_aliens.htm; http:// users.aristotle.net/~bhuie/demons.htm; http://www.sherryshriner.com/fallen_angels. htm; http://conspiracyguy.wordpress.com/category/nephilim/; http://www.stargods.org/ ReptilianDemons.htm; http://www.paradoxbrown.com/Chapter_3.htm; http:// www.stargods.org/ReptilianDemons.htm; http://www.tbm.org/origindemons.htm; http:// www.thestargates.com/artapprentice.net/httpdocs/old_webpage/anunnakiabyss/ page4.html; http://godsprofessor.com/dnmkchap3.htm; http://www.endtimeschristianity. com/cgi-bin/webbbs_files/webbbs_config.pl? noframes;read=582

[20] http://www.pr.com/press-release/83765; http://www.raidersnewsnetwork.com/ full.php?news=13899. See also: http://www.raidersnewsnetwork.com/full.php?news= 11401; http://www.eaec.org/newsletters/2000/NL2000sep.htm; http://home.flash.net/ ~saints/deceive.htm; http://www.raidersnewsnetwork.com/full.php?news=11222; http:// www.raidersnewsnetwork.com/editoral.php?feature=11035; http://lamarzulli. wordpress.com/; http://www.riseofthefallen.com/htm/nephilim.htm; http:// www.geocities.com/rebornempowered/cesario-ufo; http://gracethrufaith.com/ikvot-hamashiach/the-nephilim/#more-204; http://www.echoesofenoch.com/abductions.htm; http://www.sheepkillers.com/ufonephilimagenda.html ; http://www.khouse.org/articles/ 1996/43/; http://www.bibleprobe.com/nephilim.htm

[21] http://www.claudemariottini.com/blog/2006/03/rereading-genesis-64-were-they-really.html; http://www.sitchiniswrong.com/nephilim.pdf

[22] http://www.sitchiniswrong.com/nephilim.pdf; http://www.mysteriousworld.com/ Journal/2002/Summer/Atlantis/. See also: http://www.bibliotecapleyades.net/sumer_ anunnaki/anunnaki/anu_18.htm

[23] A. R. Fausset, *Fausset's Bible Dictionary* (Zondervan, 1949).

[24] http://www.ahrimangate.com/excerpt148.htm. See also: http:// www.jewishpath.org/parshanoach.html; http://www.truthintheword.com/ creation_pg_7.htm

[25] *Ibid.*

[26] *Ibid.*

27 http://www.new-life.net/faq014.htm

28 http://www.answersingenesis.org/articles/aid/v2/n1/who-were-the-nephilim

29 http://www.gospelofgenesis.com/downloads/GoG17.doc

30 http://www.lavistachurchofchrist.org/LVSermons/BookOfEnoch.htm

31 http://www.raidersnewsnetwork.com/full.php?news=5413, "Are the Nephilim Giants? I Say No."

32 http://www.ahrimangate.com/excerpt148.htm

33 http://www.amazon.com/review/product/091554024X?showViewpoints=1

34 http://www.logoschristian.org/nephillim.html, "The Nephilim." See also: http://www.groundzeromedia.org/dis/gibborim/gibborim.htm

35 http://en.wikipedia.org/wiki/Gibborim_(biblical)

36 http://www.raidersnewsnetwork.com/full.php?news=5413

37 http://www.answers.com/topic/oaf

38 http://www.raidersnewsnetwork.com/full.php?news=5413

39 http://www.ahrimangate.com/excerpt148.htm

40 http://en.wikipedia.org/wiki/Gibborim_(biblical)

41 http://www.answersingenesis.org/articles/aid/v2/n1/who-were-the-nephilim

Chapter 6: Why Was the Flood Sent?

1 http://www.bibletruthonline.com/2007_06_01_archive.html; http://www.love-the-truth.net/broken_deep.html; Joye Jeffries Pugh, *Eden: The Knowledge of Good and Evil: 666* (Mustang, Oklahoma: Tate Publishing, 2006), p. 35; http://groups.msn.com/GiantstheBibleandEnoch/jubileejasherenoch.msnw; http://historybizarremysterious.blogspot.com/2008/03/not-quite-human.html; http://www.worldnetdaily.com/index.php?pageId=75592; http://www.raidersnewsnetwork.com/full.php?news=9210; http://www.sheepkillers.com/ufonephilimagenda.html; http://www.bibleprobe.com/nephilim.htm; http://godsprofessor.com/dnmkchap3.htm; http://www.therain.org/appendixes/app25.html; http://gracethrufaith.com/ikvot-hamashiach/the-nephilim/#more-204; http://www.americanchronicle.com/articles/view/55796; http://www.christiandiscussionforums.org/v/showthread.php?p=3563611; http://www.abovetopsecret.com/forum/thread115484/pg1

2 http://www.stevequayle.com/Giants/Mid.East/Giants.Mid.East11.html

3 *Ibid.*

[4] http://www.flyingchariotministries.com/genesisrerevisited.htm

[5] http://www.endtimeschristianity.com/cgi-bin/webbbs_files/webbbs_config.pl?noframes;read=582. See also: http://www.ufodigest.com/news/0307/tremble2.html; Sherry Shriner, *Bible Codes Revealed: The Coming UFO Invasion* (iUniverse, Inc.: New York, 2005), p. 41; http://godsprofessor.com/dnmkchap3.htm]; http://www.freerepublic.com/focus/f-chat/1631505/posts; http://www.sheepkillers.com/ufonephilimagenda.html

[6] Joye Jeffries Pugh, *Eden: The Knowledge of Good and Evil: 666* (Mustang, Oklahoma: Tate Publishing, 2006), p. 31.

[7] *Ibid.*, p. 48. See also p. 35, 305, 312; http://www.biblestudygames.com/biblestudies/faq/noah.htm; http://www.raidersnewsnetwork.com/editoral.php?feature=5413; http://www.endtimeschristianity.com/cgi-bin/webbbs_files/webbbs_config.pl?noframes;read=582; http://www.stargods.org/ReptilianDemons.htm; http://www.wholebodycure.com/secret.html; http://www.khouse.org/articles/2003/462/; http://www.geocities.com/zacherle_hoag/sherry_shriner_interview.html; http://www.conspiracyarchive.com/UFOs/demons_aliens_clothes.htm; http://www.gotquestions.org/Nephilim.html; http://www.feri.com/dawn/nephilim.html

[8] *Ibid.*, p. 35. See also: http://www.logon.org/english/S/p154.html; http://www.gotquestions.org/Nephilim.html

[9] *Ibid.*, p. 31.

[10] http://en.wikipedia.org/wiki/Noah_in_rabbinic_literature

[11] http://www.jewishencyclopedia.com/view.jsp?artid=35&letter=O&search=Og; http://en.wikipedia.org/wiki/Noah_in_rabbinic_literature; http://www.riseofthefallen.com/htm/nephilim.htm; http://www.jewishencyclopedia.com/view.jsp?artid=318&letter=N; http://www.chabad.org/search/keyword_cdo/kid/10729/jewish/Og.htm; http://www.torah.org/learning/rabbis-notebook/5763/devarim.html; http://www.come-and-hear.com/niddah/niddah_61.html; http://www.biblefacts.org/history/talmud/adam.html; http://ccat.sas.upenn.edu/rs/rak/publics/mrjames/jamesog.htm; http://www.jpost.com/servlet/Satellite?pagename=JPost%2FJPArticle%2FShowFull&cid=1218095194818; http://www.answering-islam.org/Shamoun/flood.htm; Phyllis Portnoy, *The Remnant: Essays on a Theme in Old English Verse* (Runetree Press, 2005), p.81.

[12] http://www.jewishencyclopedia.com/view.jsp?artid=215&letter=G; http://ccat.sas.upenn.edu/rs/rak/publics/mrjames/jamesog.htm

[13] http://www.mnteverest.net/history.html; http://answers.yahoo.com/question/index?qid=20080505174014AAvoKwI; http://www.climb.mountains.com/Photo_Gallery_files/Eight_Thousand_files/Everest.htm

[14] http://www.climb.mountains.com/Photo_Gallery_files/Eight_Thousand_files/Everest.htm

[15] http://findarticles.com/p/articles/mi_m1590/is_n10_v54/ai_20385597

[16] http://www.unmuseum.org/kpyramid.htm

[17] http://en.wikipedia.org/wiki/Taipei_101

[18] http://en.wikipedia.org/wiki/World's_tallest_structures

[19] http://bible.cc/deuteronomy/3-11.htm

[20] http://ccat.sas.upenn.edu/rs/rak/publics/mrjames/jamesog.htm. See also: http://www.jpost.com/servlet/Satellite?pagename=JPost%2FJPArticle%2FShowFull&cid=1218095194818

[21] http://www.sacred-texts.com/chr/apo/jasher/85.htm

[22] http://www.studylight.org/dic/ats/view.cgi?number=T602

[23] http://www.thewatcherfiles.com/amongus.htm. See also: http://www.bibliotecapleyades.net/sociopolitca/the_experiment/experiment13.htm

[24] Pugh, *op. cit.,* p. 71.

[25] *Ibid.*

[26] *Ibid.,* p. 312.

[27] http://www.serpentseedline.com/; http://en.wikipedia.org/wiki/Noah's_Ark; http://www.mission.org/jesuspeople/arnmuray.htm; http://mystery-babylon.org/otherfloodsurvivors.html; http://www.letusreason.org/Poptea4.htm; http://www.biblestudygames.com/biblestudies/faq/kenites.htm

[28] http://www.sherryshriner.org/sherry/serpent-seedline.htm

[29] Pugh, *op. cit.,* p. 54-55.

[30] *Ibid.*

[31] http://home.att.net/~warplover/06_the_nephilim.html#nine. See also: http://www.ufodigest.com/news/0307/tremble2.html; http://www.rainbowcircle.net/forum/topic/show?id=1986923%3ATopic%3A19499; http://thestrongdelusion.com/index.php?option=com_content&task=view&id=440&Itemid=9; http://www.raidersnewsnetwork.com/full.php?news=19591; http://mysterial.org.uk/cgi-bin/index.cgi?action=viewnews&id=1210; http://www.americanchronicle.com/articles/view/55796; http://www.sheepkillers.com/ufonephilimagenda.html; http://www.raptureready.com/soap/ac-8.html; http://www.sherryshriner.com/sherry/cain.htm;

http://www.thewatcherfiles.com/stargates/part-eleven.htm; http://www.thewatcherfiles.com/sherry/who-is-what.html; http://www.geocities.com/zacherle_hoag/sherry_shriner_interview.html

[32] http://godsprofessor.com/dnmkchap3.htm. See also: http://thestrongdelusion.com/index.php?option=com_content&task=view&id=440&Itemid=9; http://www.raidersnewsnetwork.com/full.php?news=19591; http://www.rainbowcircle.net/forum/topic/show?id=1986923%3ATopic%3A19499; http://mysterial.org.uk/cgi-bin/index.cgi?action=viewnews&id=1210

[33] Pugh, *op. cit.*

[34] William James Hughan, *Masonic Sketches and Reprints* (London, England: George Kenning, 1871), p.42; http://www.phoenixmasonry.org/mackeys_encyclopedia/l.htm

[35] http://www.emedicine.com/med/topic3236.htm; http://medical-dictionary.thefreedictionary.com/Pregnancy; http://www.medterms.com/script/main/art.asp?articlekey=14522; http://www.nlm.nih.gov/medlineplus/ency/article/002367.htm; http://www.baby2see.com/pregnancylength.html

[36] http://www.thewatcherfiles.com/sherry/cain.htm; http://www.riseofthefallen.com/htm/nephilim.htm; http://www.sherryshriner.com/sherry/cain.htm; http://www.fundamentalforums.com/showthread.php?t=8534; http://www.sherryshriner.org/sherry/serpent-seedline.htm

[37] http://www.fundamentalforums.com/showthread.php?t=8534

[38] Jobe Martin, *Evolution of a Creationist: A Laymen's (sic) Guide to the Conflict Between the Bible and Evolutionary Theory* (Rockwall, Texas: Biblical Discipleship Publishers, 2002 Edition), p. 156.

[39] http://www.biblebelievers.org.au/bb981121.htm; http://www.sherryshriner.com/sherry/cain.htm

[40] *Ibid.*

Chapter 7: "As in the Days of Noah"

[1] Joye Jeffries Pugh, *Eden: The Knowledge of Good and Evil: 666* (Mustang, Oklahoma: Tate Publishing, 2006), p. 305. See also: http://www.youtube.com/watch?v=3mitXz9FrMY; http://www.skepticfiles.org/weird/alieninv.htm; http://home.flash.net/~saints/deceive.htm; http://www.geocities.com/zacherle_hoag/sherry_shriner_interview.html; http://www.khouse.org/articles/1996/43/; http://watch.pair.com/dragon-lineage.html; http://www.endtimez.com/nephilim.html; http://www.echoesofenoch.com/abductions.htm; http://www.newswithviews.com/Horn/thomas10.htm; http://ldolphin.org/noahdays.html; http://www.geocities.com/

roswell.geo/; http://mysteriousjourneys.blogspot.com/2007/02/as-in-days-of-noah.html; http://www.geocities.com/lvegh/Noah.html

[2] http://www.amazon.com/Star-Children-Story-Alien-Offspring/dp/0806938560

[3] *Ibid.;* See also: http://www.abduct.com/books/b29.php

[4] http://selectsmart.com/twyman.html; http://en.wikipedia.org/wiki/Indigo_children; http://www.crossroad.to/articles2/05/indigo.htm

[5] http://en.wikipedia.org/wiki/Kryon

[6] http://en.wikipedia.org/wiki/Indigo_children

[7] *Ibid.;* See also: Lee Carrol and Jan Tober, *The Indigo Children: The New Kids Have Arrived* (Carlsbad, California: Hay House, Inc., 1999), p. 6, 10; http://www.metagifted.org/topics/metagifted/indigo/introduction.html.

[8] http://www.thewatcherfiles.com/sherry/who-is-what.html; http://sherryshriner.blogspot.com/2008/11/judgment-of-tare-nations-is-coming.html; http://www.freerepublic.com/focus/f-chat/1631505/posts; http://www.sherryshriner.com/sherry/joel.htm; http://www.thebereanchronicles.com/indepth_news/indigo_children.html; http://selectsmart.com/twyman.html; http://www.reconnections.net/children_oneness.htm; http://shekinahlife.ning.com/profiles/blogs/judgment-1; http://www.reconnections.net/why_are_they_called.htm; http://www.sherryshriner.com/sherry/cain.htm; http://www.theexodus.closely-encountered.com/The_Exodus_Manifesto.htm

[9] http://sherryshriner.blogspot.com/2008/11/judgment-of-tare-nations-is-coming.html; http://shekinahlife.ning.com/profiles/blogs/judgment-1; http://www.reconnections.net/why_are_they_called.htm; http://www.cbn.com/spirituallife/BibleStudyAndTheology/Perspectives/ANS_indigokids.aspx; http://www.amazon.com/Messages-Thomas-Raising-Psychic-Children/dp/1844090140; http://reconnections.net/starkids_future_hope.htm; http://www.crystalinks.com/childrensic.html; http://www.usatoday.com/news/religion/2005-05-31-indigo-kids_x.htm; http://en.wikipedia.org/wiki/Indigo_children; http://www.crystalinks.com/starseeds.html; http://www.metagifted.org/topics/metagifted/indigo/introduction.html; http://www.reconnections.net/children_oneness.htm; http://www.briansbetterworld.com/articles/indigochildren.pdf; http://www.crossroad.to/articles2/05/indigo.htm; http://www.newswithviews.com/BeritKjos/kjos40.htm; http://www.eternalpath.com/indigochildren.html; http://www.alsopreview.com/gazebo/messages/3683/16387.html?1206648666; http://patholliday.com/christograms/from_scribd/Dec-08/Can-Witches-Be-Saved.pdf; http://teenink.com/talk/showthread.php?threadid=17762; http://www.benotdeceived.net/ufo-s-aliens-f5/aliens-are-demonic-entities-t493-15.htm;

http://www.amazon.com/dp/156414948X/ref=pe_606_11251780_pe_ar_t1; http://www.reconnections.net/first_contact.htm; http://www.reconnections.net/second_coming.htm

[10] http://selectsmart.com/twyman.html

[11] http://www.usatoday.com/news/religion/2005-05-31-indigo-kids_x.htm

[12] http://www.reconnections.net/second_coming.htm

[13] http://www.thebereanchronicles.com/indepth_news/indigo_children.html

[14] http://www.serpentseedline.com/; http://www.sherryshriner.com/sherry/cain.htm

Chapter 8: What Is the "Neshama"?

[1] Joye Jeffries Pugh, *Eden: The Knowledge of Good and Evil: 666* (Mustang, Oklahoma: Tate Publishing, 2006), p. 44. See also: Personal letter from Dr. Pugh to a friend; http://ldolphin.org/nephilim.html; http://www.endtimez.com/nephilim.html; http://home.att.net/~warplover/06_the_nephilim.html#nine; http://www.shangrala.org/RELIGIONS/1Christianity/GodsCovenants.html; http://www.delusionresistance.org/christian/noah01%20-%20nephilim.html; http://www.raidersnewsnetwork.com/editoral.php?feature=11868; http://www.kingdom-gospel.com/ufo.html; http://www.tbm.org/origindemons.htm; http://www.thewatcherfiles.com/sherry/who-is-what.html; http://www.bcrevolution.ca/secret_societies.htm; http://www.rainbowcircle.net/forum/topic/show?id=1986923%3ATopic%3A19499; http://www.paradoxbrown.com/Chapter_4.htm; http://www.tbm.org/origindemons.htm; http://www.logoschristian.org/aliens.html; http://www.thewatcherfiles.com/aliens_are_coming.html; http://www.thegreatseparation.com/newsfront/2005/02/the_nephilim_bu.html; http://www.riseofthefallen.com/htm/nephilim.htm; http://thestrongdelusion.com/index.php?option=com_content&task=view&id=440&Itemid=9; http://www.raidersnewsnetwork.com/full.php?news=19591; http://mysterial.org.uk/cgi-bin/index.cgi?action=viewnews&id=1210; http://www.paradoxbrown.com/chapter_guy.htm; http://home.att.net/~warplover/06_the_nephilim.html#nine; http://www.seancasteel.com/angels_and_aliens.htm; http://users.aristotle.net/~bhuie/demons.htm; http://www.sherryshriner.com/fallen_angels.htm; http://conspiracyguy.wordpress.com/category/nephilim/; http://www.stargods.org/ReptilianDemons.htm; http://www.paradoxbrown.com/Chapter_3.htm; http://www.stargods.org/ReptilianDemons.htm; http://www.thestargates.com/artapprentice.net/httpdocs/old_webpage/anunnakiabyss/page4.html; http://godsprofessor.com/dnmkchap3.htm; http://www.endtimeschristianity.com/cgi-bin/webbbs_files/webbbs_config.pl?noframes;read=582

[2] http://www.ufodigest.com/news/0308/prophecies34.html. See also: http://www.christianityoasis.com/EndTimes/EvilSpirits.htm; http://www.stargods.org/

INTRODUCTION.htm; http://www.piney.com/LegFallAng.html; http://www.
soulwinners.com.au/5.html; http://www.truthintheword.com/creation_pg_7.htm; http://
www.sherryshriner.com/fallen_angels.htm

[3] http://www.sacred-texts.com/bib/boe/boe018.htm

[4] http://curezone.com/forums/am.asp?i=437927&s=2; http://answers.yahoo.
com/question/index?qid=20080330040656AA3XhkH; http://www.delusionresistance.org/
christian/noah01%20-%20nephilim.html; http://www.abovetopsecret.com/forum/
thread128040/pg1; http://www.kingdom-gospel.com/ufo.html. See also: http://
russianconflict.com/ufo.html; http://lfreeman.blogspot.com/

[5] Pugh, *op. cit.*, p. 358-359. See also: Personal letter from Dr. Pugh to a
friend.

[6] http://www.redicecreations.com/radio/2008/01jan/RICR-080131.php

[7] http://www.biblestudytools.net/Lexicons/Greek/grk.cgi?number=4157&
version=kjv; http://bibletools.org/index.cfm/fuseaction/Lexicon.show/ID/G4157/
pnoe.htm

[8] John Henry, http://kjv.landmarkbiblebaptist.net/KJVheritics.html

[9] http://www.babylon.com/systems/affiliates/landing/download.php?id=
55555&lang=eng

[10] Personal letter from Dr. Pugh to a friend.

Chapter 9: The Golem

[1] http://www.merriam-webster.com/dictionary/golem

[2] http://encyclopedia2.thefreedictionary.com/golem

[3] http://knowledgerush.com/kr/encyclopedia/Golem/. See also: Howard
Schwartz, Caren Loebel-Fried, Elliot K. Ginsburg, *Tree of Souls: The Mythology of
Judaism* (Oxford University Press, 2004), p. 282; http://www.jewishvirtuallibrary.org/
jsource/Judaism/Golem.html; http://baike.8883.org/what-is-a-golem.htm; http://
www.wisegeek.com/what-is-a-golem.htm; http://www.templesanjose.org/JudaismInfo/
tradition/Golem.htm; http://www.mishkan.com/agr.html; http://golem.plush.org/faq/;
http://www.jewish-theatre.com/visitor/article_display.aspx?articleID=802; http://
www.monstropedia.org/index.php?title=Golem; http://www.applet-magic.com/golem.htm;
http://www.jewishmag.com/124mag/golem_history/golem_history.htm; http://
www.levity.com/alchemy/golem.html; http://antinewworldorder.blogspot.com/2008/12/
golem.html; http://unger.myplainview.com/reviews/Golem.htm; http://www.answers.com/
topic/golem; http://www.dragon-warrior.com/Bestiary/golem.shtml; http://tvtropes.org/
pmwiki/pmwiki.php/Main/Golem; http://www.newworldencyclopedia.org/entry/Golem;

http://www.davkamusic.com/GolemScore.htm; http://curiousexpeditions.org/?p=74; http://www.mishkan.com/agr.html; http://www.jewishmag.com/124mag/golem_history/golem_history.htm; http://ejmmm2007.blogspot.com/2007_02_01_archive.html; http://scribalterror.blogs.com/scribal_terror/2007/08/the-golem-of-pr.html; http://www.flyingchariotministries.com/golemtruth.htm; http://www.endicott-studio.com/jMA0301/menMud.html

⁴ Oberon Zell-Ravenheart, Grey Council, *Grimoire for the Apprentice Wizard* (Career Press, 2004), p.319; http://books.google.com/books?id=cMuQADen69UC&pg=PA319&lpg=PA319&dq=golem+Nephilim&source=web&ots=VbYmX6KDsw&sig=izCwZJanYWtSNt67EJHhrBprg00&hl=en&sa=X&oi=book_result&resnum= 99&ct=result

⁵ http://tvtropes.org/pmwiki/pmwiki.php/Main/Golem; http://www.zsido.hu/english/community/golem.htm; http://en.wikipedia.org/wiki/Golem; http://antinewworldorder.blogspot.com/2008/12/golem.html; http://www.digitalspace.com/avatars/book/fullbook/chbi/chbi1.htm; http://www.etsy.com/view_listing.php?listing_id=19770050; http://stefan680.tripod.com/stefanstories/golem.html; http://www.ehow.com/how_2124097_make-golem.html; http://www.pep-web.org/document.php?id=ijp.023.0089d; http://www.luckymojo.com/esoteric/religion/judaism/kabbalah/cy200112golemkabbalah.txt; http://www.templesanjose.org/JudaismInfo/tradition/Golem.htm; http://aquanetsiecwodna.blogspot.com/2007/05/great-rabbi-loew-decided-that-golem.html; http://www.jewishmag.com/124mag/golem_history/golem_history.htm

⁶ http://www.geocities.com/markleeper/golem.htm. See also: http://www.monstropedia.org/index.php?title=Golem

⁷ http://www.dragon-warrior.com/Bestiary/golem.shtml. See also: http://knowledgerush.com/kr/encyclopedia/Golem/; http://tvtropes.org/pmwiki/pmwiki.php/Main/Golem

⁸ http://www.jewishvirtuallibrary.org/jsource/Judaism/Golem.html

⁹ http://emol.org/kabbalah/golem/creategolem.html

¹⁰ http://www.metanexus.net/magazine/ArticleDetail/tabid/68/id/8123/Default.aspx; http://www.answers.com/topic/golem. See also: http://www.enemies.com/illustrated-gnostic-gospels/archons-aliens-eden/adam-the-golem-2/; http://www.jewishvirtuallibrary.org/jsource/Judaism/Golem.html; http://www.applet-magic.com/golem.htm; http://www.jewishencyclopedia.com/view.jsp?letter=G&artid=334; http://aquanetsiecwodna.blogspot.com/2007/05/great-rabbi-loew-decided-that-golem.html; http://www.associatedcontent.com/article/752559/was_the_incredible_hulk_inspired_by.html?cat=2; http://en.wikipedia.org/wiki/Golem; http://petragrail.tripod.com/golem.html; Moshe Idel, *Golem: Jewish Magical and Mystical Traditions on the Artificial Anthropoid* (SUNY Press, 1990), p. 6, 18, 34, 36, 38, 42, 57, 65, 130, 137,

140, 146, 149, 210, 298; Howard Schwartz, Caren Loebel-Fried, Elliot K. Ginsburg, *Tree of Souls: The Mythology of Judaism* (Oxford University Press, 2004), p. xii, lxxxi, 127, 131; http://antinewworldorder. blogspot.com/2008/12/golem.html; http://www.jewishvirtuallibrary.org/jsource/Judaism/Golem.html

[11] Howard Schwartz, Caren Loebel-Fried, Elliot K. Ginsburg, *Tree of Souls: The Mythology of Judaism* (Oxford University Press, 2004), p. 128. See also: http://aquanetsiecwodna.blogspot.com/2007/05/great-rabbi-loew-decided-that-golem.html; http://www.answering-islam.org/Responses/Osama/90feet-adam.htm; http://www.come-and-hear.com/sanhedrin/sanhedrin_100.html; Daniel Chanan Matt, *The Zohar* (Stanford University Press, 2003), p. 293; http://www.kabbalaonline.org/Safedteachings/gor/Three_Types_of_Soul_(71).asp; Avraham Yaakov Finkel, *Kabbalah* (Targum Press, 2002), p. 256.

[12] http://www.enemies.com/illustrated-gnostic-gospels/archons-aliens-eden/adam-the-golem-2/; http://www.enemies.com/illustrated-gnostic-gospels/archons-aliens-eden/adam-the-golem-2/

[13] See: http://www.thewatcherfiles.com/amongus.htm

[14] http://www.6thatpenn.com/The%20Golem.htm; http://golem.plush.org/faq/; http://www.newworldencyclopedia.org/entry/Golem; http://antinewworldorder. blogspot.com/2008/12/golem.html; http://www.monstropedia.org/index.php?title= Golem&printable=yes; http://www.jewishmag.com/114mag/golem/golem.htm; http://www.jewishmag.com/124mag/golem_history/golem_history.htm; http://tvtropes.org/pmwiki/pmwiki.php/Main/Golem; http://www.kabbalahmadeeasy.com/prevarticles/golem.html; http://www.jewishmag.com/26MAG/GOLEM/golem.htm

[15] http://golem.plush.org/faq/

[16] http://www.newworldencyclopedia.org/entry/Golem

[17] http://www.monstropedia.org/index.php?title=Golem

[18] http://unger.myplainview.com/reviews/Golem.htm; http://encyclopedia2. thefreedictionary.com/golem; http://antinewworldorder.blogspot.com/2008/12/golem.html

[19] http://www.newworldencyclopedia.org/entry/Golem; http://tvtropes.org/pmwiki/pmwiki.php/Main/Golem; http://www.pep-web.org/document.php?id=ijp.023.0089d; http://www.metanexus.net/magazine/ArticleDetail/tabid/68/id/8123/Default.aspx; http://www.delusionresistance.org/christian/noah01%20-%20nephilim.html; http://petragrail.tripod.com/golem.html; http://www.templesanjose.org/JudaismInfo/tradition/Golem.htm; http://curiousexpeditions.org/?p=74s; http://golem.plush.org/faq/; http://www.applet-magic.com/golem.htm

[20] http://ezinearticles.com/?Alien-Invasion-of-Planet-Earth-PART-ONE&id= 60415; http://www.shangrala.org/RELIGIONS/1Christianity/GodsCovenants.html; http://www.newsguide.us/art-entertainment/books/Due-to-Increasing-Demand-Arrival-of-the-Prince-a-Progressive-Christian-Book-is-Now-Available-Via-the-AuthorHouse-Book-Return-Program/; http://antinewworldorder.blogspot.com/2008/12/golem.html; http://www.biggerbooks.com/bk_detail.aspx?isbn=9781550228304; http://www.ecwpress.com/books/tongues_dead; http://justwatchsome.tv/blog/Clash+of+the+Cavemen; http://www.abovetopsecret.com/forum/thread356138/pg1; http://www.etpv.org/2006/dotwat.html; http://www.thewatcherfiles.com/amongus.htm; http://www.mysteriousworld.com/Journal/2002/Summer/Atlantis/; http://www.stargods.org/ReptilianDemons.htm; http://gracethrufaith.com/ask-a-bible-teacher/can-nephilim-be-saved/; http://www.lovesociety.net/alien-invasion-of-planet-earth-part-one/; http://www.missionu.org/380.php

[21] http://www.burnyourwings.com/phpBB3/viewtopic.php?f=27&t=37

[22] Joye Jeffries Pugh, *Eden: The Knowledge of Good and Evil: 666* (Mustang, Oklahoma: Tate Publishing, 2006), p. 64.

[23] *Ibid.*, p. 415.

[24] *Ibid.*, p. 93.

[25] *Ibid.*

[26] *Ibid.*, p. 62.

[27] http://www.monstropedia.org/index.php?title=Chimera

[28] http://www.dragon-warrior.com/Bestiary/chimera.shtml

[29] http://www.babylon.com/systems/affiliates/landing/download.php?id= 55555&lang=eng. See also: http://www.biblestudytools.net/Lexicons/Greek/grk.cgi?number=4157&version=kjv; http://bibletools.org/index.cfm/fuseaction/Lexicon.show/ID/G4157/pnoe.htm; John Henry, http://kjv.landmarkbiblebaptist.net/KJVheritics.html.

[30] http://www.nationmaster.com/encyclopedia/Characters-of-Fullmetal-Alchemist-video-games

[31] http://en.wikipedia.org/wiki/Construct_(Dungeons_&_Dragons); http://www.dragon-warrior.com/Bestiary/golem.shtml; http://www.sdjewishjournal.com/stories/cover_oct04.html; http://www.monstropedia.org/index.php?title=Golem; http://tvtropes.org/pmwiki/pmwiki.php/Main/Golem; http://www.applet-magic.com/golem.htm; http://www.mishkan.com/agr.html; http://scifipedia.scifi.com/index.php/Frankenstein's_Monster; http://www.jewishvirtuallibrary.org/jsource/Judaism/Golem.html; http://www.nationmaster.com/encyclopedia/Golem; http://www.spout.com/

films/Der_Golem/59288/default.aspx; http://www.absoluteastronomy.com/topics/ The_Sorcerer's_Apprentice; http://www.jewishmag.com/124mag/golem_history/ golem_history.htm; http://www.mishkan.com/agr.html; http://www.geocities.com/ markleeper/golem.htm; http://www.britannica.com/EBchecked/topic/217218/ Frankenstein

[32] http://www.applet-magic.com/golem.htm; http://www.associatedcontent.com/ article/752559/was_the_incredible_hulk_inspired_by.html?cat=2

[33] *Ibid.;* http://www.answers.com/topic/the-sorcerer-s-apprentice; http:// www.monstropedia.org/index.php?title=Golem; Gad Ya'ir Michaela Soyer, *The Golem in German Social Theory* (Rowman and Littlefield, 2007), p. 13, 19, 23, 26, 152; http:// www.jewishmag.com/124mag/golem_history/golem_history.htm; http://knowledgerush. com/kr/encyclopedia/Golem/; http://www.absoluteastronomy.com/topics/ The_Sorcerer's_Apprentice; http://en.wikipedia.org/wiki/The_Sorcerer's_Apprentice; http://www.answers.com/topic/golem; http://www.mishkan.com/agr.html; http:// www.nationmaster.com/encyclopedia/The-Sorcerer's-Apprentice; http://www. mishkan.com/agr.html; http://www.nationmaster.com/encyclopedia/Golem

[34] *Ibid.;* http://www.associatedcontent.com/article/1009990/why_we_are_ obsessed_with_horror_films.html?cat=40

[35] http://www.sdjewishjournal.com/stories/cover_oct04.html; http:// www.applet-magic.com/golem.htm

[36] http://ingehaupt.wordpress.com/brief-notes-on-the-burden-of-choice/

[37] http://emol.org/kabbalah/golem/creategolem.html; http://www.pep-web.org/ document.php?id=ijp.023.0089d; http://www.burnyourwings.com/phpBB3/ viewtopic.php?f=27&t=37; http://apehatorah.org/apespirit/thegolem.html; http:// www.123exp-beliefs.com/t/00804057922/; http://www.experiencefestival.com/golem_-_ history; http://www.nytimes.com/2006/09/11/arts/11conn.html

[38] http://gracethrufaith.com/ikvot-hamashiach/the-nephilim/#more-204

[39] http://gracethrufaith.com/ask-a-bible-teacher/still-another-nephilim- question/

[40] http://petragrail.tripod.com/golem.html. See also: http://www.nazism.net/ about/ideological_theory/; http://mysteriousjourneys.blogspot.com/2007/02/as-in-days- of-noah.html; http://www.overlordsofchaos.com/html/secret_societies__ancient_ luci.html; http://cantontruth.blogspot.com/2008/04/adolf-hitlers-master-race-ideas- came.html; http://www.shatterthedarkness.net/lebensborn/page2.html; http:// www.karinya.com/lizards.html; http://www.freerepublic.com/focus/f-chat/1631505/ posts; http://blackpetalsks.tripod.com/blackpetalsissue45/; http://www.telegraph.co.uk/ news/worldnews/southamerica/brazil/4307262/Nazi-angel-of-death-Josef-Mengele-

created-twin-town-in-Brazil.html; http://www.conspiracyarchive.com/UFOs/demons_aliens_ clothes.htm; http://farahsufos.blogspot.com/2007/11/was-venusian-orthon-nazi- officer.html; http://tracyrtwyman.com/blog/?page_id=52; http://www. orgoneblasters. com/sherry/who-is-what.htm; http://simple.wikipedia.org/wiki/Master_race

⁴¹ http://remnantradio.org/Archives/articles/William%20Cooper/ Mystery%20Babylon/MB4.htm

⁴² *Ibid.*

⁴³ *Ibid.*

⁴⁴ http://petragrail.tripod.com/golem.html

⁴⁵ http://www.reptilianagenda.com/bib/b122104a.shtml; http://www. thewatcherfiles.com/sherry/who-is-what.html

⁴⁶ http://www.eaec.org/newsletters/2004/NL2004Sep.htm

⁴⁷ http://www.satansrapture.com/gen64.htm; http://www.delusionresistance.org/ christian/noah01%20-%20nephilim.html; http://conspiracyguy.wordpress.com/ category/nephilim/

⁴⁸ http://www.delusionresistance.org/christian/noah01%20-%20nephilim.html

⁴⁹ Pugh, *op. cit.,* p. 173.

⁵⁰ http://petragrail.tripod.com/golem.html

Chapter 10: What About Daniel 2?

¹ http://khouse.org/articles/1997/22/. See also: http://www.khouse.org/articles/ 2001/324/; http://www.raidersnewsnetwork.com/full.php?news=9210; http:// www.thewatcherfiles.com/stargates/part-thirteen.htm; http://www.letusreason.org/ Current21.htm

² http://gracethrufaith.com/ask-a-bible-teacher/daniel-and-the-nephilim/. See also: http://home.flash.net/~saints/deceive.htm

³ http://gracethrufaith.com/ask-a-bible-teacher/human-alien-hybrids/. See also: http:// www.echoesofenoch.com/abductions.htm; http://groups.msn.com/AbductionExposed/ daniel2.msnw

⁴ http://www.christian-forum.net/index.php?showtopic=11808. See also: http:// www.endtimeschristianity.com/cgi-bin/webbbs_files/webbbs_config.pl?noframes;read=582; http://www.delusionresistance.org/christian/noah01%20-%20nephilim.html

⁵ http://sherryshriner.blogspot.com/2004_09_01_archive.html; http://www.sherryshriner.com/sherry/lunatic-fringe.htm. See also: http://home.flash.net/~saints/deceive.htm; http://www.freerepublic.com/focus/f-chat/1631505/posts

⁶ Joye Jeffries Pugh, *Eden: The Knowledge of Good and Evil: 666* (Mustang, Oklahoma: Tate Publishing, 2006), p. 404.

Chapter 11: Who Are the "Watchers"?

¹ Michael W. Ford, *Liber HVHI: Magick of the Adversary* (Houston, Texas: Succubus Publishing, 2005), p. 30; Michael W. Ford, *Black Witchcraft: Foundations of the Luciferian Path,* p. 6-7; http://www.chaostatic.com/paradigm/writings/black-witchcraft.php

² http://www.templeoftheblacklight.net/main.html

³ http://www.eris-x.com/23/fallen.html; http://www.templeoftheblacklight.net/library/rituals/the_rite_of_the_fire-bearer_azazel.html

⁴ http://www.probe.org/site/c.fdKEIMNsEoG/b.4217631/k.645D/Wicca_A_Biblical_Critique.htm; http://www.michaelgleghorn.com/documents/Wicca.pdf

⁵ *Ibid.*

⁶ *Ibid.*

⁷ Joye Jeffries Pugh, *Eden: The Knowledge of Good and Evil: 666* (Mustang, Oklahoma: Tate Publishing, 2006), p. 34.

⁸ *Ibid.,* p. 103.

⁹ *Ibid.,* p. 308.

¹⁰ http://www.bibliotecapleyades.net/bb/enoch03.htm. See also http://www.bibliotecapleyades.net/enoch/4Q227.html

¹¹ http://www.mystae.com/restricted/streams/scripts/watchers.html

¹² http://www.thewatcherfiles.com/sherry/who-is-what.html

¹³ http://www.bibliotecapleyades.net/bb/enoch03.htm. See also: http://www.raptureready.com/soap/ac-8.html; http://www.ziaabbas.com/chapters.php?title=Gods%20were%20Watchers&book=Atlantis

¹⁴ *Ibid.*

¹⁵ Pugh, *op. cit.,* p. 36. See also: Pugh, p. 43, 48, 68, 312, 314, 317, 407; http://www.ziaabbas.com/chapters.php?title=Gods%20were%20Watchers&book=Atlantis; http://www.bibliotecapleyades.net/sumer_anunnaki/anunnaki/anu_16.htm; http://

www.bibliotecapleyades.net/vida_alien/alien_watchers21.htm; http://en.wikipedia.org/wiki/Grigori; http://www.geocities.com/zacherle_hoag/sherry_shriner_interview.html; http://www.shangrala.org/RELIGIONS/1Christianity/GodsCovenants.html

¹⁶ http://www.ahrimangate.com/excerpt148.htm. See also: http://www.jewishpath.org/parshanoach.html; http://www.truthintheword.com/creation_pg_7.htm

¹⁷ http://www.youtube.com/watch?v=HqBh2s1JqtY&feature=related

¹⁸ Albert Barnes, *Albert Barnes' Notes on the Bible* (Commentary on Daniel 4:13).

¹⁹ Robert Jamieson, A. R. Fausset, David Brown, *Jamieson-Fauseet-Brown Bible Commentary* (Hendrickson Publishing, 1997).

Chapter 12: The Nephilim, Cloning, and the Antichrist

¹ http://www.khouse.org/articles/2001/314/

² http://standeyo.com/Larry_Taylor/2003.March.html

³ http://home.flash.net/~saints/deceive.htm

⁴ Sherry Shriner, *Bible Codes Revealed: The Coming UFO Invasion* (iUniverse, Inc.: New York, 2005), p. 41; http://www.watcherfiles.50megs.com/

⁵ http://www.khouse.org/articles/2001/321/

⁶ http://www.khouse.org/articles/2001/324/

⁷ Joye Jeffries Pugh, *Eden: The Knowledge of Good and Evil: 666* (Mustang, Oklahoma: Tate Publishing, 2006), p. 358-359.

⁸ *Ibid.,* p. 358.

⁹ *Ibid.,* p. 43, 115, 205, 396, 409, 423-424.

¹⁰ *Ibid.,* p. 43.

¹¹ *Ibid.,* p. 396.

¹² *Ibid.,* p. 115.

¹³ *Ibid.,* p. 205.

¹⁴ *Ibid.,* p. 358.

¹⁵ *Ibid.*

¹⁶ *Ibid.*

17 *Ibid.*, p. 357.

18 *Ibid.*, p. 264, 359, 379.

19 http://www.mail-archive.com/ctrl@listserv.aol.com/msg105356.html

20 *Ibid.*

21 http://www.bibliotecapleyades.net/merovingians/twyman/twyman.htm; http://www.bibliotecapleyades.net/esp_autor_twyman_a.htm

22 http://www.bibliotecapleyades.net/merovingians/merovingios_11.htm

23 Pugh, *op. cit.*, p. 134. See also p. 95.

24 *Ibid.*, p. 95.

25 http://en.wikipedia.org/wiki/Shroud_of_Turin; http://www.c14dating.com/k12.html; http://www.shroud2000.com/CarbonDatingNews.html; http://www.shroudstory.com/; http://www.factsplusfacts.com/; http://www.shroudstory.com/faq-carbon-14.htm

26 http://www.weneedice.com/How%20Carbon14%20Dating.pdf. See also: http://www.gnmagazine.org/issues/gn46/noahsflood_methods.htm; http://www.fsteiger.com/carbon14.html; http://contenderministries.org/evolution/carbon14.php; http://www.creation-science-prophecy.com/C14fp.htm; http://creationwiki.org/Living_snails_were_C14_dated_at_2,300_and_27,000_years_old; http://www.sciencemag.org/cgi/content/abstract/224/4644/58

27 http://vpcatholicyouth.wordpress.com/2008/04/20/is-this-the-face-of-jesus/; http://www.unsolvedmysteries.com/usm389319.html; http://findarticles.com/p/articles/mi_kmske/is_/ai_n28745527; http://www.frtommylane.com/homilies/pilgrimage/sudarium.htm; http://www.skeptiseum.org/index.php?id=7&cat=miracles; http://www.shroudstory.com/early.htm; http://www.factsplusfacts.com/resources/Edessa.htm

28 http://www.jewishencyclopedia.com/view.jsp?artid=1573&letter=A. See also: http://www.jewishencyclopedia.com/view.jsp?artid=751&letter=C

29 http://100777.com/node/275

30 Pugh, *op. cit.*, p. 118.

31 *Ibid.*, p. 159-160.

32 *Ibid.*, p. 160.

33 *Ibid.*, p. 181.

34 *Ibid.*

[35] *Ibid.,* p. 365.

[36] *Ibid.,* p. 423. See also p. 181, 365, 388.

[37] *Ibid.,* p. 377.

[38] *Ibid.,* p. 204.

[39] *Ibid.,* p. 396.

[40] *Ibid.,* p. 377.

[41] *Ibid.,* p. 264.

[42] *Ibid.,* p. 382, 388.

[43] *Ibid.,* p. 382.

[44] *Ibid.,* p. 357.

[45] *Ibid.,* p. 264, 355, 358, 379, 388, along with p. 78, 93, 94, 95, 159, 181, and 204.

[46] Martin Ralph DeHaan, *The Chemistry of the Blood* (Zondervan, 1983), p. 31.

[47] *Ibid,* p. 32.

[48] http://www.shroudstory.com/faq/Shroud-Turin-wiki20.htm; http://users.belgacom.net/gc674645/shroud/shroud1.htm; http://www.newgeology.us/presentation24.html; http://www.shroud.org/blood_man_shroud_turin_type.html; http://www.spartechsoftware.com/dimensions/mystical/ShroudOfTurin.htm; http://www.jesusisreal.org/shroudofturin/index.htm

[49] http://www.blood.co.uk/visually_impaired/vi_secrets_in_blood.html. See also: http://www.chromosomal-labs.com/files/ABOBloodGroups.pdf; http://www.helium.com/items/260698-explaining-different-blood-types; http://www.elleuk.com/beauty/diets/diet-guide/(diet)/the-blood-group-diet; *A Question of Evidence: The Casebook of Great Forensic Controversies, from Napoleon to O. J.* Colin Evans (John Wiley and Sons, 2003), p. 15; http://www.targetwoman.com/articles/blood-group-diet.html; http://www.originalzen.com/writings/oz_writings_bloodtype.htm

[50] Pugh, *op. cit.,* p. 423.

[51] http://www.blood.co.uk/visually_impaired/vi_secrets_in_blood.html; http://nbs.lightmaker.com/pages/secrets_in_blood.html; http://whatsmybloodtype.org/types.html

[52] http://www.nettyroyal.nl/newsjuly05.html; http://www.dailymail.co.uk/news/article-354051/William-tears-new-attack-Diana.html; http://www.freerepublic.com/focus/f-news/1432660/posts; http://www.strangecosmos.com/content/item/

108507.html; http://asianfanatics.net/forum/index.php?showtopic=114586; http://www.expressindia.com/news/fullstory.php?newsid=49691

[53] www.jewishencyclopedia.com

[54] Pugh, *op. cit.,* p. 364.

[55] Personal letter from Dr. Pugh to a friend.

[56] *Ibid.*

[57] Pugh, *op. cit.,* p. 264.

[58] http://judaism.about.com/library/3_askrabbi_o/bl_simmons_messiah3.htm; http://www.aish.com/spirituality/philosophy/Why_Dont_Jews_Believe_In_Jesus$.asp

[59] http://www.aish.com/spirituality/philosophy/Why_Dont_Jews_Believe_In_Jesus$.asp

[60] http://jdstone.org/cr/files/critmosh.html

[61] http://www.lucistrust.org/en/publications_store/the_beacon_magazine/reprinted_from_the_beacon/christ_as_he_is

[62] http://www.answers.com/topic/ruth-montgomery

[63] Ruth Montgomery, *Strangers Among Us* (New York: Coward, McCann & Geoghegan, 1979), p. 251.

[64] *Ibid.,* p. 251-252.

[65] http://heisback.com.au/Maitreya_and_Jesus.html. See also: http://home.sprynet.com/~eastwood01/notjesus.htm; http://www.watchman.org/Profile/maitreyapro.htm; http://www.mouontshastawisdomproject.com/Christ.ppt

[66] *Ibid.*

[67] http://www.islaam.org/Al_Mahdi/mahdi10.html; http://bdsteel.tripod.com/More/Prophecy.htm; http://www.alhafeez.org/rashid/Imammahdi.htm

Chapter 13: Is the *Book of Enoch* Scripture?

[1] http://www.christianbook.com/Christian/Books/cms_content?page=357160&sp=62141&event=62141SBF%7C608665%7C62141

[2] http://www.tbm.org/origindemons.htm

[3] http://www.raptureready.com/soap/ac-8.html

[4] http://www.new-life.net/faq013.htm; http://www.sacred-texts.com/bib/boe/boe002.htm

[5] http://en.wikipedia.org/wiki/1_Enoch; http://www.gotquestions.org/book-of-Enoch.html; http://www.newworldencyclopedia.org/entry/Book_of_Enoch; http://www.lavistachurchofchrist.org/LVSermons/BookOfEnoch.htm; http://www.jesus-is-savior.com/Bible/Edward%20F%20Hills%20-%20KJB%20Defended/kjbd_chapter_four.htm; http://www.experiencefestival.com/a/Book_of_Enoch/id/1894384; http://en.wikipedia.org/wiki/Pseudepigraphic; http://www.lavistachurchofchrist.org/LVanswers/2006/01-06.htm; http://www.christiancourier.com/articles/562-did-jude-quote-from-an-apocryphal-book; http://www.theologyweb.com/campus/archive/index.php/t-8121.html; Geoffrey Wigoder, Editor, *Encyclopedic Dictionary of Judaica*, "Apocrypha and Pseudepigrapha" (New York: Leon Amiel Publisher, 1974), p. 35.

[6] http://www.spiritualawakeningradio.com/enochcase.html; http://www.newadvent.org/cathen/14520c.htm; http://www.heaven.net.nz/writings/enoch.htm; http://reluctant-messenger.com/enoch.htm; http://www.echeat.com/essay.php?t=31251; http://www.experiencefestival.com/a/Book_of_Enoch/id/1894384; http://philologos.org/__eb-mazzaroth/204.htm; http://www.jesus-is-savior.com/Bible/Edward%20F%20Hills%20-%20KJB%20Defended/kjbd_chapter_four.htm; http://www.lavistachurchofchrist.org/LVanswers/2006/01-06.htm; http://www.tertullian.org/works/de_cultu_feminarum.htm

[7] http://www2.ida.net/graphics/shirtail/pseudepi.htm

[8] http://en.wikipedia.org/wiki/Montanism; http://sda2rc.blogspot.com/2008/10/apostolic-succession-its-about.html?showComment=1223915040000; http://www.newadvent.org/cathen/14520c.htm; http://www.infidels.org/library/modern/richard_carrier/NTcanon.html; http://www.earlychurch.org.uk/article_montanism.html; http://www.robibrad.demon.co.uk/Chapter1.htm

[9] http://www.lavistachurchofchrist.org/LVSermons/BookOfEnoch.htm

[10] http://www.heaven.net.nz/writings/enoch.htm. See also: http://www.thelostbooks.com/descrip3.htm

[11] http://www.tentmaker.org/books/Retribution/retribution10.htm; http://en.wikipedia.org/wiki/1_Enoch; http://www.thelostbooks.com/descrip3.htm; http://www.newworldencyclopedia.org/entry/Book_of_Enoch; http://www.experiencefestival.com/a/Book_of_Enoch/id/1894384; http://reluctant-messenger.com/enoch.htm

[12] http://www.raptureready.com/soap/ac-8.html

[13] http://www.lavistachurchofchrist.org/LVSermons/BookOfEnoch.htm; http://www.lavistachurchofchrist.org/LVanswers/2006/01-06.htm

[14] http://www.lavistachurchofchrist.org/LVanswers/2006/01-06.htm; http://www.lavistachurchofchrist.org/LVSermons/BookOfEnoch.htm

[15] http://en.wikipedia.org/wiki/Carmelina_Fedele; http://www.timesonline.co.uk/tol/news/world/article414766.ece

[16] http://www.tagza.com/WeiredNews/Worlds_Tallest_Man_Now_the_Worlds_Tallest_Dad/

[17] Nevill Drury, *The Watkins Dictionary of Magic: Over 3,000 Entries on the World of Magical Formulas, Secret Symbols, and the Occult* (Sterling Publishing Company, Inc., 2005), p. 92.

[18] See also: *What Is the Order of the Eastern Star?* (Newtonville, New York: HRT Ministries, Inc., n.d.), p. 2; J. Gordon Melton, *The Encyclopedia of American Religions* (Vol. 2) (Wilmington, North Carolina: McGrath Publishing Company, 1978), p. 185; Stewart Farrar, *What Witches Do: The Modern Coven Revealed* (Custer, Washington: Phoenix Publishing Company, 1983, Revised Edition), p. 121, 181; E. A. Wallis Budge, *Amulets and Superstitions* (New York, New York: Dover Publications, Inc., 1978), p. xxxviii; Nat Freedland, *The Occult Explosion* (New York: G. P. Putnam's and Sons, 1972), p. 71; J. Edward Decker, Jr., *The Question of Freemasonry* (Lafayette, Louisiana: Huntington House Publishers, 1992), p. 5; *The F.A.T.A.L. Flaw* (Issaquah, Washington: Free the Masons Ministries, n.d.), p. 6; *New Times* (March/April 1986; #862), p. 12; John Godwin, *Occult America* (Garden City, New York: Doubleday and Company, Inc., 1972), p. 292; *Self-Help Update* (Issue #27), p. 16; *Llewellyn New Times* (May/June 1987; #873), p. 6; *Llewellyn New Times* (January/February 1987; #871), p. 7; Brochure from Coleman Publishing; Joseph Wallman, *The Kabalah: From Its Inception to Its Evanescence* (Brooklyn, New York: Theological Research Publishing Company, 1958), p. 1, 205; Moshe Idel, *Kabbalah: New Perspectives* (New Haven, Connecticut: Yale University Press, 1988), p. 394; Harold Bloom, *Kabbalah and Criticism* (New York, New York: The Seabury Press, Inc., 1975), p. 15, 32; Arthur Edward Waite, *The Holy Kabbalah* (London: Williams and Norgate Ltd., 1929), p. xiii, 4, 186, 557; Mary Ann Slipper, *The Symbolism of the Eastern Star* (n.p., 1927), p. 136; David L. Carrico, *Immorals and Dogma* (Evansville, Indiana: Followers of Jesus Christ, n.d.), p. 4; Joseph Leon Blau, *The Christian Cabala* (Port Washington, New York: Kennikat Press, Inc., 1944), p. 6, 85; Rex R. Hutchens, *A Bridge to Light* (Washington, D.C.: Supreme Council, 33° Ancient and Accepted Scottish Rite of Freemasonry, Southern Jurisdiction, 1988), p. 249; Arthur Edward Waite, *The Mysteries of Magic: A Digest of the Writings of Eliphas Levi* (Chicago, Illinois: De Laurence, Scott and Company, 1909), p. 97; H. L. Haywood, *The Great Teachings of Masonry* (New York: George H. Doran Company, 1923), p. 95; Rex R. Hutchens and Donald W. Monson, *The Bible in Albert Pike's Morals and Dogma* (Washington, D.C.: Supreme Council, 33rd Degree, 1992), p. 242; Editors of Time-Life Books, *Magical Arts* (Alexandria, Virginia: Time-Life Books, 1990), p. 26; Paul Foster Case, *The Masonic Letter G* (Los Angeles, California: Builders of the Adytum, Ltd., 1981), p. 14; William O. Peterson, Editor, *Masonic Quiz Book: "Ask Me Another, Brother"* (Chicago, Illinois:

Charles T. Powner Company, 1950), p. 143, 266; Lynn F. Perkins, *Masonry in the New Age* (Lakemont, Georgia: CSA Press, 1971), p. 75; p.310; Catalog from Research Centre of Kabbalah, p. 2; Shirley Plessner, *Symbolism of the Eastern Star* (Cleveland, Ohio: Gilbert Publishing Company, 1956), p. 33, 34; Colin Wilson, *The Occult: A History* (New York: Random House, 1971), p. 104; *New Times* (1984; #884), p. 28.

[19] Colin Wilson, *The Occult: A History* (New York, Random House, 1971), p. 511, 513; Editors of Time-Life Books, *Magical Arts* (Alexandria, Virginia: Time-Life Books, 1990), p. 26, 61; John Maxson Stillman, *The Story of Alchemy and Early Chemistry* (New York, New York: Dover Publications, Inc., 1960), p. 367.

[20] *New Times* (1985; #855), p. 29.

[21] *Llewellyn New Times* (January/February 1987; #871), p. 7.

[22] Catalog from Isis, p. 35.

[23] *New Times* (1984; #884), p. 28.

[24] Frank Gaynor, Editor, *Dictionary of Mysticism* (New York: Philosophical Library, 1953), p. 92.

[25] http://www.amazon.co.uk/Aleister-Crowley-Wickedest-World-Search/dp/B000TR6BGG; http://www.aleister-crowley-666.com/HOME.html; http://www.zimbio.com/Aleister+Crowley/articles/14/Aleister+Crowley+Wickedest+Man+Alive+until; http://abstractconcept.blogspot.com/2007/10/aleister-crowley-wickedest-man-in-world.html; http://www.lycos.com/info/aleister-crowley—wickedest-man.html; http://www.disinfo.com/archive/pages/dossier/id50/pg1/index.html; http://profile.myspace.com/index.cfm?fuseaction=user.viewprofile&friendid=78212475; http://en.wikipedia.org/wiki/Aleister_Crowley; http://www.rawilsonfans.com/articles/GreatBeast.htm; http://cannonfire.blogspot.com/2006/04/george-w-bush-barbara-bush-and.html; http://www.hermetic.com/crowley/l418/aetyr6.html

[26] http://rochester92.vox.com/library/post/the-infamous-albert-pike-pt-2.html; http://rochester92.vox.com/library/post/the-infamous-albert-pike-pt-1.html

[27] http://www.blavatskyarchives.com/longseal.htm; http://en.wikipedia.org/wiki/Madame_Blavatsky; http://www.crystalinks.com/blavatsky.html; http://www.theosociety.org/pasadena/sunrise/34-84-5/th-hbpgr.htm

[28] http://www.tsl.org/messengers/Messengers.asp; http://en.wikipedia.org/wiki/Elizabeth_Clare_Prophet; http://www.tsl.org/Messengers/ecp.asp; http://www.amazon.co.uk/FALLEN-ANGELS-ORIGINS-Suppressed-Revelations/dp/0922729433

[29] http://www.komabookstore.com/natas.html

[30] http://www.near-death.com/experiences/origen049.html

[31] http://www.blavatskyarchives.com/kessinger.htm

[32] Editors of Time-Life Books, *Magical Arts* (Alexandria, Virginia: Time-Life Books, 1990), p. 54.

[33] http://www.raptureready.com/soap/ac-8.html

[34] http://www.jesus-is-savior.com/Wolves/book_of_enoch.htm

Chapter 14: Is the *Book of Jasher* Scripture?

[1] http://www.bibletruthonline.com/2007_06_01_archive.html; http://www.love-the-truth.net/broken_deep.html; http://www.worldnetdaily.com/index.php?pageId=75592; http://groups.msn.com/GiantstheBibleandEnoch/jubileejasherenoch.msnw; http://historybizarremysterious.blogspot.com/2008/03/not-quite-human.html; http://www.watchmanbiblestudy.com/Topics/HealthWatch.htm; http://www.raidersnewsnetwork.com/full.php?news=9210; http://godsprofessor.com/dnmkchap3.htm; http://www.christiandiscussionforums.org/v/showthread.php?p=3563611; http://www.abovetopsecret.com/forum/thread115484/pg1

[2] http://www.strangite.net/latterdayscriptures.html; http://answers.org/bible/jasher-book-of.html; http://www.bycommonconsent.com/2008/12/the-book-of-jasher/; http://www.johnpratt.com/items/docs/lds/meridian/2002/jasher.html; http://www.dkosopedia.com/wiki/Church_of_Jesus_Christ_of_Latter-day_Saints; http://cornishevangelist.wordpress.com/the-holy-scripture-book-of-jasher/; http://www.evangelistbillybolitho.blogspot.com/; http://billbolitho.blogspot.com/2008/09/holy-scripture-book-of-jasher.html; http://www.angelfire.com/ill/hebrewisrael/Links.htm

[3] http://farshores.org/a07neph2.htm; http://www.raidersnewsnetwork.com/archives.php; http://www.raidersnewsnetwork.com/thomas-horn.php; http://www.raidersnewsnetwork.com/full.php?news=9210; http://www.jasher.com/Realjash.htm; http://www.raidersnewsnetwork.com/full.php?news=8165; http://rapture-armageddon.com/; http://stevemchenry.blogspot.com/2007_09_01_archive.html; http://www.logoschristian.org/revealed/; http://www.ccel.org/a/anonymous/jasher/real.htm; http://www.gospelminutes.org/index.php; http://www.missiontoisrael.org/yahs-laws-1.php; http://stevenmcollins.com/WordPress/?p=238

[4] http://www.jewishencyclopedia.com/view.jsp?artid=164&letter=J. See also: http://www.bible-history.com/isbe/J/JASHAR,+BOOK+OF/

[5] http://en.wikipedia.org/wiki/Book_of_Jasher. See also: http://www.babylon.com/definition/Jasher/English; http://www.jasher.com/Forum.htm; http://www.ccel.org/a/anonymous/jasher/real.htm; http://www.sacred-texts.com/chr/apo/jasher/index.htm

⁶ http://www.sacred-texts.com/chr/apo/jasher/index.htm

⁷ http://en.wikipedia.org/wiki/Sefer_haYashar_(midrash)

⁸ http://www.johnpratt.com/items/docs/lds/meridian/2002/jasher.html

⁹ http://www.newswithviews.com/Horn/thomas10.htm; http://www.uforc.com/research/Horn-Nephilim_090807.htm; http://bibleprobe.com/nephilim.htm; http://www.wnd.com/index.php?fa=PAGE.view&pageId=75592; http://www.allbusiness.com/science-technology/biochemistry-genetic-biochemistry-dna/11593358-1.html; http://www.raidersnewsnetwork.com/thomas-horn.php; http://farshores.org/a07neph2.htm; http://www.raidersnewsnetwork.com/full.php?news=9210

¹⁰ http://www.prophetseye.com/Melchizedek.htm

¹¹ http://www.americanchronicle.com/articles/view/55796

¹² http://www.gods-kingdom-ministries.org/Birthright/Chapter2/Chapter%202.htm#Shem%20was%20Melchizedek

¹³ http://www.truediscipleship.com/Gtopics/general254.htm

Glossary

¹ http://www.thefreedictionary.com/clone

² http://encyclopedia2.thefreedictionary.com/Merkabah

³ http://www.thefreedictionary.com/Montanism

⁴ http://en.wikipedia.org/wiki/Sefer_haYashar_(midrash)

⁵ http://en.wikipedia.org/wiki/Tablets_of_Destiny

⁶ David W. Cloud, "What Is Judaism?," *O Timothy* (1988, Vol. 5, Issue 2). See also: "Midrash—What Is It?," *Despatch Magazine* (June 2000, Vol. 12, No. 2), p.82; "Be Informed About the Talmud," *Christian News* (March 5, 2001, Vol. 39, No. 10), p.7; Maureen Fiedler and Linda Rabben, Editors, *Rome Has Spoken...: A Guide to Forgotten Papal Statements, and How They Have Changed Through the Centuries* (New York, NY: The Crossroad Publishing Company, 1998), p.69; "Lieberman, Gore, and God," *Power of Prophecy* (September 2000, Vol. 2000-09), p.2; "Lieberman, The Talmud, The Noahide Laws and Judeo-Christians," *Christian News* (September 18, 2000, Vol. 38, No. 34), p.7; "Noahide Laws: Religion of a New World Order," *GANPAC Brief* (February 1992, No. 112), p.4.

⁷ "Judaism's Strange Gods," *Christian News* (October 9, 2000, Vol. 38, No. 37), p.15; http://www.cephas-library.com/israel/israel_the_talmud_against_jesus.html

⁸ "Lieberman, Gore, and God," *Power of Prophecy* (September 2000, Vol. 2000-09), p.2; http://www.cephas-library.com/israel/israel_the_talmud_against_jesus.html

INDEX

2001: A Space Odyssey 101

A

A Kabbalah for the Modern World 161
abductees 104
abduction 35, 36, 37, 38, 77, 108, 116
Abel 24, 26
Abraham 25, 48
Abraham's seed 22, 29
Adam 40, 51, 54, 58, 68, 74, 95
Adam and Eve 9, 10, 11, 53, 155
Adam and Satan participating in a homosexual act 9
Adam was created as a golem 95
Ahriman 14
Albert Barnes' Notes on the Bible 117
alchemy 100, 138, 161
Alexander the Great 61
alien 30, 77, 78, 103, 108, 120, 121, 122
alien abduction 35, 37, 77, 116, 121, 183, 184
alien agenda 113
All My Ghosts 32
Amorites 63
'anah 37, 38
angel 39, 41, 42, 44, 45, 114, 159
angel-human hybrids 32
angels do not marry 34, 52
Angels on Earth 78
Antichrist 46, 103, 121, 122, 123, 124, 126, 127, 138, 139, 142, 144, 145, 147, 148
Antichrist has the cloned body of Jesus 144
Antichrist will be Lucifer in the flesh 124
Antichrist will be Satan's seed 121
Anunnaki 183
ark 55, 59, 64, 65, 66, 72, 80, 83, 154
Aryan Nations 8
ascended masters 162
Ascending Children 78
Assemblies of God 16

astrology 116, 161, 162, 176
Augustine 150
auras 78
Azazel 14

B

Baal 31
Bailey, Mary 147
beast would possess the blood of Jesus 123
Behemoth 31
Bennett , W. H. 15
Best , Marshall W. 169
Bishop, Cardinal 30
Black, Frank 32
Black Tradition 14
Blavatsky, Helena Petrovna 162
blood source comes from the father 141
Book of Enoch 30, 53, 86, 87, 88, 114, 115, 115, 126, 149, 150, 151, 154, 156, 158, 159, 160, 161, 162, 163, 183, 185
Book of Enoch compared to the Bible 151-163
Book of Jasher 53, 62, 164, 165, 166, 167, 169, 170, 174, 179, 183, 185
Book of Jasher compared to the BIble 164-179
Book of Jubilees 53
Branham, William 8
Bride of the Devil 14
Brown, Tom 149
Bruce, James 150

C

Cabala 160, 161, 163
Cain 8, 11, 12, 14, 15, 16, 21, 23, 24, 26, 27, 28, 30, 34, 48, 52, 56, 58, 63, 68, 71, 72, 77, 114, 140, 155, 180, 184, 185, 186
Cain is missing from Adam's lineage 26
Cain was of the wicked one 23
Cain was the son of Satan 26
Cain's lineage 64, 67, 71, 141
Carroll, Lee 77, 78
Cavendish, Richard 114
Cayce, Edgar 162
centaur 54, 55
channeling 78
Chaosium 31

charms 93, 115, 184
Childhood's End 78
Children of Aids 78
children of God 19, 23
Children of Now 78
Children of Oneness 78
Children of Oz 78
children of the devil 19, 23
Children of the New Dream 78
Children of the New Times 78
Children of the Stars 78
Children of Winter 78
chimera 55, 97, 98, 99, 100, 104, 120
chimera appears as a symbol of Satanic forces 98
Christian Identity Movement 21
Church of Satan 162
clairaudience 78
clairsentience 78
clairvoyance 78
Clarke, Arthur C. 78
clone 73, 104, 123, 138, 142, 143, 148, 183
cloned image of Jesus 122, 123, 124, 125, 126, 127, 137, 148
cloning 77, 92, 103, 104, 105, 121, 124, 126, 140, 180
Cloth of Edessa 136
Collins, Steven 164
communication with the dead 154, 162, 163
conjuration 161
Couche, Timothy 164
Council of Laodicea 150
Creme, Benjamin 147
Crowley, Aleister 30, 162
Crystal Children 78
Crystalline Children 78
Cyclops 54

D

Daniel 106, 107, 110, 112, 117, 118
Daniel 2 107, 109, 110, 112, 113, 121
Daniel 4 114, 115, 117, 118
Davenport, Ralph 121
David 27, 46, 47, 49
days of Noah 77, 79, 84, 103, 108, 109, 121

Dead Sea Scrolls 11, 12, 16
deception 120
DeHaan, M. R. 141
Demigod 31
demon 32, 86, 88, 89, 90, 98, 103, 104, 147, 158
demon-alien invasion 109
demons are spirits 91
Devil's Notebook, The 162
Diablo II 31
Dictionary of Mysticism 162
Disney, Walt 101
divination 161
DNA 30, 54, 55, 70, 73, 78, 79, 109, 110, 121, 127, 138, 140, 142, 164, 183
Dragon Court 126
Dragon Quest 99
Dungeons and Dragons 94, 99

E

Edinburgh Manuscript 67, 68, 71, 183
Eleazar, R. 165
Emerald Tablets 68
Encyclopedia of Hell 162
enlightenment 127
evil spirits 32, 86, 87
evolution 54
extraterrestrial 78, 104, 121, 183, 184

F

face napkin 129, 135
Faith, Philip 71
fallen angel 14, 15, 30, 32, 33, 34, 39, 41, 45, 50, 52, 53, 54, 55, 58, 64, 65, 76, 77, 79, 81, 86, 87, 95, 97, 103, 104, 110, 114, 115, 117, 118, 119, 121, 124, 141, 142, 149, 150, 155, 162, 163, 164, 166, 180, 185, 187
false prophet 124
Fantasia 93, 101
Fausset's Bible Dictionary 35
Ferri, Lorenzo 138, 139
Fields of the Nephilim 30
flood 53, 56, 58, 60, 63, 66, 67, 68, 70, 72, 74, 75, 76, 77, 80, 82, 83, 84, 86, 89, 90, 101, 103, 110, 116
Ford, Michael 14, 30, 114
Frankenstein 100

G

Garden of Eden 8, 53, 115, 180, 186
genetic modification 53, 55
Gentry, Jerry 11
giant 14, 30, 32, 45, 48, 49, 51, 53, 54, 56, 62, 63, 64, 73, 77, 86, 94, 95, 97, 98, 101, 102, 103, 110, 114, 115, 116, 121, 158, 167, 185
gibborim 34, 45, 46, 48, 49, 50, 121, 183
Ginzberg, Louis 15
Gnostic Scriptures 8
Gnosticism 95
gods do not dwell with flesh 112
golem 92, 94, 93, 95, 96, 97, 99, 100, 101, 102, 104, 120, 180, 183
golem had no soul 102
Goliath 46, 47, 49, 52, 97
Gonzalez-Wippler, Migene 161
Gospel message 181
Gothic 30, 71
Greek Melodic Death Metal 31
greys 46, 184
Grimassi, Raven 114
Grimoire for the Apprentice Wizard 93

H

Hage, Olaf 104
half-demon 48
Ham 64, 67, 68, 69, 71, 72, 73, 74, 75
Harris, Nathaniel 15, 30
Heiser, Michael S. 12
Henry, Matthew 16
Heron, Patrick 45, 46, 47, 86, 89, 116, 149, 151, 163
Hitler, Adolph 8, 21, 101, 102
Hoggard, Michael 108
Holy Grail 138
homosexual act 9, 72, 73, 74, 75
Horn, Thomas 16, 35, 38, 45, 48, 108, 116, 149, 164, 166
humanoid 54, 103, 184
Hunchback of Notre Dame, The 101
hybrid 32, 35, 38, 45, 46, 52, 55, 64, 65, 77, 78, 79, 86, 88, 97, 98, 100, 103, 104, 109, 115, 116, 121, 163, 167, 184
Hyles, Martin Luther 73

I

Identity 8
Imam Mahdi 147
incantations 96
incest 75
Incredible Hulk, The 101
Indigo 78
Indigo Child, The 77
Indigo Children 77, 78, 79
Institute of Jewish Studies 45
iysh 51, 52, 184

J

J. H. Parry and Company 165
Jacob 27
James, Terry 32
Jamieson-Fausset-Brown Bible Commentary 117
Jerome 150
Jesus and Satan are brothers 126
Jesus is a hybrid 98
Jesus is not the Christ 147
Jesus was a chimera 97, 98, 99
Jewish Encyclopedia 60
Jews don't believe in Jesus 146
Johanan, R. 165
Jones, Stephen E. 169
Joseph 26, 27
Joshua 46, 47, 48, 89
Jude 150

K

Kabalah 94, 160, 161
Kabbala 160
Kazwini 60
Kelley, Jack 108
Kenite 27, 28, 29
KKK 8
Knights Templar 132, 136, 138
Kohler, Kaufmann 15
Koran 30
Kryon 78

L

laqach 35
Laurence, Richard 150
LaVey, Anton 162
Lehman, Helena 169
levitation 101
Lewis, Clyde 45
Liber HVHI 14
Lilith 14, 21, 184, 185
Lilith-Az 15
local flood 66
Loew, Judah 93, 94
long hair 130, 131
Lot 81, 82, 83, 84
Lucifer 14, 15, 53, 87, 109, 114, 124, 127
Luciferian 14, 30, 114, 127, 185
Lucifer's crown 127
Lucis Trust 147

M

magic 30, 93, 96, 112, 114, 115, 161, 162
Magic: The Gathering 31
Magical Arts 163
Mahdi 148
Maitreya 147
Man-God 102
marriage 35
Martin, Dr. Jobe 74
Martin, Willie 16, 21
Marzulli, Lynn 149
Mason 68, 162
master race 101
Masters 78
Melchizedek 169, 170
Merkabah 160, 184
Merkava 184
Messiah 123, 137, 140, 145, 147, 148
Messiah will be born of human parents 146
Metagifted Children 78
Midrash 184
Millennium Children 78

mind control 101
mind reading 101
mingle themselves with the seed of men 107, 108, 109, 110, 111, 121
minotaur 54, 55
Missler, Chuck 108, 121
Montanism 150, 185
Montanus 185
Montgomery, Ruth 147
Moon, Sun Myung 8, 21
Mormon 5, 164, 165, 166
Morning Star 127
Moses 29, 48, 61, 62, 69, 173, 174
Mount Ararat 64
Mount Everest 60
Murray, Arnold 16, 65
Muslims 148
Mystic Children 78
mysticism 161
mythology 93, 101, 115, 161

N

naphal 33, 34
Nation of Yahweh 21
National Blood Society 142
National Socialism 102
Nazarite vow 131
Nazarites 130
Nazis 101, 102
Nebuchadnezzar 106, 107, 109, 110, 111, 112, 114, 116, 118, 119
necromancy 97, 176
Neo Preterhumans 109
neo-Nazis 8
Nephilim 14, 30, 31, 32, 33, 38, 39, 45, 46, 48, 50, 52, 53, 54, 55, 56, 58, 62, 63, 66,
    67, 69, 70, 71, 72, 73, 76, 77, 79, 81, 88, 89, 90, 92, 94, 95, 97, 99, 101, 102, 103,
    104, 108, 114, 115, 116, 120, 121, 148, 149, 150, 154, 163, 167, 180, 185
neshama 88, 89, 90, 92, 99, 100, 122, 123, 185
New Age 30, 78, 123, 147, 161, 162
New Children 78
New Hybrid Race 109
new man 102
New Order 32
New Super Humans 109

no soul 89, 103, 123, 125, 144, 180
Noah 27, 28, 51, 55, 58, 59, 60, 63, 64, 65, 66, 68, 69, 70, 72, 73, 74, 75, 77, 79, 80, 81, 82, 83, 152, 154, 170
Noah's wife 59, 75
numerology 161
Nurse's Handbook of Obstetrics 141

O

occult 30, 56, 86, 99, 102, 116, 126, 127, 161, 162, 163, 179
Og 60, 61, 62, 64, 71
Ordo Lapsit Exillis 126, 127
Origen 150
out of body experiences 101

P

pagan 161, 179
Pandera 186
paranormal 31
Pegasus 54
Peguy, Charles 126
Pharaoh 171, 172, 175, 176, 177, 178
Pike, Albert 162
pneuma 90, 92, 100, 185
Pratt, John 167
prayer of forgiveness 182
Prince Charles 143
Prince Harry 143
Prince William 138, 139, 141, 142, 143, 145
Prince William is a Clone 140
Prince William is Satan in the flesh 139, 144
Prince William was cloned from the Shroud of Turin 141
Prophet, Elizabeth Clare 162
Pseudepigrapha 12, 149, 185
psychic 78, 162
Psychic Children 78
Pugh, Dr. Joye Jeffries 11, 26, 32, 56, 57, 58, 63, 65, 67, 68, 71, 77, 86, 87, 88, 89, 90, 92, 97, 104, 110, 111, 114, 116, 117, 122, 123, 124, 125, 127, 129, 132, 134, 135, 136, 137, 138, 139, 140, 141, 142, 143, 144, 145, 148, 149

Q

Qabala 160
Quayle, Steve 53, 76
Queen of Demons 15

R

racism 8
Randles, Jenny 77
reincarnation 161
remote viewing 101
Reuel 28
rock group 30
role-playing game 31, 94

S

Samael 11, 12, 14, 184, 185
Satan 8, 9, 11, 12, 14, 16, 21, 23, 25, 26, 30, 46, 51, 56, 57, 58, 67, 69, 73, 86, 87, 102, 109, 110, 114, 122, 123, 124, 125, 126, 137, 140, 141, 142, 162, 180, 184, 185, 186
Satan and Jesus share the same blood 126
Satan has a seed 16, 19, 46, 59, 103
Satan is the Antichrist 123
Satan Speaks 162
Satan will live in the cloned body of Jesus 137
Satanic Bible, The 162
Satanic Rituals, The 162
Satanic Screen, The 162
Satanic Witch, The 162
Satanism 15, 114
Satanist 30, 162, 163
Satan's son 58
satyr 54, 55
Schoene, Robert 60
Secret Life of a Satanist 162
Sefer haYashar 59, 186
Septic Flesh 31
Septuagint 90
serpent seed 8, 11, 16, 21, 23, 24, 25, 26, 27, 29, 58, 59, 69, 70, 72, 75, 79, 121, 180, 186
Set 14
Seth 15, 27, 40, 58, 63, 68, 71, 141
sexual magick 15
Shem 69, 171
Shem was the Melchizedek 169
Shepherd's Chapel 66
Shriner, Sherry 8, 11, 16, 63, 79, 103, 109
Shroud of Turin 124, 126, 127, 128, 129, 130, 132, 134, 135, 136, 138, 140, 141, 142, 145, 148, 180

Simmons, Rabbi 146
Simpson, Wayne 164
Sitchin, Zecharia 33
sons of God 30, 39, 40, 41, 45, 51, 56, 87, 116, 121, 159, 167
sorcerers 112
Sorcerer's Apprentice 93, 101
soul 88, 99, 100, 104, 122, 123, 125, 158, 185
soulless 97, 103
spells 94, 163
Spielberg, Steven 78
spirit 41, 42, 43, 44, 53, 54, 77, 98, 163
spirit entities 163
spirit guide 147
spirit world 112
Star Children 77, 78, 79
Star Kids 78
Star People 78
Star Seed 78
Stone that fell from Heaven 127
Sudarium 129
Sumerian Clay Tablets 64, 65, 186
Super Psychic Children 78

T

Tablet of Destinies 186
Taken 78
Talmud 88, 92, 99, 122, 186
Tappe, Nancy Ann 78
Targum 12, 13, 187
Targum Pseudo-Jonathan 12
tarot 161
tartaroo 39, 187
Taylor, Larry 121
Templars 134, 137
Temple of the Black Light 114
Tertullian 149, 150
thaumaturgy 161
Theosophical Society 162
theosophy 161
Tober, Jan 77
Tomb Raider 32
Torell, John 103

tree of life 10, 11
Tree of Souls 95
tree of the knowledge of good and evil 8, 9, 10
Two Pillars 68
Twyman, Tracy R. 126

U

UFO 46, 77, 108, 184
undead 123, 125
unequally yoked 40
Unification Church 8, 21
University of Washington 60

V

Vampires 31
Vatican 138
Venus 127
vipers 24, 25
virgin birth 141, 146, 180

W

Walther, Harry 103
Ward, Chris 165
watchers 14, 35, 64, 113, 114, 115, 116, 117, 118, 119, 180
Weiland, Ted 164
Whitaker, Stephanie Michelle 45
Wiccan 114
witchcraft 15
witches 161, 184

Y

yarad 33
Ye are of your father the devil 21, 22, 29, 180
Ye Olde Magick Shoppe 179
yoga 161
Yulish, Dr. 54

Z

zera 17, 187
Ziusudra 63, 64

CAPTIVATING AND UNIQUE!!!

Discover the most fascinating and in-depth meanings behind the symbols used by the Masons, occultists, witches, New Agers, Satanists, and others.

Dr. Burns uncovers the hidden meanings behind the symbols that we see around us every day. In this well-documented book you will see hundreds of illustrations along with their explanations. You will find many organizational logos, hand signals, tarot cards, zodiac signs, talismans, amulets, and humanist symbols, as well as the meaning of the peace symbol, hexagram, pentagram, yin/yang, circle, all-seeing eye, caduceus, oroboros, ankh, triskele, and the triangle. Also revealed in this book are numerous Masonic and Eastern Star symbols, such as the clasped hands, point within a circle, broken column, gavel, obelisk, pomegranate, and the cornucopia.

Only $21.95 • 552 pages (with Index) • ISBN-13: 9781891117121

SHOCKING TRUTH REVEALED

HIDDEN SECRETS OF MASONRY

Dr. Cathy Burns

√ Does Masonry promote astrology and reincarnation?

√ Are Masonry and Christianity compatible?

√ What do the Masonic symbols represent?

√ Who is the **REAL** god of Masonry?

Discover hidden meanings, sexual overtones, the god they conceal, and much more. Fully documented with 276 footnotes and includes an Index.

80 pages • $6.95 (plus $1.25 postage) • ISBN-13: 9780005405123

Intriguing Mysteries Exposed!

♦ *Who founded the Eastern Star and **WHY**?*

♦ *Is it a secret society shrouded in obscurity?*

♦ *Is it compatible with Christianity?*

♦ *What is the meaning of the Cabalistic Motto?*

♦ ***WHO** is represented by the Star in the East?*

♦ *Is there a **GODDESS** connection?*

Over 100 pictures are included as well as 1453 footnotes, many taken directly from Eastern Star and Masonic sources.

This book takes you inside the Lodge room and on a journey through the five degrees. Secret passwords are revealed as well as the hidden meaning of symbols, colors, flowers, and gems, and the significance of the lambskin apron.

A special section is included on the *Rainbow Girls*.

For your gift of only $15.95 plus $1.55 shipping and handling.

512 pages (with Index) • ISBN-13: 9780005021811

Mormonism, Masonry, and Godhood

Dr. Cathy Burns

Can Angels Be Trusted?

The Church o f Jesus Christ of Latter-day Saints (Mormons) began on April 6, 1830. In this book Dr. Burns covers many of the key Mormon doctrines as well as looking closely at Mormonism's founder, Joseph Smith.

This well-documented book answers questions such as the following:

— What **talisman** was found on Joseph Smith when he died?
— Was Joseph Smith involved in **magical and occultic practices?**
— Is there a **Masonic connection?**
— What takes place inside the Mormon Temple?
— Was God once a man?
— Is **polygamy** necessary to attain heaven?
— How can a Mormon attain **godhood?**
— What does Mormonism teach about **baptism for the dead?**
— Was Jesus married?
— Was Jesus crucified because He was a polygamist?

132 pages • $6.95 plus $1.25 postage • ISBN-13: 9781891117015

This important book looks at the issue of speaking in tongues from a Biblical perspective. The chapters are: 1. Do All Speak in Tongues?; 2. Baptism in the Holy Ghost; 3. Sinful Lives and Tongues; 4. Signs and Wonders; 5. Prosperity and Riches; 6. The Power of Words; 7. Can We Create Our Own Reality?; 8. What Is Visualization?; 9. A Look at Inner Healing; 10. Are You a God?; 11. Misfits Removed; 12. Renegades Excluded!; 13. Thy Kingdom Come!; and 14. Will the Church Be Raptured?

For your gift of only $8.95 plus $1.25 postage and handling.

ISBN-13: 9781891117183

A NEW WORLD ORDER IS COMING

"Peace, peace, we must have peace at any cost," is the cry being heard from every quarter today. If we don't soon agree to have a peaceful world, we may all die in a nuclear holocaust. So, what will it take to have a peaceful co-existence? The answer given is the establishment of a one world government. In addition to a one world government, there will be a one world religion and a one world economy. What is also needed in a one world government is a leader. Who will this leader be?

In spite of many plans for this one world government, there is still one obstacle in the way. What—or **WHO**—is this obstacle?

Each of these topics is discussed in detail in this book and then compared to the Bible to see how prophecy is being fulfilled.

For your gift of $5.95 plus $1.25 postage and handling.
116 pages • ISBN-13: 9781891117008

Pathway to Peace

This book has been prepared to help souls find the way to salvation and to find rest and true peace through applying God's never-failing words to our hearts. A great witnessing tool!

For your gift of $2.50 plus $1.25 postage and handling.
50 books for $50.00 plus $6.00 postage and handling.
72 pages • ISBN-13: 9781891117145

SECURE IN CHRIST

In this most fascinating and Scripturally-oriented book you will find approximately 1000 Bible verses to meditate upon. It will enlighten you as you search the Scriptures and will encourage a closer walk with the Lord.

This book will also strengthen your spiritual outlook on life as you see how the Lord wants you to cast all your care upon Him and walk hand in hand in fellowship with Him as He leads you into the deep truth of His Word.

"Now unto Him that is able to keep you from falling, and to present you faultless before the presence of His glory with exceeding joy" (Jude 1:24).

For your gift of $6.95 plus $1.25 postage and handling.

136 pages • ISBN-13: 9781891117107

A SCRIPTURAL VIEW OF HELL

Dr. Cathy Burns

Does the Bible teach soul sleep?
Is Hell eternal?
Is Hell the grave?
Are the wicked annihilated?
Is there fire in Hell?
Is Hell a place of torment?
All of these questions are answered Scripturally in this small book.

For your gift of $4.95 plus $1.05 postage and handling.

40 pages • ISBN-13: 9781891117114

* Who is the Higher Power of AA?
* Were AA's founders Christians or occultists?
* How is the New Age involved?
* Is there a "Rockefeller connection"?
* Who are AA's "godparents"?
* How successful is AA's treatment program?
* Is alcoholism a sin or a disease?

Don't you think it's time to learn about Bill Wilson's adulterous affairs, LSD experimentation, as well as his and Dr. Bob Smith's interest in seances and spiritualism?

320 pages • $11.95 • ISBN-13: 9781560434498

Billy Graham
and His Friends

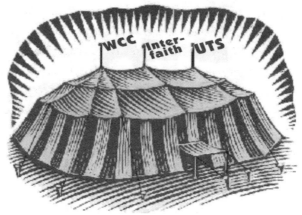

This fasincating book covers many aspects of Billy Graham's life that cannot be found elsewhere. You will discover some little known facts about one of the most well-known men of the 20th century—as well as several of his influential friends. This adventure will take us inside Graham's tent meetings and crusades, his visits to other countries, and his friendship with many Presidents and national leaders.

While Graham has been a beacon of hope in spiritually turbulent times and the source of comfort and solace to many in times of tragedy, we find that others have questioned his connection with the National and World Council of Churches, as well as the ecumenical movement. Using many of his own quotes, you will be able to find out about the other side of Billy Graham and find out about some things that have taken place "behind the scenes." This is your opportunity to take a look at this unusual man.

This book also gives brief reports (appx. 1 to 3 pages each) on dozens of people and subjects such as: Martin Luther King, Jr., Dietrich Bonhoeffer, Bishop Fulton Sheen, Amy Grant, Nelson Mandela, Al Gore, Henry Luce, Laurance Rockefeller, the Alpha Course, Prince of Egypt, Harry Potter, Vatican II, Jesse Jackson, Mikhail Gorbachev, Pope Paul VI, Pope John Paul II, Harry Ward, E. V. Hill, Bishop James Pike, Elvis Presley, Billy Kim, Chuck Colson, C. S. Lewis, Madeleine L'Engle, Archbishop George Carey, Mother Teresa, John R. W. Stott, Tony Campolo, John Marks Templeton, WCC/FCC/NCC, Robert Schuller, John Foster Dulles, Andrew Young, Desmond Tutu, Norman Vincent Peale, Virginia Ramey Mollenkott, Teilhard de Chardin, Armand Hammer, National Endowment for the Arts, United Bible Societies, United Nations Meditation Room, Union Theological Seminary, etc., etc.

For your gift of $21.95 plus $2.20 postage and handling.

800 pages (with Index) Over 4400 footnotes • ISBN-13: 9781891117176

ORDER BLANK

BOOKS:

____ *A New World Order Is Coming!* (128 pages).............$ 5.95

____ *A Scriptural View of Hell* (40 pages)...........................$ 4.95

____ *Alcoholics Anonymous Unmasked* (320 pages)..........$ 11.95

____ *Billy Graham and His Friends* (800 pages)..................$21.95

____ *Hidden Secrets of Masonry* (80 pages).........................$ 6.95

____ *Hidden Secrets of the Eastern Star* (512 pages)............$15.95

____ *Masonic and Occult Symbols Illustrated* (552 pages)..$21.95

____ *Mormonism, Masonry, and Godhood* (132 pages).......$ 6.95

____ *Nephilim, Fallen Angels, and Aliens* (240 pages)........$11.95

____ *Pathway to Peace* (72 pages)...................................$2.50

____ *Secure in Christ* (136 pages)...................................$ 6.95

____ *Tongues, Prosperity, and Godhood* (192 pages)............$8.95

BOOKLETS: ....$ .50 each

____ Astrology and Your Future

____ Different Types of Friendship

____ Dowsing Is in the Bible!

____ Eastern Star Goddesses

____ Explanation of Some Occult Terms

____ Hidden Dangers of Reflexology

____ Hypnosis: Cure or Curse?

____ Questions and Answers About the New Age Movement

____ To Catholics with Love

____ What Is Your I.Q.?

ARTICLES: ....$ .50 each

____ Chart Your Course with Orion International

____ Divination

____ I Have Sinned

____ Jason Winters and His Herbal Tea

____ March for Jesus (WHICH Jesus?)

_____ New Age Love

_____ Should We Name Names?

_____ The Rapture—When Will It Occur?

_____ Unity or D-i-v-i-s-i-o-n?

_____ What Is Miscegenation?

_____ Witchcraft in the Church

_____ Ye Shall Not Surely Die

MORE ARTICLES:

_____ Masons Pay Tribute to Billy Graham!..........................$1.00

_____ Unholy Laughter? (2 part series)................................$1.00

_____ Jay Gary: The Millennium Doctor..............................$4.00

_____ Little Known Facts About Focus on the Family..........$4.00

TRACTS: ....$ .05 each

_____ A Perfect Church (Malcolm Burns)

_____ ABC's of Salvation

_____ Divorce and Remarriage

_____ I've Been Cheated! (Jean Burns)

_____ My God Cannot Do Everything

_____ Treasure of All Ages (Jean Burns)

_____ What Are You Missing? (Jean Burns)

_____ What Is Sin?

_____

_____ **SUBTOTAL**

_____ **POSTAGE** (12% of order [$1.50 mininum; $9.00 maximum])

_____ **ADDITIONAL DONATION**

_____ **TOTAL ENCLOSED**

For orders, or a complete list of literature available, write to:

SHARING

212 East Seventh Street (N-1)

Mt. Carmel, PA 17851-2211